**The Mysteries of the Faith
By St. Alphonsus De Liguori
Translated by Robert Coffin**

THE MYSTERIES OF THE FAITH.

CONTAINING
REFLECTIONS, MEDITATIONS, AND DEVOTIONS ON THE PASSION OF OUR LORD JESUS CHRIST,
AND THE NOVENA OF THE SACRED HEART.
BY
ST. ALPHONSUS MARIA DE LIGUORI,
bishop of St. Agatha, and founder of the congregation of the most holy redeemer.
Translated from the Italian
and edited by
ROBERT A. COFFIN,
priest of the congregation of the most holy redeemer.

RESCRIPT OF HIS HOLINESS PIUS IX

(translation.)

"Most Holy Father,

"The Bishop of Southwark in England, in representing to your Holiness how the Redemptorist Fathers have had the consolation to see an immense good result from the condescension with which your Holiness was pleased to praise the *German* edition of the works of St Alphonsus, humbly begs to be authorised to bless, in the name of your Holiness, the translation already commenced, and in part published, of the pious works of St Alphonsus *in English*.

"In an audience with his Holiness on the 13th November 1858, our most holy Lord, by Divine Providence, Pope Pius IX., at the request of me, the undersigned Secretary of the Sacred Congregation for the Propagation of the Faith, was graciously pleased to grant the above petition; charging, however, the conscience of the petitioner with faithfulness in the translation.

"Given at Rome, from the Palace of the Sacred Congregation, on the day and in the year as above.

"Gratis, &c. &c.   Al. Babnabo, Secretary."

Imprimatur.

N. CARD. WISEMAN.

Westm., die 2 Feb, 1861.

TO

THE RIGHT REVEREND
MONSIGNORE HENRY EDWARD MANNING, D.D.
PROTONOTARY APOSTOLIC, AND PROVOST OF WESTMINSTER,

This Volume,
on the subject which formed the special devotion and constant meditation of his patron

ST. CHARLES,

is most affectionately dedicated.

NOTICE.

The present volume, so long promised, so earnestly expected, but unavoidably delayed, contains nearly all the Devotional Treatises of St. Alphonsus on the Passion of Jesus Christ.

In order not to increase the volume to an inconvenient size, it has been thought well to omit the " Reflections on the Passion," which were newly translated, and published in the *Catholic Practical Library* by Mr. Burns in 1849, before the present edition was undertaken. These, together with a set of " Eight Meditations" taken from them, and "Sixteen Reflections simply explained from the Holy Evangelists," the Editor proposes to give in a future volume.

The *Love of Souls* is the work already known under the titles, *Jesus has loved us,* or *The Clock of the Passion,* given to former translations of it.

Robert Aston Coffin, C.SS.R.

St. Mary's, Clapham,
   Feast of St. Charles, 1860.

THE PASSION OF JESUS CHRIST.

ON THE POWER OF THE PASSION OF JESUS CHRIST

TO ENKINDLE THE DIVINE LOVE IN EVERT HEART.

Father Balthassar Alvarez, a great servant of God, used to say that we must not think we have made any progress in the way of God until we have come to keep Jesus crucified ever in our heart. And St. Francis of Sales said that ' the love which is not the offspring of the Passion is feeble.' Yes, because we cannot have a more powerful motive for loving God than the Passion of Jesus Christ, by which we know that the Eternal Father, to manifest to us His exceeding love for us, was pleased to send His only-begotten Son upon earth to die for us sinners. Whence the Apostle says that God, through the excess of love wherewith He loved us, willed that the death of His Son should convey life to us : " for His exceeding charity wherewith He loved us, even when we were dead in sins, hath quickened us together in Christ" (Ephes. ii. 5). And this was precisely the expression used by Moses and Elias on Mount Tabor, in speaking of the Passion of Jesus Christ. They did not know how to give it any other appellation than an excess of love : " And they spoke of His excess, which He should consummate in Jerusalem" (St. Luke ix. 31).

When our Saviour came into the world, the shepherds heard the Angels singing, " Glory to God in the highest" (St. Luke ii. 14). But the humiliation of the Son of God in becoming man, through His love for man, might have seemed rather to obscure, than to manifest the Divine glory : but no ; there was no means by which the glory of God could have been better manifested to the world than by Jesus Christ dying for the salvation of mankind, since the Passion of Jesus Christ has made us know the perfection of the Divine attributes. It has made us know how great is *Hie mercy of God,* in that a God was willing to die to save sinners, and to die moreover by a death so painful and ignominious. St. John Chrysostom says, that the Passion ef Jesus Christ was not an ordinary suffering, nor His death a simple death like that of other men.

It has made us know the Divine *wisdom.* Had our Redeemer been merely God, He could not have made satisfaction for man ; for God could not make satisfaction to Himself in place of man ; nor could God make satisfaction by means of suffering, being impassible. On the other hand, had He been merely man, man could not have made satisfaction for the grievous injury done by him to the Divine Majesty. What, then, did God do ? He sent His own very Son, true God with the Father, to take human flesh, that so as man He might by His death pay the debt due to the Divine justice, and as God might make to it full satisfaction.

It has, moreover, made us know how great is the Divine *justice.* St. John Chrysostom says, that God reveals to us the greatness of His justice, not so much by hell in which He punishes sinners, as by the sight of Jesus on the Cross ; since in Hell creatures are punished for sins of their own, but on the Cross we behold a God cruelly treated in order to make satisfaction for the sins of men. What obligation had Jesus Christ to die for us ? "He was offered, because it was His own will" (Is. liii. 7). He might have justly abandoned man to his perdition ; but His love for us would not let Him see us lost : wherefore He chose to give Himself up to so painful a death in order to obtain for us salvation : " He hath loved us, and delivered Himself up for us" (Ephes. v. 11). From all eternity He had loved man : "I have loved thee with an everlasting love" (Jer. xxxi. 3). But then, seeing that His justice obliged Him to condemn him, and to keep him at a distance separated from Himself in hell, His mercy urged Him to find out a way by which He might be able to save him. But how ? By making satisfaction Himself to the Divine justice by His own death. And consequently He willed that there should be affixed to the Cross whereon He died the sentence of condemnation to eternal death which man had merited, in order that it might remain there cancelled in His Blood. "Blotting out the writing of the decree that was against us, which was contrary to us. He hath taken the same out of the way, fastening it to the Cross" (Colos. ii. 14). And thus, through the merits of His own Blood, He pardons all our sins : "Forgiving you all offences" (ib. 13). And at the same time He spoiled the devils of the rights they had acquired over us, carrying along with Him in triumph as well our enemies as ourselves who were their prey. " And despoiling the principalities and powers, He hath exposed them confidently in open show, triumphing over them in Himself (ib. 15). On which Theophylact comments, "As a conqueror in triumph, carrying with him the booty and the enemy."

Hence, when satisfying the Divine justice on the Cross, Jesus Christ speaks but of mercy. He prays His Father to have mercy on the very Jews who had contrived His death, and on His murderers who were putting Him to death : " Father, forgive them, for they know not what they do" (St. Luke xxiii. 34). While He was on the Cross, instead of punishing the two thieves who had just before reviled Him,—"And they that were crucified with Him reviled Him" (St. Mark xv. 32),—when He heard one of them asking for mercy,—" Lord, remember me when Thou shalt come into Thy kingdom" (St. Luke xxiii. 41), — overflowing with mercy, He promises him Paradise that very day : " This day thou shalt be with Me in Paradise" (ib. 43). Then, before He expired, He gave to us, in the person of John, His own Mother to be our Mother : " He saith to the disciple, Behold thy Mother" (St. John xix. 24). There upon the Cross He declares Himself content in having done everything to obtain salvation for us, and He makes perfect the sacrifice by His death : "Afterwards Jesus, knowing that all things were now accomplished, ... said, It is consummated ; and bowing His head, He gave up the ghost" (ib. 28, 30). And behold, by the death of Jesus Christ, man is set free from sin and from the power of the devil ; and, moreover, is raised to grace, and to a greater degree of grace than Adam lost : " And where sin abounded," says St. Paul, "grace did more abound" (Rom. v. 20). It remains therefore for us, writes the Apostle, to have frequent recourse with all confidence to this throne of grace, which Jesus crucified exactly is, in order to receive from His mercy the grace of salvation, together with aid to overcome the temptations of the world and of hell í "Let us go therefore with confidence to the throne of grace, that we may obtain mercy, and find grace in seasonable aid" (Heb. iv. 16).

Ah, my Jesus, I love Thee above all things, and whom would I wish to love if I love not Thee, who art infinite goodness, and who hast died for me? Would that I could die of grief every time I think how I have driven Thee away from my soul by my sins, and separated myself from Thee, who art my only good, and who hast loved me so much : "Who shall separate me from the charity of Christ?" It is sin only that can separate me from Thee. But I hope in the Blood Thou hast shed for me, that Thou wilt never allow me to separate myself from Thy love, and to lose Thy grace, which I prize more than every other good. I give myself wholly to Thee. Do Thou accept me, and draw all my affections to Thyself, that so I may love none but Thee.

Does Jesus Christ perhaps claim too much in wishing us to give ourselves wholly to Him, after He has given to us all His blood and His life, in dying for us upon the cross ? " The charity of Christ presseth us" (2 Cor. v. 14). Let us hear what St. Francis of Sales says upon these words : ' To know that Jesus has loved us unto death, and that the death of the Cross, is not this to feel our hearts constrained by a violence which is the stronger in proportion to its loveliness?' And then he adds : ' My Jesus gives Himself all to me, and I give myself all to Him. On His bosom will I live and die. Neither death nor life shall ever separate me from Him.'

It was for this end, says St. Paul, that Jesus Christ died, that each of us should no longer live to the world nor to himself, but to Him alone who has given Himself wholly to us : " And Christ died for all, that they who live may not now live to themselves, but unto Him who died for them" (ib. *15).* He who lives to the world, seeks to please the world ; he who lives to himself, seeks to please himself ; but he who lives to Jesus Christ, seeks only to please Jesus Christ, and fears only to displease Him. His only joy is to see Him loved ; his only sorrow, to see Him despised. This is to live to Jesus Christ ; and this is what He claims from each one of us. I repeat, does He claim too much from us, after having given us His Blood and His life ?

Wherefore, then, O my God, do we employ our affections in loving creatures, relations, friends, the great ones of the world, who have never suffered for us scourges, or thorns, or nails, nor shed one drop of blood for us ; and not in loving a God who for love of us came down from heaven, and was made man, and has shed all His blood for us in the midst of torments, and finally died of grief upon a Cross, in order to win to Himself our hearts : and, further, in order to unite Himself more closely with us, has left Himself, after His death, upon our altars ; where He makes Himself one with us, that we might understand how burning is the love wherewith He loves us ? ' He hath mingled Himself with us,' exclaims St. John Chrysostom, ' that we may be one and the same thing ; for this is the desire of those who ardently love.' And St. Francis of Sales, speaking of the Holy Communion, adds : 'There is no action in which we can think of our Saviour as more tender or more loving than this, in which He, as it were, annihilates Himself, and reduces Himself to food, in order to unite Himself to the hearts of His faithful.'

But how comes it, O Lord, that I, after having been loved by Thee to such an excess, have had the heart to despise Thee, according to Thy just reproach, " I have nourished and brought up children, and they have despised Me"? (Is. i. 2.) I have dared to turn my back upon Thee, in order to gratify my senses : "Thou hast cast Me behind thy back" (Ezech. xxiii. 35). I have dared to drive Thee from my soul : " The wicked have said to God, Depart from us" (Job xxi. 14). I have dared to afflict that Heart of Thine which has loved me so much. And what, then, am I now to do ? Ought I to be distrustful of Thy mercy?

I curse the days wherein I have dishonoured Thee. Oh, would that I had died a thousand times, O my Saviour, than that I had ever offended Thee ! O Lamb of God, Thou hast bled to death upon the Cross to wash away our sins in Thy Blood. O sinners, what would you not pay on the day of judgment for one drop of the Blood of this Lamb? O my Jesus, have pity on me, and pardon me ; but Thou knowest my weakness ; take, then, my will, that it may never more rebel against Thee. Expel from me all love that is not for Thee. I choose Thee alone for my treasure and my only good. Thou art sufficient for me ; and I desire no other good apart from Thee : " The God of my heart, and God is my portion forever."

O little sheep, beloved of God (so used St. Teresa to call the Blessed Virgin), who art the Mother of the Divine Lamb, recommend me to thy Son. Thou, after Jesus, art my hope ; for thou art the nope of sinners. To thy hands I intrust my eternal salvation. *Spes nostra, salve.*

A SWEET ENTERTAINMENT

FOR SOULS THAT LOVE GOD AT THE SIGHT OF JESUS CRUCIFIED.

Jesus on the Cross ! O stupendous sight for heaven and earth of mercy and of love ! To see the Son of God dying through pain upon a gibbet of infamy, condemned as a malefactor to so bitter and shameful a death in order to save sinful men from the penalty that was due to them ! This sight has ever been, and will always be, the subject of the contemplation of the Saints, and has led them willingly to renounce all the goods of the earth, and to embrace with great courage sufferings and death, that they might make themselves more pleasing to a God who died for love of them. The sight of Jesus despised between two thieves has made them love contempt far more than worldlings have loved the honours of the world. Beholding Jesus covered with wounds upon the Cross, they hold in abhorrence the pleasures of sense, and have endeavoured to afflict their flesh in order to unite their sufferings to the sufferings of the Crucified. Beholding the patience of our Saviour in His death, they have joyfully accepted the most painful sicknesses, and even the most cruel torments which tyrants can inflict. Lastly, from beholding the love of Jesus Christ in being willing to sacrifice His life for us in a sea of sorrows, they have sought to sacrifice to Him all that they had,—possessions, children, and even life itself.

St. Paul, in speaking of the love which the Eternal Father has borne towards us, in that, when He saw us dead by reason of sin, He willed to restore life to us by sending His Son to die for us, calls it *too great* a love. " But God (who is rich in mercy), for His *exceeding* charity [niniam char-tatem] wherewith He loved us, hath quickened us together in Christ" (Ephes. ii. 4, 5). And in the same way ought we to call the love wherewith Jesus Christ has willed to die for us *too great* a love. Hence the same Apostle says : "We preach Christ crucified, unto the Jews indeed a stumbling-block, and unto the Gentiles foolishness" (1 Cor. i. 23). St. Paul says that the death of Jesus Christ appeared to the Jews a stumbling-block, because they thought that He should have appeared on earth full of worldly majesty, and not indeed as one condemned to die like a criminal upon a cross ; on the other hand, to the Gentiles it seemed a folly that a God should be willing to die, and by such a death too, for His creatures. On this subject St. Laurence Justinian remarks : 'We have seen Him who is wise infatuated through an excess of love.' We have beheld Him who is the Eternal Wisdom Itself, the Son of God, become a fool for us, by reason of the *too great* love which He bore towards us.

And does it not seem folly for a God, almighty and supremely happy in Himself, to be willing of His own accord to subject Himself to be scourged, treated as a mock king, buffeted, spit upon in the face, condemned to die as a malefactor, abandoned by all upon a Cross of shame, and this to save the miserable worms He Himself had created ? The loving St. Francis, when he thought on this, went about the country exclaiming with tears : ' Love is not loved ! Love is not loved ! And hence St. Bonaventure says, that he who wishes to keep his love for Jesus Christ, ought always to represent Him to himself hanging upon the Cross, and dying there for us : ' Let him ever have before the eyes of his heart Christ dying upon the Cross.'

Oh, happy is that soul which frequently sets before its eyes Jesus dying on the Cross, and stops to contemplate with tenderness the pains which Jesus has suffered, and the love wherewith He offered Himself to the Father, while He lay agonising on that bed of sorrow. Souls that love God, when they find themselves more than usually harassed by temptations of the devil and by fears about their eternal salvation, derive great comfort by considering in silence and alone Jesus hanging upon the Cross, and shedding Blood from all His wounds. At the sight of the Crucifix, all desires for the goods of this world flee utterly away. From that Cross exhales a heavenly breath, which causes us to forget all earthly objects, and enkindles within us a holy desire of quitting all things, in order to empty all our affections in loving that Lord who was pleased to die through love for us.

Isaias foretold that our Redeemer would be a man of sorrows : " And we have seen Him . . . . despised, and the most abject of men, a man of sorrows" (Is. liii. 2, 3). Now let him who wishes to behold this man of sorrows foretold by Isaias look on Jesus Christ dying upon the Cross. There, nailed by His hands and feet, He hangs, the whole weight of His body pressing on His wounds in all His members, which are every one of them torn and bruised. He suffers continual and excruciating pain ; whichever way He turns, so far from finding relief, His pain but increases more and more, until it deprives Him of life ; and thus this man of sorrows is condemned by the Father to die of sheer sufferings on account of our sins.

What Christian, then, O my Jesus, knowing by faith that Thou hast died upon the Cross for love of him, can live without loving Thee ? Pardon me, then, O Lord, first of all, this great sin of having lived so many years in the world without loving Thee. My beloved Saviour, the thought of death fills me with dread, as being the moment when I shall give an account to Thee of all the sins I have committed against Thee ; but that Blood which I see flowing from Thy wounds causes me to hope for pardon from Thee, and at the same time the grace of loving Thee for the future with my whole heart, in virtue of those merits Thou hast earned by so many pains. I give myself wholly to Thee ; I will no longer be my own ; I desire to do all, I desire to suffer, in order to please Thee. I will die for Thee who hast died for me. I will say to Thee, with St. Francis : 'May I die for love of the love of Thee, who didst vouchsafe to die for love of the love of me.'

"Father, into Thy hands I commend My spirit." These words, uttered by Jesus Christ upon the Cross when He was on the point of death, bring great comfort to the dying, who find themselves engaged in that last combat with hell, and are about to pass into eternity. My beloved Jesus, I will not wait for the moment of my death to recommend my soul to Thee. From this moment I recommend it to Thee. By that Blood shed for me, permit it not to be separated from Thee. Henceforth I will be Thine, and all Thine without reserve. If Thou seest that I should ever turn my back upon Thee, as I have in times past, I beseech Thee, let me die in this moment in which I hope to be in Thy grace. " In Thee, O Lord, have I hoped ; I shall not be confounded forever." O faithful soul, lift up thine eyes, and look at the Cross of thy Redeemer, now dead for the love of thee. Say to Him, O my Jesus, in Thy flesh lacerated and torn by the scourges, the thorns, and nails, I behold the burning love Thou hast borne me, and the ingratitude I have shown Thee ; but Thy Blood is my hope. Wretch that I am, how often have I renounced Thy grace, and have myself willed to condemn myself to hell ! What would become of me if Thou hadst not chosen to die for me ? I could die of grief every time I think of having despised Thine infinite goodness, and of having of my own accord banished and separated Thee from my soul. But no ; from henceforth, with the help of Thy grace, I will leave all. Enough for me to be united to Thee, my God and my All.

O men, O men, how can you show such contempt for a God who has suffered so much for love of you ? Behold Him on that Cross ! how He sacrifices Himself by death to pay for your sins and to gain your affections ! My Jesus, I will lire no longer ungrateful for such goodness. O Wounds of Jesus, wound me with love ! O Blood of Jesus, inebriate me with love ! O Death of Jesus, make me die to every affection which is not for Jesus ! I love Thee more than myself, O my Jesus, and there is no pain which causes me more sorrow than the thought of having so often despised Thy love. Accept me ; in Thy mercy reject me not, now that I give myself to Thee without reserve.

Behold, lastly, how our Saviour, overwhelmed with sufferings upon the Cross, bows His head, and breathes forth His soul : "And, bowing His head, He gave up the ghost" (St. John xix. 30). Eternal God, I, a wretched sinner, have dishonoured Thee by my evil life ; but Jesus Christ, in making satisfaction for me by His death, has abundantly restored Thy honour. By the merits of Thy Son, who has died for me, have pity on me.

O Jesus, my Saviour, I see Thee now dead upon this Cross. Thou speakest no more ; Thou breathest no more ; because Thou hast life no longer, having willed to lose it to give life to our souls. Thou hast no longer any Blood ; for Thou has shed it all, by dint of torments, to wash away our sins. In one word, Thou hast abandoned Thyself to death through Thy love for us. " He hath loved us, and delivered Himself for us." ' Let us consider,' writes St. Francis of Sales, ' this Divine Saviour stretched upon the Cross, as upon His altar of honour, where He is dying of love for us ; but a love more painful than that very death. Ah, why, then, do we not in spirit throw ourselves upon upon Him, to die upon the Cross with Him, who has willed to die there for love of us ? I will hold Him, we ought to say, and will never let Him go. I will die with Him, and be burned up in the flames of His love. One and the same fire shall consume this Divine Creator and His miserable creature. My Jesus is all mine, and I am all His. I will live and die upon His breast ; neither death nor life shall ever separate Him from me.'

Yes, my sweet Redeemer, I embrace with tenderness Thy pierced feet ; and, filled with confidence in beholding Thee dead tor love of me, I repent of having despised Thee, and I love Thee with my whole soul. At the foot of Thy Cross I leave Thee my heart and my will. Do Thou Thyself nail it to this Cross, so that it may never be separated from Thee, and from henceforth may have no other desire than to please Thee alone. St. John writes that our Saviour, in order to make His disciples understand the death He was to suffer upon the Cross, said : " And I, if I be lifted up from the earth, will draw all things to Myself. Now this He said, signifying what death He should die" (St. John xii. 32, 33).

And, in fact, by exhibiting Himself crucified and dead, how many souls has Jesus drawn to Himself, so that they have left all to give themselves up entirely to His Divine lore. Ah, my Jesus ! draw my soul to Thyself, which was one time lost ; draw it by the chains of Thy love, so that it may forget the world to think of nothing else but of loving and pleasing Thee. " Draw me after Thee by the odour of Thine ointments." O my Lord, Thou knowest my weakness and the offences which I have committed against Thee. Draw me out of the mire of my passions ; draw all my affections to Thyself, that so I may attend to nothing but Thy pleasure only, O my God most lovely. Hear me, O Lord, by the merits of Thy death, and make me wholly Thine.

St. Leo tells us, that he who looks with confidence upon Jesus dead upon the Cross is healed of the wounds caused by his sins : 'They who with faith behold the death of Christ are healed from the wounds of sin.' Every Christian, therefore, should keep Jesus crucified always before his eyes, and say with St. Paul, " I judged not myself to know anything among you, but Jesus Christ and Him crucified" (1 Cor. ii. 2). In short, the Apostle says, that he did not desire any other knowledge in this world than that of knowing how to love Jesus Christ crucified. My beloved Saviour, to obtain for me a good death Thou hast chosen a death so full of pain and desolation. I cast myself into the arms of Thy mercy. I see that since many years I ought to have been in hell, separated from Thee forever, for having at one time despised Thy grace ; but Thou hast called me to penance, and I hope hast pardoned me ; but if through my fault Thou hast not yet pardoned me, pardon me at this moment. I repent, O my Jesus, with all my head), for haying turned my back upon Thee, and driven Thee from my soul. Restore me to Thy grace. But that is not enough : give me strength to love Thee with all my soul during my whole life. And when I come to the hour of my death, let me expire burning with love for Thee, and saying, My Jesus, I love Thee, I love Thee, to continue to love Thee for all eternity. From this moment I unite my death to Thy holy death, through which I hope for my salvation. "In Thee, O Lord, have I hoped; I shall not be confounded forever." O great Mother of God, thou after Jesus art my hope. 'In thee, O Lady, have I hoped ; I shall not be confounded forever.' O devout souls, when the devil would make us distrustful about our salvation by the remembrance of our past sins, let us lift up our eyes to Jesus dead upon the Cross, in order to deliver us from eternal death. After a God has made us know by means of the holy faith the desire He has of our salvation, having sacrificed even His life for us, if we are resolved really to love Him for the remainder of our lives, cost what it may, we should be on our guard against any weakness of confidence in His mercy. After His having given us so many signs of His love for us, and of His desire for our salvation, it is a kind of sin against Him not to put our whole confidence and hope in His goodness.

Full, then, of holy confidence, let us hope for every good from the hands of a God so liberal and so loving ; and at the same time let us give ourselves to Him without reserve, and thus pray to Him : O Eternal God, we are sinners, but Thou who art Almighty canst make us saints ; grant that henceforth we may neglect nothing that we know to be for Thy glory, and may do all to please Thee. Blessed shall we be if we lose all to gain Thee the infinite Good. Grant that we may spend the remainder of our lives in pleasing Thee alone. Punish us as Thou wilt for our past sins, but deliver us from the chastisement of not being able to love Thee ; deprive us of all things save Thyself. Thou hast loved us without reserve; we also will love Thee without reserve, O infinite Love, O infinite Good ! O Virgin Mary, draw us wholly to God ; thou canst do so, do so for the love thou hast for Jesus Christ.

Let us finish this little treatise with the prayer of St. Francis of Sales, saying : O Eternal Love, my soul seeks Thee, and chooses Thee for all eternity. Come, O Holy Spirit, and kindle in our hearts the fire of Thy love. To die and to love: to die to everything, in order to live eternally for the love of Jesus. O Saviour of our souls, grant that we may sing for ever and ever : Live, Jesus! I love Jesus. Live, Jesus, whom I love! I love Jesus, who liveth and reigneth for ever and ever. Amen.

Ah ! my Jesus, and who, seeing that Thou, the Son of God, hast willed to end Thy life by so bitter a death for lore of us, will be so hard and ungrateful of heart as to be able to love anything in the world but Thee, or to prefer before Thee any of the miserable good things of earth ? My God and my all, I prefer Thee before all the knowledge, all the wealth, all the riches, all the glories and hopes, and all the gifts Thou canst bestow upon me. Thou art all my good. Thou art infinitely amiable ; and how can I love any. but Thee ? Every gift, therefore, which is not Thyself, is not sufficient for me, does not satisfy me ; Thee only do I desire and nothing more. And if for my sins it be Thy will to punish me, punish me by the deprivation of everything, but deprive me not of Thyself. Thou alone art sufficient for me : I repeat, I desire Thee alone, and nothing more.

I desire to spend the remainder of my life in loving and pleasing Thee. What have the Saints not done to please Thee? They have stripped themselves of all their possessions, have renounced the greatest dignities of the world, and have welcomed as treasures contempt, torments, and the most cruel deaths which the cruelty of tyrants could contrive.

O Lord, I now understand that Thou hast created us to love and please Thee. In past time I was wretched enough, instead of pleasing Thee, to cause Thee so much displeasure. What do I say ? I could die of grief at the very thought. I hope that now Thou hast pardoned me for Thy mercy's sake. Since Thou hast now pardoned me, I give Thee my whole will, my whole self. Take possession of me forever ; make me all Thine. Draw me ever closer within Thy heart. Banish from me every love that is not Thee, who art my only Good, my only Love. O Mary, Mother of God, thou after Jesus art my hope. I ask of God the grace to be wholly His ; this is His only desire for us. Thou canst do all things with God ; thou must obtain for me this grace.

O Divine Love, how is it Thou art so despised by men ? O men, look at the Son of God upon that Cross, who like a lamb is sacrificing Himself by a painful death to pay for your sins, and so to gain your love ; look at Him, and love Him.

My Jesus, worthy of infinite love, let me not live any longer ungrateful for such goodness. In past time I have thought but little of corresponding to the love Thou hast borne me ; for the future I will only think of loving and pleasing Thee. Let us strip ourselves of all self-love, and of all earthly affections, to give our will wholly, wholly to God without reserve. O Lord, dispose of me and of all belonging to me for life and death as Thou wilt : I only will what Thou willest. My only desire is to love Thee always in this life and for all eternity. "And what will I but Thee alone, O God of my heart ?"

O Blood of Jesus, inebriate me with the love of Jesus ! O Wounds of Jesus, pierce me with the love of Jesus I O Death of Jesus, make me die to every love which is not for Jesus! My Jesus, I love Thee above all things : I love Thee with my whole soul ; I love Thee more than myself. My beloved Lord, give me Thy love, and make me all Thine. O Mary, my Mother, again I beg of thee, make me all for Jesus. Thou canst do so ; I hope it from thee.

DEVOUT ASPIRATIONS.

O loving Heart of Jesus, inflame this poor heart of mine. My Jesus, when shall I begin to love Thee as Thou hast loved me ?

My God, when shall I die to everything to live to Thee alone ?

My beloved One, make me love Thee even in sufferings.

Thou hast loved me without reserve : I also will love Thee without reserve.

My Jesus, make Thyself known and loved by all.

My Jesus, grant that I may die, saying, I love Thee, I love Thee.

My God, suffer me not to lose Thee forever. Give me the grace to love Thee, and then do with me what Thou wilt.

At this hour I might have been in hell; but now I love Thee, and I hope always to love Thee.

And what else do I wish for, O my God, but Thee, who art my chief, my only Good.

My Jesus, in the Day of Judgment do not separate me from Thee.

My Jesus, how lovely art Thou, but by how few art Thou loved !

Oh, that I could die of grief every time that I think of having voluntarily lost Thee.

My Jesus, grant me Thy love, and I ask Thee for nothing more.

Thou hast died for me ; I wish also to die for Thee. O Death of Jesus, from Thee I hope for a good death. O Blood of Jesus, from Thee I hope for the pardon of all my sins.

O Wounds of Jesus, from Thee I hope to love Thee forever.

O Agony of Jesus, from Thee I hope to bear peacefully the agony of my death.

O Sorrows of Jesus, from Thee I hope for patience in all contradictions.

O Scourges of Jesus, deliver me from everlasting despair.

O Tears of Mary, obtain for me sorrow for my sins.

My own St. Joseph, by thy happy death obtain for me a good death.

O ye holy Apostles, by your blessed death obtain for me the grace to die in the love of God.

And what wish I, either in this life or in the next, but Thee alone, my God ?

My Jesus, had I died in sin, I could no more love Thee; now I desire to love Thee, and Thee alone.

My God, I love Thee, and I will love none but Thee.

St. Teresa, St. Philip Neri, my advocates, make me burn with love for Jesus, as you yourselves did burn.

My Jesus, by the pain Thou didst endure when Thy left hand was pierced with the nail, give me a true sorrow for my sins

My Jesus, by the pain Thou didst endure when Thy right hand was pierced with the nail, give me perseverance in Thy grace.

My Jesus, by the pain Thou didst endure when Thy left foot was pierced with the nail, deliver me from the pains of hell.

My Jesus, by the pain Thou didst endure when Thy right foot was pierced with the nail, give me the grace to love Thee eternally in heaven.

My Jesus, by the wound that was made in Thy Sacred Heart, give me the grace to love Thee always in this life and in the next.

Live, Jesus, our Love,
And Mary, our Hope.

DARTS OF FIRE; OR PROOFS THAT JESUS CHRIST HAS GIVEN US OF HIS LOVE IN THE WORK OF REDEMPTION.

To anyone who considers the immense love which Jesus Christ has shown us in His life, and especially in His death, it is impossible not to be stirred up and excited to love a God who is so enamoured of our souls. St. Bonaventure calls the wounds of our Redeemer wounds which pierce the hardest hearts, and kindle Divine love in the coldest souls.

Therefore in this short examination of the love of Jesus Christ let us consider, according to the testimony of the Divine Scriptures, how much our loving Redeemer has done to make us understand the love that He bears us, and to oblige us to love Him.

1. "He hath loved us, and hath delivered Himself for us" (Ephes. v. 2). God had conferred so many blessings on men, thereby to draw them to love Him, but these ungrateful men not only did not love Him, but they would not even acknowledge Him as their Lord. Scarcely in one corner of the earth, in Judea, was He recognised as God by His chosen people ; and by them He was more feared than loved. He, however, who wished to be more loved than feared by us, became man like us, chose a poor suffering and obscure life, and a painful and ignominious death; and why? to draw our hearts to Himself. If Jesus Christ had not redeemed us, He would not have been less great or less happy than He has always been ; but He determined to procure our salvation at the cost of so many labours and sufferings, as if His happiness depended on ours. He might have redeemed us without suffering; but no ; He willed to free us from eternal death by His own death ; and though He was able to save us in a thousand ways, He chose the most humiliating and painful way, of dying on the Cross of pure suffering to purchase the love of us, ungrateful worms of the earth. And what indeed was the cause of His miserable birth and His most sorrowful death, if not the love He had for us? Ah, my Jesus, may that love which made Thee die for me on Calvary destroy in me all earthly affections, and consume me in the fire which Thou art come to kindle on the earth. I curse a thousand times those shameful passions which cost Thee so much pain. I repent, my dear Redeemer, with all my heart for all the offences I have committed against Thee. For the future I will rather die than offend Thee ; and I wish to do all I can to please Thee. Thou hast spared nothing for my love, neither will I spare anything for Thy love. Thou hast loved me without reserve, I also without reserve will love Thee. I love Thee, my only Good, my Love, my All.

2. " God so loved the world, as to give His only-begotten Son" (St. John iii. 16). Oh, how much does that little word *so* mean ! It means that we shall never be able to comprehend the extent of such a love as this, which made a God send His Son to die that lost man might be saved. And who would ever have been able to bestow on us this gift of infinite value but a God of infinite love ?

I thank Thee, O Eternal Father, for having given me Thy Son to be my Redeemer ; and I thank Thee, O great Son of God, for having redeemed me with so much suffering and love. What would have become of me, after the many sins I have committed against Thee, if Thon hadst not died for me ? Ah, that I had died before I had offended Thee, my Saviour ! Make me feel some of that detestation for my sins which Thou hadst while on earth, and pardon me. But pardon is not sufficient for me, Thou dost merit my love ; Thou hast loved me even to death, unto death will I also love Thee. I love Thee, O infinite Goodness, with all my soul; Hove Thee more than myself; in Thee alone will I place all my affections. Do Thou help me ; let me no longer live ungrateful to Thee, as I have done hitherto. Tell me what Thou wouldst have of me, for, by Thy grace, all, all will I do. Yes, my Jesus, I love Thee ; I will always love Thee, my Treasure, my Life, my Love, my All.

3. " Neither by the blood of goats, or of calves, bat by His own blood, entered once into the Holies, having obtained eternal redemption" (Heb. ix. 12). And of what worth would the blood of all goats, or even of all men, be, if they were sacrificed to obtain Divine grace for us? It ia only the Blood of this Man-God which would merit for us pardon and eternal salvation. But if God Himself had net devised this way to redeem us, as He did by dying to save us, whoever would have been able to think of it ? His love alone designed it and executed it. Therefore holy Job did well to cry out to this God who loves man so much, "What is man, O Lord, that Thou dost so exalt him ? why is Thy heart so intent upon loving him ? what is man, that Thou shouldst magnify him? or why dost Thou set Thy heart upon him ?" ,

Ah, my Jesus, one heart is but little to love Thee with ; if I loved Thee even with the hearts of all men it would be too little. What ingratitude, then, would it be if I were to divide my heart between Thee and creatures ? *No,* my Love, Thou wouldst have it all, and well dost Thou deserve it ; I will give it all to Thee. If I do not know how to give it Thee as I ought, take it Thyself, and grant that I may be able to say to Thee with truth, 'God of my heart.' Ah, my Redeemer, by the merits of the abject and afflicted life that Thou hast willed to live for me, give me true humility, which will make me love contempt and an obscure life. May I lovingly embrace all infirmities, affronts, persecutions, and interior sufferings, and all the crosses which may come to me from Thy hands. Let me love Thee, and then dispose of me as Thou wilt. O loving Heart of my Jesus, make me love Thee by discovering to me the immense good that Thou art. Make me all Thine before I die. I love Thee, my Jesus, who art worthy to be loved. I love Thee with all my heart, I love Thee with all my soul.

4. " The goodness and kindness of God our Saviour appeared" (Tit. iii. 4). God has loved man from all eternity. "I have loved thee with an everlasting love" (Jer. xxxi. 3). 'But,' says St. Bernard, 'before the Incarnation of the Word the Divine power appeared in creating the world; and the Divine wisdom in governing it; but when the Son of God became Man, then was made manifest the love which God had for men.' And in fact, after seeing Jesus Christ go through such an afflicted life and such a painful death, we should be offering Him an insult if we doubted the great love which He bears us. Yes, He does surely love us ; and because He loves us, He wishes to be loved by us. " And Christ died for all, that they also who live may not now live to themselves, but for Him who died for them and rose again" (2 Cor. v. 15).

Ah, my Saviour, when shall I begin to understand the love which Thou hast had for me ? Hitherto, instead of loving Thee, I have repaid Thee with offences and contempt of Thy graces, but since Thou art infinite in goodness I will not lose confidence. Thou hast promised to pardon him who repents ; for Thy mercy's sake fulfil Thy promise to me. I have dishonoured Thee by putting Thee aside to follow my own pleasures; but now I grieve for it from the bottom of my soul, and there is no sorrow that afflicts me more than the remembrance of having offended Thee, my Sovereign Good ; pardon me, and unite me entirely to Thee by an eternal bond of love, that I may not leave Thee any more, and that I may only live to love Thee and to obey Thee. Yes, my Jesus, for Thee alone will I live, Thee only will I love. Once I left Thee for creatures, now I leave all to give myself wholly to Thee. I love Thee, O God of my soul, I love Thee more than *my*self. O Mary, Mother of God, obtain for me the grace to be faithful to God till death.

5. " By this hath the charity of God appeared towards us, because God hath sent His only-begotten Son into the world that we might live by Him" (1 St. John iv. 9). All men were dead by sin, and they would have remained dead if the Eternal Father had not sent His Son to restore them to life by His death. But how? what is this? A God to die for man ! A God ! And who is this man ? ' Who am I ?' says St. Bonaventure. 'O Lord, why hast Thou loved me so much ?' But it is in this that the infinite love of God shines forth. "By this hath the charily of God appeared." The Holy Church exclaims on Holy Saturday, ' O wonderful condescension of Thy mercy towards us ! O inestimable affection of charity ! that Thou mightest redeem a slave, Thou didst deliver up Thy Son.' O immense compassion ! O prodigy ! O excess of the love of God ! to deliver a servant and a sinner from the death which he deserves, His innocent Son is condemned to die.

Thou, then, O my God, hast done this that we might live by Jesus Christ, "that we might live by Him." Yes, indeed, it is but meet that we should live for Him, who has given all His Blood and His life for us. My dear Redeemer, in the presence of Thy wounds and of the Cross on which I see Thee dead for me, I consecrate to Thee my life and my whole will. Ah, make me all Thine ; for from this day forward I seek and desire none but Thee; I love Thee, infinite Goodness ; I love Thee, infinite love ; while I live may I always repeat, *My God, I love Thee, I love Thee;* let my last words in death be, *My God, I love Thee, I love Thee.*

6. " Through the bowels of the mercy of our God, in which the Orient from on high hath visited us" (St. Luke i. 78). Behold, the Son of God comes on earth to redeem us, and He comes stimulated alone by the bowels of His mercy. But, O God, if Thou hast compassion on lost man, is it not enough that Thou shouldst send an angel to redeem him ? No, says the Eternal Word, I will come Myself, that man may know how much I love him. St. Augustine writes, 'For this reason chiefly did Jesus Christ come, that man should know how much God loves him.' But, my Jesus, even now that Thou hast come, how many men are there who truly love Thee ? Wretch that I am, Thou knowest how I have hitherto loved Thee ; Thou knowest what contempt I have had for Thy love. Oh, that I might die of grief for it ! I repent, my dear Redeemer, of having so despised Thee.

Ah, pardon me, and at the same time give me grace to love Thee. Let me no longer remain unmindful of that great affection which Thou hast borne me. I love Thee now, though I love Thee but little. Thou dost merit an infinite love. Grant me at least that I may love Thee with all my strength. Ah, my Saviour, my Joy, my Life, my All, who should I love if I love not Thee, the infinite Good ? I consecrate all my wishes to Thy will, at the sight of the sufferings Thou hast undergone for me. I offer myself te suffer as much as it shall please Thee. Take away from me all occasions in which I might offend Thee. " Lead us not into temptation, but deliver us from evil." Deliver me from sin, and then dispose of me as Thou wilt. I love Thee, infinite Good, and I am content to receive any punishment, even to be annihilated, rather than to live without loving Thee.

7. "And the Word was made flesh" (St. John i. 14). God sent the Archangel Gabriel to ask Mary's consent that He should become her Son ; Mary gives her consent, and behold the Word is made man. O wonderful prodigy, at which the heavens and all nature stand in astonishment. The Word made flesh ! A God made man ! What if we were to see a king become a worm to have the life of a little worm of earth by his death ? So, then, my Jesus, Thou art my God, and not being able to die as God, Thou hast been pleased to become man capable of dying in order to give Thy life for me.

My sweet Redeemer, how is it that, at the sight of such mercy and love Thou hast shown towards me, I do not die of grief? Thou didst come down from heaven to seek me, a lost sheep ; and how many times have I not driven Thee away, preferring my miserable pleasures before Thee ! But since Thou dost wish to have me, I leave all; I wish to be Thine, and will have none other but Thee. Thee do I choose for the only object of my affections. "My Beloved to me and I to Him." Thou dost think of me, and I will think of none but Thee. Let me always love Thee, and may I never leave off loving Thee. Provided I can love Thee, I am content to be deprived of all sensible consolation, and even to suffer all torments. I see that Thou dost indeed wish me to be all Thine, and I wish to belong entirely to Thee. I know that everything in the world is a falsehood, a deceit ; nothing but smoke, filth, and vanity. Thou alone art the true and only Good, therefore Thou alone art sufficient for me. *My God, I wish for Thee alone, and nothing else* ; Lord hear me, *for Thee alone do I wish, and nothing else.*

8."He emptied Himself" (Phil. ii. 7). Behold the only-begotten Son of God, omnipotent and true God, equal to the Father, born a little Infant in a stable. " He emptied Himself, taking the form of a servant, being made to the likeness of men." If anyone would see a God annihilated, let him enter into the cave of Bethlehem, and he will find Him as a little Infant, bound in swaddling clothes, so that He cannot move, weeping and trembling with cold. Ah, holy faith, tell me whose Son is this poor Child ? Faith answers, He is the Son of God, and He is true God. And who has brought Him to such a miserable condition ? It was the love He had for men. And yet there are men to be found who do not love this God ! Thou, then, my Jesus, hast spent all Thy life amidst sorrows to make me understand the love Thou dost bear me, and I have spent my life in despising and displeasing Thee by my sins! Ah, make me know the evil I have committed, and the love which Thou desirest to have. But since Thou hast borne with me till now, permit me not to give Thee any more cause for sorrow. Inflame me altogether with Thy love, and remind me always of all Thou hast suffered for me, that from this day forth I may forget everything, and think of nothing but loving and pleasing Thee. Thon didst come on earth to reign in our hearts ; take, then, from my heart all that could prevent Thee from possessing it entirely ! Make my will to be wholly conformed to Thy will ; may Thine be mine, and may it be the rule of all my actions and desires.

9. " For a Child is born to us, and a Son is given to us" (Isaias ix. 6). Behold the end for which the Son of God will be born an Infant, to give Himself to us from His Childhood, and thus to draw to Himself our love; Why (writes St. Francis of Sales) does Jesus take the sweet and tender form of an Infant, if it be not to provoke us to love Him and to confide in Him *?* St. Peter Chrysologus had said before, ' Thus He willed to be born, because He wished to be loved.'

O dear Child Jesus, my Saviour, I love Thee; in Thee do I trust, Thou art all my hope and all my love. What would have become of me if Thou hadst not come down from heaven to save me ? I know the hell which Would have awaited me for the offences I have offered Thee. Blessed be Thy mercy, because Thou art ever ready to pardon me if I repent of my sins. Yes, I repent with all my heart, my Jesus, of having despised Thee. Receive me into Thy favour, and make me die to myself to live only to Thee, my only Good. Destroy in me, O thou consuming fire, everything which is displeasing in Thine eyes, and draw all my affections to Thee. I love Thee, O God of my soul ; I love Thee, my Treasure, my Life, my AU. I love Thee, and I wish to die saying, My God, I love Thee; and begin then to love Thee with a perfect love which shall have no end.

10. For so many years the holy Prophets desired the coming of the Saviour. They said, " Drop down dew, O ye heavens, from above, and let the clouds rain the just". (Is. xlv. 8). "Send forth the Lamb, the Ruler of the earth" (Is. xvi. 1). "Grant us Thy salvation" (Ps. lxxxiv. 8). The same prophet Isaias said, " Oh, that Thou wouldst rend the heavens, and wouldst come down : the mountains would melt away at Thy presence, . . . the waters would burn with fire" (Is. lxiv. 1,2). Lord, he said, when men shall see that Thou hast come on earth out of love for them, the mountains shall be made smooth; that is, men in serving Thee will conquer all the difficulties which at first appeared to them insuperable obstacles. " The waters would burn with fire," and the coldest hearts will feel themselves burning with Thy love, at the sight of Thee made man. And how well has this been verified in many happy souls !—in a St. Teresa, in a St. Philip Neri, a St. Francis Xavier, who even in this life were consumed by this holy fire. But how many such are there ? Alas, but too few.

Ah, my Jesus, amongst these few I also wish to be. How many years ought I not already to have been burning in hell, separated from Thee, hating and cursing Thee forever. But no; Thou hast borne with me with so much patience, that Thou mightest see me burn, not with that unhappy flame, but with the blessed fire of Thy love ; for this end Thou hast given me so many illuminations, and hast so often wounded my heart while I was far from Thee ; finally, Thou hast done so much, that Thou hast forced me to love Thee by Thy sweet attractions. Behold, I am now Thine. I will be Thine always and altogether. It remains for Thee to make me faithful, and this I confidently hope from Thy goodness. O my God, who could ever have the heart to leave Thee again, and to live even a moment without Thy love ? I love Thee, my Jesus, above all things; but this is little. I love Thee more than myself; but this is little also. I love Thee with all my heart; and this also is little. My Jesus, hear me, give me more love, more love, more love. O Mary, pray to God for me.

11. "Despised, and the most abject of men" (Is. liii. 3). Behold what was the life of the Son of God made man, " the most abject of men." He was treated as the vilest, the least of men. To what extreme of meanness could the life of Christ be reduced greater than that of being born in a stable ? of living as a servant in an unknown and despised shop ? of being bound as a criminal? Scourged as a slave ? struck, treated as a mock king, having His face spit upon ? and finally, of dying condemned as a malefactor on an infamous gibbet? St. Bernard exclaims, 'Oh, lowest and highest !' A God, Thou art the Lord of all, and how art Thou contented to be the most despised of all ? And I, my Jesus, when I see Thee so humiliated for me, how can I wish to be esteemed and honoured by all ?   A sinner to be proud !

Ah, my despised Redeemer, may Thy example inspire me with love of contempt and of an obscure life ; from this time forward I hope, with Thy help, to accept from my heart all the opprobrium I may have to suffer for the love of Thee, who hast endured so much for the love of me. Pardon me the pride of my past life, and give me love in its place. I love Thee, my despised Jesus. Go before with Thy Cross, I will follow Thee with mine, and I will not leave Thee till I die crucified for Thee, as Thou didst die crucified for me. My Jesus, my despised Jesus, I embrace Thee ; in Thy embrace will I live and die.

12. " A man of sorrows" (Is. liii. 3).   What was the life of Jesus Christ ? A life of sorrows ; a life of internal and external sorrows from the beginning to the end. But what most afflicted Jesus Christ during the course of His life, was the sight of the sins and ingratitude with which men repaid the pains He had suffered with so much love for us. This thought made Him the most afflicted amongst all men who had ever lived on the earth. So, then, my Jesus, I also added to the affliction Thou didst suffer during the whole of Thy life by my sins. And why do not I also say, as did St. Margaret of Cortona, who, when exhorted by her confessor to calm her grief and not to weep anymore because God had pardoned her, redoubled her tears and answered, 'Ah, my father, how can I leave off weeping when I know that my sins afflicted say Jesus throughout the whole of His life?' Oh, that I could die of grief, my Jesus, whenever I think of all the bitter anguish I have caused Thee every day of my life! Alas, how many nights have I slept deprived of Thy grace! How many times hast Thou pardoned me, and I have again turned my back upon Thee ! My dear Lord, I repent above all things for having offended Thee. I love Thee with all my heart, I love Thee with all my soul. Ah, my sweet Jesus, permit me not to be separated any more from Thee! Let me die rather than betray Thee afresh. O Mary, Mother of perseverance, obtain for me the gift of holy perseverance.

13. " Having loved His own who were in the world, He loved them unto the end" (St. John xiii. 1). The love of friends increases at the time of death, when they are on the point of being separated from those they love ; and it is then, therefore, that they try more than ever, by some pledge of affection, to show the love they bear to them. Jesus during the whole of His life gave us marks of His affection ; but when He came near the hour of His death He wished to give us a special proof of His love. For what greater proof could this loving Lord show us than by giving His Blood and His life for each of us ? And not content with this, He left this very same Body, sacrificed for us upon the Cross, to be our food, so that each one who should receive It should be wholly united to Him, and thus love should mutually increase. O infinite goodness! O infinite love ! Ah, my enamoured Jesus, fill my heart with Thy love, so that I may forget the world and myself, to think of nothing but of loving and pleasing Thee. I consecrate to Thee my body, my soul, my will, my liberty. Up to this time I have sought to gratify myself to Thy great displeasure ; I am exceedingly sorry for it, my crucified Love ; from henceforth I will seek nothing but Thee, ' my God and my All.' My God, Thou art my All, I wish for Thee alone and nothing more. Oh, that I could spend myself all for Thee, who hast spent Thyself all for me ! I love Thee, my only Good, my only Love. I love Thee, and abandon myself entirely to Thy holy will. Make me love Thee, and then do with me what Thou wilt.

14. " My soul is sorrowful even unto death" (St. Matt, xxvi. 38). These were the words that proceeded from the sorrowful Heart of Jesus Christ in the Garden of Gethsemani, before He went to die. Alas, whence came this extreme grief of Hie, which was so great that it was enough to kill Him? Perhaps it was on account of the torments He saw He should have to suffer ? No ; for He had foreseen these torments from the time of His Incarnation. He had foreseen them, and had accepted them of His own free-will : " He was offered because it was His own will" (Is. liii. 7). His grief came from seeing the sins men would commit after His death. It was then, according to St Bernardine of Sienna, that He clearly saw each particular sin of each one of us. ' He had regard to every individual fault.

It was not, then, my Jesus, the sight of the scourges, of the thorns, and of the Cross which so afflicted Thee in the Garden of Gethsemani ; it was the sight of my sins, each one of which so oppressed Thy Heart with grief and sadness that it made Thee agonise and sweat Blood. This is the recompense I have made Thee for the love Thou hast shown me by dying for me. Ah, let me share the grief Thou didst feel in the Garden for my sins, so that the remembrance of it may make me sad for all ray life. Ah, my sweet Redeemer, if I could but console Thee as much now by my grief and love as I then afflicted Thee ! I repent, my Love, with all my heart for having preferred my own miserable satisfaction to Thee. I am sorry, and I love Thee above all things. Although I have despised Thee, yet I hear Thee ask for my love. Thou wouldst have me love Thee with all my heart;. " Love the Lord thy God with all thy heart, and with all thy soul." Yes, my God, I love Thee with all my heart, I love Thee with all my soul. Do Thou give me the love Thou requirest of me. If I have hitherto sought myself, I will now seek none but Thee. And seeing that Thou hast loved me more than others, more than others will I love Thee. Draw me always more, my Jesus, to Thy love by the odour of Thy ointments, which are the loving attractions of Thy grace. Finally, give me strength to correspond to so much love which God has borne to an ungrateful worm and traitor. Mary, Mother of mercy, help me by thy prayers.

15. "They took Jesus and bound Him" (St. John xviii. 12). A God taken and bound! What could the Angels have said at seeing their King with His hands bound, led between soldiers through the streets of Jerusalem! And what ought we to say at the sight of our God, who is content for our sakes to be bound as a thief, and to be presented to the judge who is to condemn Him to death? St. Bernard laments, saying, ' What hast Thou to do with chains?' What have malefactors and chains to do with Thee, O my Jesus, Thou who art infinite Goodness and Majesty? They should belong to us sinners, guilty of hell, and not to Thee, who art innocent and the Holy of holies. St. Bernard goes on to say, on seeing Jesus guilty of death, ' What hast Thou done, most innocent Saviour, that Thou shouldst be thus condemned?' O my dear Saviour, Thou art innocence itself ; for what crime hast Thou been thus condemned? 'Ah, I will tell Thee,' he replies ; ' the crime Thou hast committed is the too great love Thou hast borne to men. Thy sin is love.'

My beloved Jesus, I kiss the cords that bind Thee, for they have freed me from those eternal chains which I have deserved. Alas, how many times have I renounced Thy friendship and made myself a slave of Satan, dishonouring
Thy infinite Majesty! I grieve above all things for having so grievously insulted Thee. Ah, my God, bind my will to Thy feet with the sweet cords of Thy holy love, that it may wish for nothing but what is pleasing to Thee. May I take Thy will for the sole guide of my life. As Thou hast had so great a care for my good, may I not care for anything but to love Thee. I love Thee, my Sovereign Good ; I love Thee, the only object of my affections. I know that Thou alone hast loved me truly, and Thee alone will I love. I renounce everything. Thou alone art sufficient for me.

16. "But He was wounded for our iniquities, He was bruised for our sins" (Isaias liii. 5). One single blow suffered by this Man-God was sufficient to satisfy for the sins of the whole world ; but Jesus Christ was not content with that ; He wished to be "wounded and bruised" for our iniquities, which means to say, wounded and torn from head to foot, so that there should be no whole part remaining in His sacred Body. Hence the same Prophet beheld Him full of sores like a leper. "And we have thought Him as it were a leper, and as one struck by God and afflicted" (ib. 4).

O Wounds of my sorrowful Jesus, you are all living evidences of the love which my Redeemer preserves for me ; with tender words do you force me to love Him for the many sufferings He has undergone for the love of me. Ah, my sweet Jesus, when shall I give myself all to Thee, as Thou hast given Thyself all to me? I love Thee, my Sovereign Good. I love Thee, my God, Lover of my soul. O God of love, give me love. By my love let me atone to Thee for the bitterness I have given Thee in times past. Help me to drive from my heart everything that does not tend to Thy love. Eternal Father, " look at the face of Thy Christ," look at the wounds of Thy Son, which seek pity for me, and for their sake pardon me the outrages I have committed against Thee ; take my heart entirely to Thyself that it may neither love, seek, nor sigh after any other but Thee. I say to Thee, with St. Ignatius, ' Give me only love of Thee and Thy grace, and I am rich enough.' Behold, this is all I ask of Thee, O God of my soul; give me Thy love, together with Thy grace, and I desire nothing else. O Mary, Mother of God, intercede for me.

17. " Hail, King of the Jews" (St. Matt, xxvii. 29). Thus was our Redeemer scornfully saluted by the Roman soldiers. After having treated Him as a false king, and having crowned Him with thorns, they knelt before Him and called Him King of the Jews, and then, rising up with loud cries and laughter, they struck Him and spit in His face. St. Matthew writes, "And platting a crown of thorns, they put it upon His head. . . . And bowing the knee before Him, they mocked Him, saying, Hail, King of the Jews ; and spitting upon Him they took the reed and struck His head." And St. John adds, "And they gave Him blows" (St. John xix. 3). O my Jesus, this barbarous crown that encircles Thy head, this vile reed that Thou dost hold in Thy hand, this torn purple garment that covers Thee with ridicule, make Thee known indeed as a King, but a King of love. The Jews will not acknowledge Thee for their King, and they say to Pilate, " We have no king but Caesar." My beloved Redeemer, if others will not have Thee for their King, I accept Thee, and desire that Thou shouldst be the only King of my sou. To Thee do I consecrate my whole self ; dispose of me as Thou pleasest. For this end hast Thou endured such contempt, so many sorrows, and death itself, to gain our hearts and to reign therein by Thy love. " For to this end Christ died,. . . . that He might be Lord both of the dead and of the living" (Rom. xvi. 9). Make Thyself therefore Master of my heart, O my beloved King, and reign and exercise Thy sway there forever. Formerly I refused Thee for my Lord, that I might serve my passions ; now I will be all Thine, and Thee alone will I serve. Ah, bind me to Thee by Thy love, and make me always remember the bitter death Thou hast willed to suffer for me. Ab, my King, my God, my Love, my All, what do I wish for if not for Thee alone ! " Thee, God of my heart and my portion forever." O God of my heart, I love Thee; Thou art my portion, Thou art my only Good.

18. " And bearing His own Cross, He went forth ta that place which is called Calvary" (St. John xix. 17). Behold, the Saviour of the world has now set out on His journey with His Cross on His shoulders, going forth to die in torments for the love of men. The Divine Lamb allows Himself to be led without complaining to be sacrificed upon the Cross for our salvation. Go thou also, my soul ; accompany and follow thy Jesus, who goes to suffer death for thy love, to satisfy for thy sins. Tell me, my Jesus and my God, what dost Thou expect from men by giving Thy life for their sake? St. Bernard answers, Thou dost expect nothing but to be loved by them : ' When God loves, He wishes for nothing but to be loved in return.'

Is it, then, my Redeemer, at so great a cost that Thou hast desired to gain our love? And shall there be any among men who believe in Thee, and not love Thee ? I comfort myself with the thought that Thou art the love of all the souls of the Saints, the love of Mary, and the love of Thy Father ; but, O my God, how many are there who will not know Thee, and how many that know Thee and yet will not love Thee! Infinite Love, make Thyself known, make Thyself loved. Ah, that I could by my blood and my death make Thee loved by all. But alas ! that I have lived so many years in the world while I knew Thee, but did not love Thee. But now at last Thou hast drawn me to love Thee by Thy so great goodness. At one time I was so unhappy as to lose Thy grace ; but the grief I now feel for it, the desire I have of being all Thine, and still more the death Thou hast suffered for me, give me a firm confidence, O my Love, that Thou hast already pardoned me, and that now Thou dost love me. Oh, that I could die for Thee, my Jesus, as Thou hast died for me ! Although no punishment awaited those who love Thee not, I would never leave off loving Thee, and I would do all I could to please Thee. Thou, who givest me this good desire, give me strength to follow it out. My Love, my Hope, do not abandon me ; make me correspond, during the remainder of my life, to the especial love Thou hast borne me. Thou desirest to have me for Thine own, and I wish to be all for Thee. I love Thee, my God, my Treasure, my All. I will live and die always repeating, I love Thee, I love Thee, I love Thee.

19. " And shall be dumb as a lamb before his shearer, and He shall not open His mouth" (Is. liii. 7). This was precisely the passage which the eunuch of Queen Candace was reading ; but not understanding of whom it was written, St. Philip, inspired by

God, got up into the carriage in which the eunuch was, and explained to him that these words referred to our Redeemer Jesus Christ. Jesus was called a Lamb because He was first dragged into the praetorium of Pilate, and then led to death just like an innocent lamb. Therefore the Baptist calls Him a Lamb. " Behold the Lamb of God, behold Him who taketh away the sins of the world." A Lamb who suffers and dies a victim on the Cross for our sins : " Surely He hath borne our infirmities, and carried our sorrows" (Is. liii. 4). Miserable are those who do not love Jesus Christ during their life. In the last day the sight of this Lamb in His wrath will make them say to the mountains, "Fall upon us, and hide us from the face of Him that sitteth upon the throne, and from the wrath of the Lamb" (Apoc vi. 16).

No, my Divine Lamb, if in times past I have not loved Thee, now I will love Thee forever. Before I was blind; but now that Thou hast enlightened me, and hast made me know the great evil I have done in turning my back upon Thee, and the infinite love which is due to Thee for Thy goodness and for the love Thou hast borne me, I repent with all my heart for having offended Thee, and I love Thee above all things. O Wounds, O Blood of ray Redeemer, how many souls have you not inflamed with love! inflame my soul also. Ah, my Jesus, continually call to my remembrance Thy Passion and the pains and ignominies Thou hast suffered for me, that I may detach my affections from earthly goods and place them all on Thee, my only and infinite Good. I love Thee, Lamb of God, sacrificed and annihilated on the Cross for my sake. Thou hast not refused to suffer for me, I will not refuse to suffer for Thee whatever Thou requirest. I will no longer complain of the crosses Thou dost send me. I ought to have been in hell these many years; how, then, can I complain? Give me grace to love Thee, and then do with me what Thou wilt.   "Who shall separate me from the love of Christ?" Ah, my Jesus, sin alone can separate me from Thy love. Ah, let it not be; rather let me die a thousand times ; this I beg of Thee by Thy sacred Passion. I beseech thee, O Mary, by thy sorrows deliver me from the death of sin.

20. " My God, My God, why hast Thou forsaken Me?" (St. Matt, xxvii. 46.) O God, who shall not compassionate the Son of God, who for love of men is dying of grief on a cross ? He is tormented externally in His body by innumerable wounds, and internally He is so afflicted and sad that He seeks solace for His great sorrow from the Eternal Father ; but His Father, in order to satisfy His Divine justice, abandons Him, and leaves Him to die desolate and deprived of every consolation.

O desolate Death of my loving Redeemer, Thou art my hope. O my abandoned Jesus, Thy merits make me hope that I shall not remain abandoned and separated from Thee forever in hell. I do not care to live in consolation in this earth, I embrace all the pains and desolations Thou mayest send me. He is not worthy of consolation who by offending Thee has merited for himself eternal torments. It is enough for me to love Thee and to live in Thy grace. This alone do I beg of Thee, let me never more see myself deprived of Thy love. Let me be abandoned by all; do not Thou abandon me to this extremity. I love Thee, my Jesus, who didst die abandoned for me. I love Thee, my only Good, my only Hope, my only Love.

21. " They crucified Him, and with Him two others, one on each side, and Jesus in the midst" (St. John xix. *18)*. The Incarnate Word was called by the sacred spouse "all lovely; such is my Beloved" (Cant. v. 16). At whatever period of His life Jesus Christ presents Himself to us, He appears altogether desirable and most worthy of love—whether we see Him as an Infant in the stable, as a Boy in the shop of St. Joseph, as a Solitary meditating in the desert, or bathed in sweat as He walked about preaching throughout Judea. But in no other form does He appear more loving than when He is nailed to the Cross on which the immense love He bears us forced Him to die.   St. Francis of Sales has said, the mount of Calvary is the hill of lovers. All love which does not take its rise from the Passion of the Saviour is weak. How miserable is the death where there is no love of the Redeemer ! Let us stop, then, and consider that this Man, nailed to the tree of shame, is our true God, and that He is here suffering and dying for nothing but for love of us. Ah, my Jesus, if all men would stand still and contemplate Thee on the Cross, believing with a lively faith that Thou art their God, and that Thou hast died for their salvation, how could they live far from Thee and without Thy love? And how could I, knowing all this, have displeased Thee so often ? If others have offended Thee, they have at least sinned in darkness ; but I have sinned in the light. But these pierced Hands, this wounded Side, this Blood, these Wounds which I see in Thee—make me hope for pardon and Thy grace. I am grieved, my Love, for having ever so despised Thee. But now I love Thee with all my heart, and my greatest grief is the remembrance of my having despised Thee. This grief, however, which I feel, is a sign that Thou hast pardoned me. O burning Heart of my Jesus, inflame my poor heart with Thy love. O my Jesus, dead, consumed with sorrow for me, make me die, consumed with sorrow for having offended Thee, and with the love Thou dost merit, I sacrifice myself entirely to Thee, who hast sacrificed Thyself entirely for me. O sorrowful Mother Mary, make me faithful in loving Jesus.

22. " And bowing His head, He gave up the ghost" (St. John xix. 30). Behold, my Redeemer, to what Thy love for man has brought Thee—even to die of sorrow on a cross, drowned in a sea of grief and ignominy ; as David had predicted of Thee, "I am come into the depth of the sea, and a tempest hath overwhelmed me" (Ps. lxviii. 3). St. Francis of Sales writes thus : ' Let us contemplate this Divine Saviour stretched on the Cross, as upon the altar of His glory, on which He is dying of love for us. Ah, why, then, do we not in spirit throw ourselves upon Him to die upon the Cross with Him who has chosen to die there for love of us? I will hold Him, we ought to say ; I will never let Him go. I will die with Him, and will burn in the flames of His love ; one and the same fire shall devour this Divine Creator and His miserable creature. My Jesus is all mine, and I am all His. I will live and die on His bosom. Neither life nor death shall ever separate me from my Jesus.'

Yes, my dear Redeemer, I hold fast by Thy Cross ; I kiss Thy pierced Feet, touched with compassion, and confounded at seeing the affection with which Thou hast died for me. Ah, accept me, and bind me to Thy Feet, that I may no more depart from Thee, and may from this day forward converse with Thee alone, with Thee consult on all my thoughts ; in a word, may I henceforth direct, all my affections so as to seek nothing but to love Thee and please Thee, always longing to leave this valley of dangers to come and love Thee face to face with all my strength in Thy kingdom, which is a kingdom of eternal love. In. the mean time let me always live grieving for the offences I have committed against Thee, and always burning with love for Thee, who for love of me hast given Thy life. I love Thee, my Jesus, who hast died for me. I love Thee, O infinite Lover; I love Thee, O infinite Love; I love Thee, infinite Goodness. O Mary, Mother of beautiful love, pray to my Jesus for me.

23. "He was offered because it was His own will" (Is. liii. 7). The Incarnate Word, at the moment of His conception, saw before Him all the souls He was to redeem. Then thou also, my soul, wast presented with the guilt of all thy sins upon thee, and for thee did Jesus Christ accept all the pains He suffered in life and death ; and in doing so did He obtain for thee thy pardon, and all the graces thou hast received from God—the lights, the calls to His love, the helps to overcome temptations, the spiritual consolations, the tears, the compassionate feelings thou hast experienced when thinking of the love which He has had for thee, and the sentiments of sorrow in remembering how thou hast offended Him. Thou didst, then, my Jesus, from the very beginning of Thy life, take upon Thee all my sins, and didst offer Thyself to satisfy for them by Thy sufferings. By Thy death Thou hast delivered me from eternal death. " But Thou hast delivered my soul that it should not perish ; Thou hast cast all my sins behind Thy back" (Is. xxxviii. 17). Thou, my Love, instead of punishing me for the insults which I have added to those Thou hadst already received, hast gone on

adding to Thy favours and mercies towards me, in order to win my heart one day to Thyself; My Jesus, this day is come ; I love Thee with all my soul. Who should love Thee if I do not ? This is the first sin, my Jesus, that Thou hast to forgive me, that I have been so many years in the world without loving Thee. But for the future I will do all I can to please Thee. I feel by Thy grace a great desire to live to Thee alone, and to detach myself from all created things. I have also a great compunction for the displeasure I have caused Thee. This desire and this sorrow, I see, my Jesus, are all Thy gift. Continue, then, my Love, to keep me ever faithful in Thy love; for Thou knowest my weakness. Make me all Thine, as Thou hast made Thyself all mine. I love Thee, my only Good ; I love Thee, my only Love ; I love Thee, my Treasure, my All. My Jesus, I love Thee, I love Thee, I love Thee. Help me, O Mother of God.

24. "God sending His own Son in the likeness of sinful flesh, even of sin, hath condemned sin in the flesh" (Rom. viii. 3). God, then, has sent His Son to redeem us clothed in human flesh, like to the sinful flesh of other men, " in the likeness of sinful flesh." "Christ hath redeemed us from the curse of the law, being made a curse for us, for it is written : Cursed is every one that hangeth on a tree" (Gal. iii. 13). So that Jesus Christ willed to appear in the world as a guilty and accused man, hanging on the Cross to deliver us from eternal malediction. O Eternal Father, for the love of this Son so dear to Thee, have pity on me. And Thou, Jesus, my Redeemer, who by Thy death hast liberated me from the slavery of sin in which I was born, and of the sins I have committed since my baptism, ah, change the miserable chains which once bound me a slave to Satan into chains of gold, which may bind me to Thee with a holy love. Arise, and show forth in me the efficacy of Thy merits, by changing me a sinner into a saint.

I have deserved to be burning in hell for many years past ; but I hope by Thy infinite mercy, for the glory of Thy death, to burn with Thy love, and to be all Thine. I wish that my heart should love none but Thee. "Thy kingdom come." Reign, my Jesus ; reign over my whole soul. May it obey Thee alone, Thee alone seek, Thee alone desire. Away from my heart, ye earthly affections ! and come, O ye flames of Divine love ; come, and remain alone to possess and consume me for that God of love who didst die consumed for me. I love Thee, my Jesus ; I love Thee, O infinite Sweetness and my true Lover. I have no one who has loved me more than Thou ; and therefore I give and consecrate myself to Thee, my Treasure and my All.

25. " He hath loved us, and washed us from our sins in His own blood " (Apoc. i. 5). So, then, my Jesus, in order to save my soul, Thou hast prepared a bath of Thine own Blood wherein to cleanse it from the filth of its sins. If, then, our souls have been bought by Thy Blood,—" For you are bought with a great price " (1 Cor. vi. 20),—it is a sign that Thou lovest them much; and as Thou dost love them, let us pray thus to Thee, 'We therefore pray Thee help Thy servants, whom Thou hast redeemed with Thy precious Blood.' It is true that by my sins I have separated myself from Thee, and have knowingly lost Thee. But remember, my Jesus, that Thou hast bought me with Thy Blood. Ah, may this Blood not have been given in Vain for me, which was shed with so much grief and so much love.

By my sins have I driven Thee, my God, from my soul, and have merited Thy hatred ; but Thou hast said that Thou wouldst forget the crimes of a repentant sinner. " But if he do penance . . . . I will not remember all his iniquities" (Ez. xviii. 21,22). Thou hast further said, " I love them that love Me" (Prov. viii. 17). I pray Thee, therefore, my Jesus, to forget all the injuries I have offered Thee, and love me; whilst I also will now love Thee more than myself, and repent above all things for having offended Thee. Ah, my beloved Lord, for the sake of that Blood which Thou hast shed for the love of me, hate me no longer, but love me. It is not enough for me that Thou shouldst only forgive me the chastisement I deserve, I desire to love Thee and to be loved by Thee. O God, who art all love, all goodness, unite me and bind me to Thyself, and permit not that I should ever be separated from Thee any more, and that thus I should again deserve Thy hatred. No, my Jesus, my Love, let it not be ; I will be all Thine, and I desire that Thou shouldst be all mine.

26. " He humbled Himself, becoming obedient unto death ; even the death of the cross" (Phil. ii. 8). What great thing is it that the martyrs have done in giving their lives for God, while this God has humbled Himself to the death of the Cross for their love? To render a just return for the death of a God, it would not be sufficient to sacrifice the lives of all men; the death of another God for His love would alone compensate for it. O my Jesus, allow me, a poor sinner, to say to Thee, with Thy true lover St. Francis of Assisi, 'May I die, O Lord, for the love of Thy love, as Thou didst deign to die for the love of my love.'

It is true, my Redeemer, that hitherto for the love of my own pleasures, unhappy that I am ! I have renounced Thy love. Would that I had died before, and had never offended Thee ! I thank Thee that Thou givest me time to love Thee in this life, that I may afterwards love Thee throughout all eternity. Ah, remind me continually, my Jesus, of the ignominious death Thou hast suffered for me. that I may never forget to love Thee in consideration of the love Thou hast borne me. I love Thee, infinite Goodness ; I love Thee, my supreme Good ; to Thee I give myself entirely, and by that love which caused Thee to die for me, do Thou accept my love, and let me die, destroy me, rather than ever permit me to leave off loving Thee. I will say to Thee with St. Francis of Sales, O Eternal Love, my soul seeks Thee and chooses Thee for all eternity. Come, O Holy Spirit, inflame our hearts with Thy love. Either to love or to die. To die to all other affections, to live only to the love of Jesus.

27. "For the charity of Christ presseth us" (2 Cor. v. 14). How tender and full of unction are the words with which St. Francis of Sales comments on this passage in his book of the Divine love. Hear, Theotimus, he says, nothing forces and presses the soul of man so much as love. If a man knows he is loved by any one, he feels himself forced to love him ; but if a peasant is loved by a lord, he is still more strongly forced ; and if by a monarch, how much more so! Know, then, that Jesus, the true God, has loved us so far as to suffer death, even the death of the Cross, for us. Is not this to have our hearts put under a press, and to feel them squeezed and crushed so as to force out our love with a violence which is all the stronger for being so loving.

Ah, my Jesus, since Thou dost desire to be loved by me, remind me always of the love Thou hast borne me, and of the pains Thou hast suffered to show me this love. May the remembrance of them be ever present in my mind and in the minds of all men; for it is impossible to believe what Thou hast suffered to oblige us to love, and yet not to love Thee. . Till now the cause of my negligent and wicked life has been, that I have not thought on the affection which Thou, my Jesus, hast had for me. All the while, however, I knew the great displeasure my sins gave Thee, and nevertheless I went on multiplying them. Every time I remember this I should wish to die of grief for it, and I should not now have courage to ask Thy pardon, if I did not know that Thou didst die to obtain forgiveness for me. Thou hast borne with me in order that at the sight of the wrong I have done Thee, and of the death Thou hast suffered for me, my sorrow and love towards Thee should be increased. I repent, my dear Redeemer, with all my heart for having offended Thee, and I love Thee with all my soul. After so many signs of Thy affection, and after the many mercies Thou hast shown me, I promise Thee that I will love none but Thee. Thee will I love with all my strength. Thou art, my Jesus, my Love, my All. Thou art my Love, because in Thee I have placed all my affection. Thou art my All, because I will have none but Thee. Grant, then, that always, both in life and death and throughout all eternity, I may ever call Thee my God, my Love, and my All.

28. " The charity of Christ presseth us" (2 Cor. v. 14). Let us consider anew the force of these words. The Apostle means to say that it is not so much the thought of all Christ has suffered for us that should constrain us to love Him, as the thought of the love He

has shown us in willing to suffer so much for us. This love made our Saviour say, while He was yet alive, that He was dying with the desire that the day of His death should draw near, to make us know the boundless love He had for us. "I have a baptism wherewith I am to be baptised, and how am I straitened till it be accomplished" (St. Luke xii. 50). And this same love made Him say the last night of His life, " With desire I have desired to eat this pasch with you before I suffer" (St. Luke xxii. 15).

So great, then, O my Jesus, was the desire Thou hadst to be loved by us, that all through Thy life Thou didst desire nothing but to suffer and to die for us, and so to put us under the necessity of loving Thee at least out of gratitude for so much love. Dost Thou so thirst after our love? How is it, then, that we so little desire Thine. Alas, that I should have been up to this time so foolish! Not only have I not desired Thy love, but I have brought down upon myself Thy hatred by losing my respect for Thee. My dear Redeemer, I know the evil that I have done, I detest it above all my other sins, and am sorry from the bottom of my heart. Now I desire Thy love more than all the goods of the world. My best and only Treasure, I love Thee above all things, I love Thee more than myself, I love Thee with all my soul, and I desire nothing but to love Thee and to be loved by Thee. Forget, my Jesus, the offences I have committed against Thee ; do Thou also love me, and love me exceedingly, that I may exceedingly love Thee. Thou art my Love, Thou art my Hope, Thou knowest well how weak I am ; help me, Jesus, my Love ; help me, Jesus, my Hope. Succour me also with thy prayers, O Mary, great Mother of God.

29. " Greater love than this no man hath, that a man lay down his life for his friends" (St John xv. 13). What more, O my soul, could thy God do than to give His life in order to make thee love Him ? To give his life is the greatest mark of affection which a man can give to another man who is his friend. But what love must that have been which our Creator has shown for us, in choosing to die for us His creatures !   This is what St. John was considering when he wrote, " In this we have known the charity of God, because He hath laid down His life for us" (1 St. John iii. 16). Indeed, if faith did not teach us that a God has willed to die to show us His love, who would ever have been able to believe it ? Ah, my Jesus, I believe that Thou hast died for me, and therefore I confess that I deserve a thousand hells for having repaid with insults and ingratitude the love which Thou hast borne me in giving Thy life for me. I thank Thy mercy, which has promised to forgive those that repent. Trusting, then, in this sweet promise, I hope for pardon from Thee, repenting, as I do, with all my heart for having so often despised Thy love. But since Thy love has not abandoned me, overcome by Thy love I consecrate myself all to Thee. Thou, my Jesus, hast finished Thy life by dying in agony on a cross ; and what recompense can I, a miserable creature, make Thee? I consecrate to Thee my life, accepting with love all the sufferings which shall come to me from Thy hand both in life and death. Softened and confounded at the great mercy Thou hast used towards me, I hold fast Thy Cross ; at Thy feet thus will I live and die. Ah, my Redeemer, by the love Thou hast borne me in dying for me, do not permit me ever to separate myself from Thee again. Make me always live and die in Thy embrace. My Jesus, my Jesus, I repeat, make me always live and die united to Thee.

30. " I, if I be lifted up from the earth, will draw all things unto Myself (St. John xii. 32). Thou hast said, then, my Saviour, that when hanging on the Cross Thou wouldst draw all our hearts unto Thyself ; why is it that for so many years my heart has gone far away from Thee? Ah, it is not Thy fault. How many times hast Thou called me to Thy love and I have turned a deaf ear ? How many times too hast Thou pardoned me, and affectionately warned me by remorse of conscience not to offend Thee again, and I have repeated my offence? Ah, my Jesus, send me not to hell, because there I shall be cursing forever these graces which Thou hast given me ; so that these graces, the illuminations Thou hast given me, Thy calls, Thy patience in bearing with me, the Blood Thou didst shed to save me, would be the most cruel of all the torments of hell. But now I hear Thee call me again, and Thou dost say to me, with the greatest love, as if I had never offended Thee, " Love the Lord thy God with all thy heart." Thou dost command me to love Thee, and to love Thee with all my heart. But if Thou didst not command me, O Jesus, how could I live without loving Thee, after so many proofs of Thy love ? Yes, I love Thee, my supreme Good, I love Thee with all my heart. I love Thee because Thou dost command me to love Thee. I love Thee because Thou art worthy of infinite love. I love Thee, and desire nothing eke but to love Thee, and nothing else do I fear except being separated from Thee, and living without Thy love. Ah, my crucified Love, permit not that I ever leave off loving Thee. Ever call to my remembrance the death Thou hast undergone for me. Remind me of the endearments Thou hast used towards me ; and may the remembrance of them incite me more and more to love Thee, and to spend myself for Thee, who hast spent Thyself as a victim of love on the Cross for me.

31. "He that spared not His only Son, but delivered Him up for us all, how hath He not also . . . given us all things" (Rom. viii. 32). What flames of love ought not these words to enkindle in our hearts, " delivered Him up for us all" ! Divine justice, offended by our sins, must be satisfied ; what, therefore, does God do ? To pardon us, He wills that His Son should be condemned to death, and should Himself pay the penalty due from us : " He spared not His only Son." O God, if the Eternal Father were capable of suffering, what grief would He. not have experienced in condemning to death, for the sins of His servants, His well-beloved and innocent Son ! Let us imagine we see the Eternal Father, with Jesus dead in His arms, and saying, " For the wickedness of My people have I struck Him" (Is. liii. 8). Rightly did St. Francis of Paula exclaim, in ecstasy of love, when meditating on the death of Jesus Christ, ' O Love ! O Love ! O Love!' On the other hand, with what confidence ought not the following words to inspire us, " How hath He not also, with Him, given us all things?"   And how, my God, should I fear that Thou shouldst not give me pardon, perseverance, Thy love, Thy Paradise, and all the graces that I can hope for, now that Thou hast given me that which is most dear to Thee, even Thine own Son ? I know what I must do to obtain every good from Thee,—I must ask for it for the love of Jesus Christ; of this Jesus Christ Himself assures me : " Amen, amen, I say to you, if you ask the Father anything in My name, He will give it *you.*"

My supreme and eternal God, · I have hitherto despised Thy majesty and goodness : now I love Thee above all things ; and because I love Thee, I repent with all my heart of having offended Thee, and I would rather accept any chastisement than ever more offend Thee. Pardon me, and grant me those graces which I now ask of Thee, confiding in the promise of Jesus Christ. In the name of Jesus Christ I beseech Thee to give me holy perseverance to death ; give me a pure and perfect love towards Thee ; give me an entire conformity with Thy holy will ; give me finally Paradise. I ask for all, and hope for all, from Thee, through the merits of Jesus Christ. I deserve nothing ; I am worthy of punishment, not of graces ; but Thou dost deny nothing to those who pray to Thee for the love of Jesus Christ. Ah, my good God, I see that Thou dost wish me to be all Thine ; I also wish to be Thine, and will not fear that my sins should prevent my being all Thine,— Jesus Christ has already satisfied for them,—and Thou, besides, art ready, for the love of Jesus Christ, to give me all I desire. This is my desire, and my request ; my God, hear me ! I wish to love Thee, to love Thee exceedingly ; and to be altogether Thine.   Most holy Mary, help me.

32. " But we preach Christ crucified, unto the Jews indeed a stumbling-block, and unto the Gentiles foolishness" (1 Cor. i. 23). St. Paul assures us that the Gentiles, hearing it preached that the Son of God had been crucified for the salvation of mankind, reckoned it folly : " but unto the Gentiles foolishness as if they said, Who can believe such folly, that a God should have willed to die

for the love of His creatures !' It seems a foolish thing,' says St. Gregory, 'that a God should will to die for the salvation of man.' St. Mary Magdalen of Pazzi, also wrapt in love, exclaims in an ecstasy, 'Do you not know, my sisters, that my Jesus is nothing but love? rather He is mad with love. I say that Thou art mad with love, my Jesus, and I will always say so.'

My beloved Redeemer, oh, that I could possess the hearts of all men, and with them love Thee as Thou deservest to be loved ! O God of love, why after Thou hast shed all Thy blood in this world and given Thy life for the love of mankind,—why, I say, are there so few men who burn with Thy love? For this end didst Thou come, namely, to kindle in our hearts the fire of Thy love, and Thou desirest nothing but to see it enkindled. " I am come to cast fire on the earth, and what will I but that it be kindled ?" (St. Luke xii. *id.*) I pray, then, with the Holy Church, in my name and in the name of every one living, kindle in them the fire of Thy love ; enkindle them, en-kindle them, enkindle them! My God, Thou art all goodness, all love, all infinite sweetness, boundless in love ; make Thyself known to all, make Thyself loved. I am not ashamed of praying thus to Thee,—although up to this time I have been more guilty than others in despising Thy love, —because now enlightened by Thy grace, and wounded by the many arrows of love Thou hast shot forth from Thy burning and loving Heart into my soul, I am determined no longer to be ungrateful to Thee as I have hitherto been ; but I will love Thee with all my strength, I desire to burn with Thy love, and this Thou hast to grant me. I look not for sensible consolations in loving Thee, I do not deserve them, neither do I ask for them ; it is enough for me to love Thee. I love Thee, my sovereign Good j I love Thee, my God and my All.

33. " The Lord hath laid on Him the iniquity of us all. . . . And the Lord was pleased to bruise Him" (Isaias liii. 6, 10). Behold the extent of Divine love towards man ! The Eternal Father loads the shoulders of His Son with our sins ; "and He was pleased to bruise Him." He willed that His own Son should suffer with the utmost rigour ail the punishment due to us, making Him die on an ignominious cross overwhelmed with torments. The Apostle is just; then, when speaking of this love, to call it too much love to ordain that we should receive life through the death of His beloved Son. " For His exceeding charity wherewith He loved us, even when we were dead in sins, hath quickened us together in Christ" (Eph. ii. 4, 5).

Thou hast, then, my God, loved me too much, and I have been too ungrateful in offending Thee and turning my back upon Thee. Ah, Eternal Father, look upon Thine Only-Begotten mangled and dead on that cross for me, and for the love of Him pardon me and draw my heart wholly to Thyself to love Thee. "A contrite and humble heart, O God, Thou wilt not despise." For the love of Jesus Christ who died for our sins Thou canst not despise a soul that humbles itself and repents. I know myself to be deserving of a thousand hells, but I repent with my whole heart for having offended Thee, the supreme Good. Reject me not, but have pity on me. But I am not content with a simple pardon ; I desire that Thou shouldst give me a great love towards Thee, that I may compensate for ail the offences I have committed against Thee. I love Thee, infinite Goodness. I love Thee, O God of love. It is but little if I should die and annihilate myself for Thy sake. I desire to know how to love Thee as Thou deservest. But Thou knowest I can do nothing; do Thou make me grateful for the immense love Thou hast had for me. I beg this of Thee for the love of Jesus Thy Son. Grant that I may overcome everything in this life to please Thee, and that in death I may expire entirely united to Thy will, and so come to love Thee face to face with a perfect and eternal love in Paradise.

34. " I am the Good Shepherd. The good shepherd giveth his life for his sheep" (St. John x. 11). My Jesus, what dost Thou say ? What shepherd would ever give his life for his sheep ? Thou alone, because Thou art a God of infinite love, canst say, " And I lay down My life for My sheep" (St. John x. 15). Thou alone hast been able to show to the world this excess of love, that being our God and our Supreme Lord, Thou hast yet willed to die for us. It was of this excess of love that Moses and Elias spoke on Mount Tabor : " They spoke of His decease that He should accomplish in Jerusalem" (St. Luke ix. 31). Hence S& John exhorts us to love a God who was the first to love us : " Let us therefore love God, because God first hath loved us" (1 St. John iv. 19). As if he said, If we will not love this God for His infinite goodness, let us love Him at least for the love which He has borne us in suffering willingly the pains that were due to us. Remember, then, my Jesus, that I am one of those sheep for whom Thou hast given Thy life. Ah, cast on me one of those looks of pity with which Thou didst regard me once when Thou wast dying on the Cross for me ; look on me, change me, and save me. Thou hast called Thyself the loving Shepherd who, finding the lost sheep, takes it with joy and carries it on his shoulders, and then calls his friends to rejoice with him : "Rejoice with me, because I have found my sheep that was lost" (St. Luke xv. 6). Behold, I am the lost sheep; seek me and find me : "I have gone astray like a sheep that is lost ; seek Thy servant" (Ps. cxviii. 176).

If through my fault Thou hast not yet found me, take me now and unite me and bind me to Thee, that Thou, mayest not lose me again. The bond must be that of Thy love ; if Thou dost not bind me with this sweet chain, Thou wilt again lose me. Ah, it is not Thou who hast been wanting in binding me by holy love ; but I, an ungrateful wretch, who have continually fled from Thee. But now I pray Thee, by that infinite mercy which caused Thee to come down to the earth, to find me. Ah, bind me ; but bind me with a double chain of love, that Thou mayest not lose me again, and that I may no more lose Thee. I renounce all the goods and pleasures of the world, and offer myself to suffer every pain, every death, provided that I live and die always united to Thee. I love Thee, my sweet Jesus ; I love Thee, my good Shepherd, who hast died for Thy lost sheep ; but know that this sheep now loves Thee more than himself, and desires nothing but to love Thee and to be consumed by Thy love. Have pity on him, then, and permit him not ever again to be separated from Thee.

35. " I lay down My life.....................No man taketh it away from Me ; but I lay it down of Myself" (St. John x. 17, 18). Behold, then, the Word Incarnate, urged alone by the love He preserves towards us, accepts the death of the Cross to give to man the life he had lost. Behold, says St. Thomas, a God does for man more than He could have done if man had been (so to speak) His god, and as if God could never have been happy without man : 'As if,' these are the words of the saint, 'man had been God's god, as if God could not be happy without him.' We sinned, and by sinning merited eternal punishment; and what does Jesus do? He takes upon Himself the obligation of satisfaction, and He pays for us by His sufferings and His death : " Surely He hath borne our infirmities and carried our sorrows" (Is. liii. 4).

Ah, my Jesus, since I have been the cause of all the bitterness and anguish Thou didst suffer while living on this earth, I pray Thee make me share the grief Thou didst feel for my sins, and give me confidence in Thy Passion. What would have become of me, my Lord, if Thou hadst not deigned to satisfy for me ? O Infinite Majesty, I repent with my whole heart for having outraged Thee ; but I hope for pity from Thee, who art infinite goodness. Arise, O Saviour of the world, and apply to my soul tho fruit of Thy death, and from an ungrateful rebel make me become such a true son as to love Thee alone, and to fear nothing but to displease Thee. May that same love which made Thee die on the Cross for me, destroy in me all earthly affections. My Jesus, take my whole body to Thyself in such a way that it may only serve to obey Thee; take my heart, that it may desire nothing but Thy pleasure ; take my whole will, that it may wish for nothing but what is according to Thy will. I embrace Thee, and press Thee to my heart, my Redeemer. Ah, do not disdain to unite Thyself to me. I love Thee, O God of love. I love Thee, my only Good. How could I have the heart to leave Thee again, now that Thou hast taught me how much Thou hast loved me, and how many mercies Thou hast shown me, changing the punishments that were due to me into graces and caresses? O holy Virgin, obtain for me the grace of being grateful to thy Son.

36. " Blotting out the handwriting of the decree that was against us, which was contrary to us. And He hath taken the same out of the way, fastening it to the cross" (Colos. ii. 14). The sentence was already recorded against us that was to condemn us to eternal death, as rebels of the offended Majesty of God. And what has Jesus Christ done? With His Blood He has cancelled the writing of the condemnation, and, to deliver us from all fear, He has fastened it to His own Cross, on which He died to satisfy for us to the Divine justice. My soul, behold the obligation thou art under to thy Redeemer; and hear how the Holy Spirit now reminds thee: " Forget not the kindness of thy Surety" (Ecclus. xxix. 19). Forget not the kindness of thy Surety, who, taking upon Himself thy debts, has paid them for thee, and behold, the pledge of the payment has been already fixed to the Cross. When, therefore, thou dost remember thy sins, look upon the Cross, and have confidence; look on that sacred wood stained with the Blood of the Lamb of God sacrificed for thy love, and hope in and love a God who has loved thee so much.

Yes, my Jesus, I hope everything from Thy infinite goodness. It is a property of thy Divine Nature to render good for evil to those who repent of their sins, are sorry for having committed them, and who love Thee. Yes, I am sorry above all things, my beloved Redeemer, for having so much despised Thy goodness, and, wounded by Thy love, I love Thee, and I ardently desire to please Thee in everything that is Thy will. Alas! when I was in sin, I was the servant of the devil, and he was my master. Now that I hope to remain in Thy grace, Thou alone, my Jesus, art the only Lord of my heart, and my only Love. Take possession of me, then; keep me always, possess me entirely; for Thine only do I desire to be. No, never more will I forget the pains Thou hast suffered for me; so shall I be more and more inflamed, and increase in Thy love. I love Thee, my most dear Redeemer; I love Thee, O Word Incarnate; my Treasure, my AU, I love Thee, I love Thee.

37. " But if any man sin, we have an Advocate with the Father, Jesus Christ the Just, and He is the propitiation for our sins" (1 St. John ii. 1, 2). Oh, what great confidence do these words give to penitent sinners! Jesus Christ is in heaven, advocating their cause, and He is certain to obtain pardon for them. The devil, when a sinner has escaped from his chains, tempts him to be diffident of obtaining pardon. But St. Paul encourages him, saying, "Who is He that shall condemn? Jesus Christ that died, . . . who also maketh intercession for us" (Rom. viii. 34). The Apostle means to say, If we detest the sins we have committed, why do we fear? Who is He who will condemn us? It is Jesus Christ, the same who died that we might not be condemned, and who is now in heaven, where He is advocating our cause. He goes on to say, "Who then shall separate us from the love of Christ?" (Rom. viii. 35.) As if he would say, But after we have been pardoned with so much love by Jesus Christ, and have been received into His grace, who could have the heart to turn their back upon Him, and separate himself from His love?

No, my Jesus, I no longer rely upon myself so as to live separated from Thee and deprived of Thy love. I weep over the unhappy days when I lived without Thy grace. Now I hope that Thou hast pardoned me. I love Thee, and Thou lovest me. But Thou dost love me with a boundless love, and I love Thee so little; give me more love. Infinite Goodness, I repent above all things for having hitherto so ill-treated Thee; now I love Thee above all things, I love Thee more than myself; and I take more delight, my God, in knowing that Thou art infinitely blessed than in my own happiness, because I love Thee better—being, as Thou art, worthy of infinite love—than myself, who deserve nothing but hell. My Jesus, I wish for nothing from Thee, but Thyself.

38. " Come to Me, all you that labour, and are burdened, and I will refresh you" (St. Matt. xi. 28). Let us listen to Jesus Christ, who, from the Cross to which He is nailed, and from the Altar where He dwells under the sacramental species, calls us poor afflicted sinners to console us and enrich us with His graces. Oh, what two great mysteries of hope and love to us are the Passion of Jesus and the Sacrament of the Eucharist! — mysteries which, if faith did not make us certain of them, would be incredible. That God should deign to shed even the very last drop of His Blood! (for this is the signification of the word "effundetur"). "This is My Blood, which shall be shed for many" (St. Matt. xxvi. 28). And why? To atone for our sins. And then to will to give His own Body as food for our souls,—that Body which had been already sacrificed on the Cross for our salvation! These sublime mysteries must surely soften the hardest hearts, and raise up the most desperate sinners. Finally, the Apostle says that in Jesus Christ we are enriched with every good, so that no grace is wanting to us: " In all things you are made rich in Him. . . . . So that nothing is wanting to you in any grace" (1 Cor. i. 5, 7). It is enough that we invoke this God for Him to have mercy on us; and He will abound mu grace to all who pray to Him, as the same Apostle assures us: " Rich unto all who call upon Him" (Rom. x. 12).

If, then, my Saviour, I have reason to despair of pardon for the offences and treacheries I have been guilty of towards Thee, I have still greater reason to trust in Thy goodness. My Father, I have forsaken Thee, like an ungrateful son; but I now return to Thy feet, full of sorrow and covered with confusion for the many mercies Thou hast shown me; and I say with shame, " Father, I am not worthy to be called Thy son." Thou hast said there is rejoicing in heaven when a sinner is converted: " There shall be joy in heaven upon one sinner that doth penance." Behold, I leave all, and turn to Thee, my crucified Father; I repent with my whole heart for having treated Thee with such contempt as to turn my back upon Thee. Receive me again to Thy grace, and inflame me with Thy holy love, so that I may never leave Thee again. Thou hast said: "I am come that they may have life, and may have it more abundantly" (St. John x. 10). Wherefore I hope to receive from Thee, not only Thy grace as I enjoyed it before I offended Thee, but a grace more abundant, which shall make me become all on fire with Thy love. Oh, that I could love Thee, my God, as Thou dost deserve to be loved! I love Thee above all things. I love Thee more than myself. I love Thee with all my heart; and I aspire after heaven, where I shall love Thee for all eternity. "What is there to me in heaven, and besides Thee what have I desired on the earth? O God, God of my heart and my portion forever." Ah, God of my heart, take and keep possession of all my heart, and drive from it every affection that does not belong to Thee. Thou art my only Treasure, my only Love. I wish for Thee alone, and nothing more. O Mary, my hope, by thy prayers draw me all to God.

MEDITATIONS ON THE PASSION OF JESUS CHRIST FOR EACH DAY OF THE WEEK. MEDITATION FOR SUNDAY. ON THE LOVE OF JESUS IN SUFFERING FOR US.

1. The time since the coming of Jesus Christ is no longer a time of fear, but a time of love, as the prophet foretold : " Thy time is a time of lovers" (Ezech. xvi. 8), because a God has been seen to die for us : " Christ hath loved us, and hath given Himself up for us" (Eph. v. 2). Under the old law, before that the Word was made flesh, man might, so to speak, have doubted whether God loved him with a tender love ; but after having seen Him suffer a bloody and ignominious death for us on a cross of infamy, we can no longer possibly doubt that He loves us with the utmost tenderness. And who will ever arrive at comprehending what was the excess of the love of the Son of God in being willing to pay the penalty of our sins ? And yet this is ' of faith.' " Truly He hath borne our griefs and carried our sorrows. He was wounded for our iniquities ; He was bruised for our sins" (Isaias liii. 4, 5). All this was the work of the great love which He bears us : "He hath loved us, and hath washed us in His Blood" (Apoc. i. 5). In order to wash us from the defilements of our sins, He was willing to empty His veins of all His Blood, to make of it for us, as it were, a bath of salvation. O infinite mercy ! O infinite love of a God!

Ah, my Redeemer, too surely hast Thou obliged me to love Thee ; too surely should I be ungrateful to Thee, if I did not love Thee with my whole heart. My Jesus, I have despised Thee, because I have lived in forgetfulness of Thy love ; but Thou hast not forgotten me. I have turned my back on Thee ; but Thou hast come near to me. I have offended Thee, and Thou hast so many times forgiven me. I have returned to offend Thee ; Thou hast returned to pardon me. Ah, my Lord, by that affection with which Thou lovedst me on the Cross, bind me tightly to Thee by the sweet chains of Thy love ; but bind me in such wise that I may never more see myself separated from Thee. I love Thee, Q my chief Good; and I desire to love Thee ever for the time to come.

2. That which ought most to inflame our love for Jesus Christ is not so much the death, the sorrows, and the ignominies which He suffered for us, as the end which He had in view in suffering for us so many and such great pains—and that was, to show us His love and to win our hearts : " In this have we known the charity of God, because He hath laid down His life for us" (1 St. John iii. 16). For it was not absolutely necessary in order to save us that Jesus should suffer so much and die for us; it were enough that He should pour forth but one drop of blood, should shed but one tear only for our salvation; this drop of blood, this tear shed by a Man-God, were sufficient to save a thousand worlds : but He willed to pour out all His Blood, He willed to lose His life in a sea of sorrows and contempt, to make us understand the great love which He has for us, and to oblige us to love Him. " The charity of Christ urgeth us," says St. Paul (2 Cor. v. 14). He says not the Passion or the death, but the love of Jesus Christ constrains us to love Him. And what were we that Thou, O Lord, wert willing at such a great price to purchase our love? " Christ died for all, that they too who live should not now live to themselves, but to Him who died for them" (2 Cor. v. 14,15). Hast Thou, then, my Jesus, died for us, that we might live wholly for Thee alone, and for Thy love? But, my poor Lord (permit me so to call Thee), Thou art so full of love that Thou hast suffered so much in order to be loved by men. But, after all, what is the number of those who love Thee? I see all these intent on loving,—some their riches, some honours, some pleasures, some their relations, some their friends, some, in fine, the beasts; but of those who truly love Thee, who alone art worthy of love, oh, how few such do I see! O God, how few they are ! Among these few, nevertheless, I too desire to be, who at one time, just like the rest, offended Thee by loving filth ; now, however, I love Thee above every other good. O my Jesus, the pain which Thou hast suffered for me urgently obliges me to love Thee ; but that which the more binds me to Thee and enkindles me to love Thee, is hearing of the love which Thou hast shown in suffering so much, to the end that Thou mayest be loved by me. Yes, O my Lord, most worthy of love, Thou, through love, hast given Thyself wholly to me ; I through love give myself wholly to Thee. Thou for love of me didst die; I for love of Thee am willing to die when and as it shall please Thee. Accept of my loving Thee, and help me by Thy grace to do so worthily.

3. There is no means which can more surely kindle in us Divine love than to consider the Passion of Jesus Christ. St. Bonaventure says that the Wounds of Jesus Christ, because they are wounds of love, are darts which wound hearts the most hard, are flames which set on fire souls the most cold : ' O Wounds, wounding stony hearts, and inflaming frozen minds!' It is impossible that a soul which believes and thinks on the Passion of the Lord should offend Him and not love Him, nay, rather that it should not run into a holy madness of love, at seeing a God as it were mad for love of us : ' We have seen,' says St. Laurence Justinian, 'Wisdom infatuated by too much love.' Hence it is that the Gentiles, as the Apostle says, when hearing him preach the Passion of Jesus crucified, thought it a folly : " We preach Christ crucified, to the Jews indeed a scandal, but to the Gentiles foolishness" (1 Cor. i. 25). How is it possible (said they) that a God, almighty and most happy, such as He who is preached to us, could have been willing to die for His creatures ?

Ah, God enamoured of men, how is it possible (let us say this who by faith believe that He really died for love of us),—how is it possible that a goodness so great, that such a love, should remain so badly corresponded to by men? It is wont to be said that love is repaid with love; but Thy love—with what manner of love can it be ever repaid ? it would be necessary that another God should die for Thee, to make recompense for the love which Thou hast borne towards us in dying for us. O Cross, O Wounds, O Death of Jesus, you bind me closely to love Him. O God, eternal and infinitely worthy of love, I love Thee, I desire to live only for Thee, only to please Thee ; tell me what Thou willest with me, and I will wholly to do it. Mary, my hope, pray to Jesus for me.

MEDITATION FOR MONDAY. ON THE SWEAT OF BLOOD, AND THE AGONY OF JESUS IN THE GARDEN.

1. Our loving Redeemer, as the hour of His death waft approaching, went away into the Garden of Gethsemani, in which of His own Self He made a beginning of His own most bitter Passion, by giving free way to fear and weariness and sorrow, which came to torment Him: " He began to fear, and to be heavy ; to grow sorrowful, and to be sad" (St. Mark xiv. 33 ; St. Matt. xxvi. 37). He began, then, to feel a great fear and weariness of death, and of the pains which must accompany it. At that moment there were represented to His mind most vividly the scourges, the thorns, the nails, the cross, which then, not one after the other, but all together, came to afflict Him; and specially there stood before Him that desolate death which He must endure, abandoned by every comfort, human and Divine ; so that, terrified by the sight of the horrid apparatus of such torments and ignominies, He besought His Eternal Father to be freed from them : " My Father, if it is possible let this chalice pass from Me" (St. Matt, xxvi. 39). But how is this ? Was it not this same Jesus who had so much desired to suffer and die for men, saying, " I have a baptism to be baptised with, and how am I straitened until it be accomplished"? (St. Luke xii. 50.) How, then, does He fear these pains and this death? Nay, it was with good will He was going to die for us: but to the end we might not suppose that through any virtue of His Divinity He could die without pain, for this it Was He made this prayer to His Father, to make us know that He not only died for love of us, but that the death He died was so tormenting as to greatly terrify Him.

2. And then to torment the Lord thus afflicted was added a great sorrowfulness—such that, as He said, it was enough to cause death: "My soul is sorrowful even unto death" (St. Matt. xxvi. 38). But, Lord, to deliver Thyself from the death which men are preparing for Thee, is in Thy hands, if it so please Thee: why, then, afflict Thyself? Ah, it was not so much the torments of His Passion as our sins which afflicted the Heart of our loving Saviour. He had come on earth to take away our sins ; but then seeing that, after all His Passion, there would yet be committed such iniquities in the world, this was the pang which before dying reduced Him to death, and made Him sweat living blood in such abundance that the ground all round about Him was bathed therewith : "And His sweat became as drops of blood running down on the earth" (St. Luke xxii. 44). Yes, this precisely it was,—because Jesus then saw before Him all the sins which men were going to commit after His death, all the hatred, the impurities, thefts, blasphemies, sacrileges ; and because then each sin, with its own malice, came like a cruel wild-beast to rend His Heart. So that He seemed to be saying, Is this, then, O men, the recompense which you make to My love ? Ah, if I could see you grateful to Me, with what gladness should I now go to die ; but to see, after so many pains of Mine, so many sins ; after such great love, such great ingratitude, —this it is which causes Me to sweat blood.

Were they then my sins, my beloved Jesus, which in that hour so greatly afflicted Thee ? If, then, I had sinned less, Thou wouldst have suffered less. The more pleasure I have taken in offending Thee, so much the more horror I then caused Thee. How is it that I do not die of grief in thinking that I have repaid Thy love by increasing Thy pain and sorrow ? Have I, then, afflicted that Heart which has so much loved me ? With creatures I have been grateful enough ; with Thee only have I been ungrateful. My Jesus, pardon me ; I repent with all my heart.

3. At seeing Himself burdened with our sins, Jesus " fell down on His face" (St. Matt. xxvi. 39). He prostrated Himself with His face on the earth, as ashamed to lift up His eyes to heaven, and lying in the agony of death He prayed a long time : " Being in an agony He prayed."

At that time, my Lord, Thou didst pray for me to the Eternal Father to pardon me, offering Thyself to die in satisfaction for my sins.

O my soul, how is it that thou dost not surrender thyself to such great love? How, believing this, canst thou love aught else than Jesus? Come ! cast thyself at the feet of thy Saviour in His Agony, and say to Him, My dear Redeemer, how is it that Thou couldest love one who had so offended Thee ? How couldest Thou suffer death for me, seeing my ingratitude? Make me, I pray Thee, partaker of this sorrow which Thou didst feel in the Garden. Now I abhor all my sins, and unite this abhorrence with that which Thou then hadst for them. O love of my Jesus, Thou art my Love ! Lord, I love Thee, and for love of Thee I offer myself to suffer every pain, any death. Ah, by the merits of the Agony which Thou didst suffer in the Garden, give me holy perseverance ! Mary, my hope, pray to Jesus for me.

MEDITATION FOR TUESDAY. OF THE IMPRISONMENT OF JESUS, AND HIS BEING LED AWAY TO THE JEWS.

1. Judas arrives at the Garden, and when he had betrayed his Master with a kiss, there fell on Jesus those insolent servants, and bound Him as a malefactor : " They took Jesus and bound Him" (St. John xviii. 12). A God bound ? and wherefore ? and by whom ? By His own very creatures. Angels of heaven, what say you to this ? And Thou, my Jesus, why cause Thyself to be bound? 'O King of kings' (mourns St. Bernard), ' what hast Thou to do with chains ! What can the bonds of slaves and of the guilty have to do with Thee, the King of kings, and the Saint of saints ? But if men dare to bind Thee, Thou who art Almighty, why dost Thou not deliver and free Thyself from the torments which these barbarous men provide for Thee ? Ah, but it is not these ropes which tie Thee. Thy love towards us is it which binds Thee and condemns Thee to death.

Look, O man, says St. Bernard, how these dogs ill-treat Jesus : one drags Him, another pushes Him, another binds Him, another smites Him. And look how Jesus, like to a gentle lamb, without resistance suffers Himself to be led to the sacrifice. And you, disciples, what are you doing ? Why do you not run up to rescue Him out of the hands of His enemies ? Why at least do you not accompany Him to defend His innocence before His judges? Ah, my God, even His disciples too, at seeing Him taken and bound, take to flight and abandon Him : " Then His disciples leaving Him, all fled" (St Mark xiv. 50). O my Jesus, thus abandoned, who shall ever undertake Thy defence, if these Thy most dear disciples forsake Thee? But, alas, to think that this injury ended not with Thy Passion ! How many souls after having consecrated themselves to follow Thee, and after having received from Thee many special graces, have through some passion of vile interest, or human respect, or defiling pleasure, abandoned Thee. Unhappy me, of the number of these ungrateful ones am I. My Jesus, pardon me, for I wish never more to leave Thee. I love Thee, and desire sooner to lose my life than ever again to lose Thy grace.

2. When brought before Caiaphas, Jesus was questioned by him about His disciples and His doctrine. Jesus answered that He had not spoken in private but in public, and that those very persons who were standing round Him well knew what He had taught : "I spoke openly to the world: lo, these know what I said" (St. John xviii. 20, 21). But at this answer one of the servants, treating Him as if too bold, gave Him a horrible blow on the cheek, saying to Him, " Dost Thou answer the high-priest so?" (St. John xviii. 22.) O the patience of my Lord!

How did an answer so gentle deserve an insult so great in the presence of so many people and of the high-priest himself, who, instead of reproving this insolent servant, rather by his silence applauds him? Ah, my Jesus, Thou didst suffer all this to pay the penalty for those affronts which I in my rashness have done to Thee. My Love, I thank Thee for it. O Eternal Father, pardon me through the merits of Jesus. My Redeemer, I love Thee more than myself.

Next, the iniquitous high-priest asked Him whether He were truly the Son of God. Jesus, through respect for the Divine Name, affirmed that this was the truth; and then Caiaphas rent his clothes, saying that Jesus had blasphemed, and they all cried out that He was worthy of death : " But they answering said, He is guilty of death" (St Matt. xxvi. 66). Yes, my Saviour, truly art Thou guilty of death, since Thou art bound to make satisfaction for me who am guilty of eternal death. But because Thou by Thy death hast acquired life for me, it is but just that I should spend my life wholly for Thee. I love Thee, and desire nothing else than to love Thee. And since Thou, who art the greatest of all kings, wert willing, through love of me, to be despised more than all men, I, for love of Thee, am willing to suffer every affront which can befall me. Give me, I pray Thee, strength to bear them through the merits of the insults done to Thee.

3. The council of priests having declared Jesus Christ guilty of death, the rabble set itself to ill-treat Him all the night through with blows and kicks, and spitting on Him as a man already declared infamous : " Then did they spit in His face, and buffeted Him" (St. Matt. xxvi. 67). And then they mocked Him, saying, " Prophesy to us, O Christ, who it is that struck Thee" (Ibid. 68). Ah, my dear Jesus, these buffet Thee, and spit in Thy face, and Thou art silent ; and as a lamb without complaining Thou sufferest all for us: "As a lamb before the shearer He shall be dumb, and shall not open His mouth" (Is. liii. 7). But if these know Thee not, I confess Thee for my God and Lord, and protest that I well understand that how much soever Thou innocently sufferest, it is all for love of me. I thank Thee for it, my Jesus, and love Thee with all my heart.

When day was come they led Jesus Christ to Pilate to have Him condemned. Pilate, nevertheless, declared Him innocent; but to rid himself of the Jews, who followed to make a tumult, he sent Him to Herod, who, desiring to see some miracle through mere curiosity, began to question Him about divers things. But Jesus, not deigning to answer this wicked one, was silent and gave him no answer. Wherefore this proud one offered Him many insults, and especially made them clothe Him as a madman in a white robe. O eternal Wisdom, O my Jesus, there lacked only this other injury, that Thou shouldst be treated as a fool ! O God, that even I in time past should have, like Herod, thus despised Thee. Do not, I pray Thee, chastise me, as Thou didst Herod, by depriving me of Thy voice. Herod knew Thee not for what Thou art ; but I confess Thee for my God: Herod repented not of having injured Thee; but I repent of it with all my heart : Herod loved Thee not; but I love Thee above everything. Ah, deny me not the voice of Thy inspirations. Tell me what Thou wouldst have of me, for by Thy grace I am willing to do all.   Mary, my hope, pray to Jesus for me.

MEDITATION FOR WEDNESDAY. THE SCOURGING OF JESUS CHRIST.

1. Pilate, seeing that the Jews ceased not to demand the death of Jesus, condemned Him to be scourged : " Then therefore Pilate took Jesus and scourged Him" (St. John xix. 1). The unjust judge thought by this to quiet His enemies; but this resource turned out the more grievous for Jesus Christ. The Jews, however, discovering that Pilate after thus punishing Him wished to let Him go free, —as indeed he had already sufficiently indicated, "I will chastise Him therefore, and release Him ;" " I will chastise Him therefore, and let Him go" (St. Luke xxiii. 16, 22),— they bribed the executioners to scourge Him to such a degree that He might die under the torment. Enter, O my soul, into the judgment-hall of Pilate, made on this day the horrible theatre of the pain and ignominies of thy Redeemer, and see how Jesus, when He had arrived there, of His own accord strips Himself of His clothes (as was revealed to St. Bridget) and embraces the column ; thereby giving to men a most clear testimony how voluntarily He submitted for their sakes to pains the most unmerciful, and how much He loved them. Look how this innocent Lamb goes with head bent down, and, as if all blushing through modesty, awaits this great torment. Lo, how these barbarians, like rabid dogs, already fly at Him. Behold there these pitiless executioners ; look how among them one strikes His breast, another His shoulders, another His thighs, and another other parts of His Body; even His Sacred Head and beautiful Face escape not from the blows. Alas ! already flows that Divine Blood from every part ; already are the scourges saturated with blood, and the hands of the executioners, the column, and even the earth. O God, the smiters, no longer finding any whole part to strike, add wound to wound, and lacerate all over that most holy Flesh : " And they have added to the grief of My wounds" (Ps. lxviii. 27). O my soul, how couldst thou offend a God who was scourged for thee? And Thou, my Jesus, how couldst Thou suffer so much for one so ungrateful? O Wounds of Jesus, you are my hope. O my Jesus, Thou art the only love of my soul.

2. Exceedingly tormenting was this scourging for Jesus Christ, because there were sixty executioners (as was revealed to St. Mary Magdalen of Pazzi) succeeding one another. The scourges chosen for this work were the most severe, and every blow made a wound. The strokes, besides, reached to many thousand ; so that even the very bones of the sides of our Lord were laid bare, as was revealed to St. Bridget. In a word, such was the havoc they made, that Pilate thought to be able to move even His enemies to compassion; wherefore he showed Him to them on the balcony, saying, " Behold the man" (St. John xix. 5). And well did the prophet Isaias foretell to us the pitiful state to which our Saviour was to be reduced by His scourging, saying that His Flesh was to be all rent : " He was bruised for our sins" (Is. liii. 5); and His blessed Body to become like the body of one leprous—all sores: " And we accounted Him one leprous" (Ibid. 4).

Ah, my Jesus, I thank Thee for Thy great love. It grieves me that I too joined in scourging Thee. I curse all my sinful pleasures which cost Thee so much pain. Make me often remember, O Lord, the love which Thou hast borne me, to the end that I may love Thee, and never offend Thee any more. Alas, what a special hell should there be fer me if, after having known Thy love, and after Thou hast so often forgiven me, I should miserably offend Thee afresh, and damn myself ! Ah, this very love and pity would be for me another hell still more tormenting. No, my Love, permit it not I love Thee, O my highest Good. I love Thee with all my heart, and will love Thee forever.

3. To pay the penalty, then, for our crimes, and specially of impurity, Jesus was willing to suffer this great torment in His innocent Flesh : " He was wounded for our iniquities" (Is. liii. 5). Is it we, then, O Lord, who have offended God, and Thou who hast been willing to pay the penalty? For ever blessed be Thine infinite charity. What would have been my lot, my Jesus, if Thou hadst not made satisfaction for me ? Oh, that I had never offended Thee ! But if by sinning I have despised Thy love, now I have no other desire than to love Thee and to be loved by Thee. Thou hast said that Thou lovest him who loveth Thee. I love Thee above everything, I love Thee with my whole soul : do Thou make me worthy of Thy love. Yes, I hope that Thou hast already pardoned me, and that at present Thou of Thy goodness lovest me. Ah, my dear Redeemer, bind me ever more indissolubly to Thy love : suffer me not to separate myself ever from Thee. Lo, I am all Thine ; chastise me as Thou willest, but permit me not to remain deprived of Thy love. Make me to love Thee, and then dispose of me as pleaseth Thee. Mary, my hope, pray to Jesus for me.

MEDITATION FOR THURSDAY. ON THE CROWNING WITH THORNS, AND ON THE WORDS, "ECCE HOMO," "BEHOLD THE MAN" (ST. JOHN XIX. 5).

1. Not content with having horribly torn the flesh of the Sacred Body of Jesus Christ with the scourging, these barbarous servants, instigated by devils and by the Jews, wished to treat Him as a mock king, and put upon His back a ragged scarlet robe to imitate a royal mantle, a reed in His Hand by way of sceptre, and on His Head a bundle of thorns plaited together instead of a crown: and in order that this crown might be not only for a mockery, but also cause Him great pain, with that same reed (as St. Matthew says, ch. xxvii. 30, " and they took the reed and struck His head") they struck the thorns till they pierced far into the head; insomuch that the thorns, as says St. Peter Damian, penetrated to the very brain, and so copious was the blood which flowed from the wounds, that, as it was revealed to St. Bridget, it filled the beard, the eyes, and all the hair of Jesus Christ. This torment of the crowning was very painful to Him, and was also the longest, since the pain of it was prolonged even till His death : and every time that the crown on His Head came to be touched, the torture was always renewed.

Ah, ungrateful thorns, what are you doing? Is it thus that you torment your Creator ? But what thorns ? O my soul, it was thou, with thy depraved consenting to sin, who didst wound the Head of thy Lord. My dear Jesus, Thou art the King of heaven ; but now Thou art become the King of reproaches and sufferings. Behold whither the love of Thy little sheep has brought Thee. O my God, I love Thee ; but alas ! as long as I live I stand in peril of forsaking and denying Thee, my Love, as I have done in time past. My Jesus, if Thou seest that I would ever turn to offend Thee, let me, I pray Thee, die now, since I hope to die in Thy grace. Suffer me not, I beseech Thee, ever to lose Thee again ; by my faults I should worthily deserve this misfortune, but of a surety Thou deservest not to be abandoned anew by me. No, my Jesus, I desire never more to lose Thee.

2. This vile crowd, not content with having so barbarously crowned Jesus Christ, wished to mock Him, and to multiply fresh insults and torments ; and so they bent the knee before Him, and deridingly saluted Him, " Hail, Bang of the Jews;" they spat in His Face, they struck Him with the palms of their hands; with cries and ridicule and contempt they vilely insult Him : " And bending the knee before Him, they mocked Him, saying, Hail, King of the Jews ; and spitting on Him, they gave Him blows" (St. Matt, xxvii. 29, 30; St. John xix. 3). Ah, my Lord, to what art Thou reduced ? O God, if anyone had chanced to pass that way, and had seen this Man thus disfigured, covered with these purple rags, with this sceptre in Hie Hand, with this crown on His Head, thus derided and ill-treated by this rabble, for what could he ever have accounted Him but for a man the most infamous and wicked in all the world. Behold, then, the Son of God become the mockery of Jerusalem !

Ah, my Jesus, if I look on Thy Body without, I see nothing but wounds and blood. If within, in Thy Heart, I find nothing else but bitterness and anguish, which make Thee suffer the agonies of death. Ah, my God, who but infinite goodness, such as Thou art, could ever have humbled Himself to suffer so much for His creatures ?—but creatures beloved of God, because Thou art God. These wounds which I see in Thee are all tokens of the love which Thou bearest to us. Oh, if all men could have contemplated Thee in the condition in which on that day Thou wast a spectacle of sorrow and reproach to all Jerusalem, who would not have been seized by love of Thee ? Lord, I love Thee, and give myself wholly to Thee. Behold, my blood, my life, all I offer Thee. Behold me ready to suffer and die as it pleaseth Thee. And what can I deny to Thee who hast not denied to me Thy blood and life ? Deign to accept the sacrifice which a miserable sinner makes of himself, who now loves Thee with all his heart.

3. Pilate, when Jesus was brought back to him, showed Him from a balcony to the people, saying, " Behold the man." As though he would say, Behold that man whom you have brought before my tribunal, accusing Him of having pretended to make Himself a king ; behold, this fear is at an end ; now that you have reduced Him, as you see to such a state that but little life can remain in Him, suffer Him to go and die in His own house ; oblige me not to condemn one innocent.   But the Jews, being infuriated, as they had at first cried out in their frenzy, " His blood be upon us" (St. Matt, xxvii. 25), so now they cried out, "Crucify Him, crucify Him. . . . Away, away with Him, crucify him" (St. John xix. 6, 15).   But just as then Pilate was from the balcony showing Jesus to the people, so the Eternal Father from heaven was pointing out to us His Son, saying in like manner, Behold the man ! He who was promised by Me as your Redeemer, and was by you so much desired ; He who is My only Son, beloved by Me even as Myself. Behold Him for the love of you become man, the most afflicted and despised among all men. Ah, meditate on Him, and love Him.

Ah, my God, be it so that I look upon Thy Son, and love Him; but do Thou, too, look on Him, and by the merit of His sorrows and insults pardon me all the offences which I have done against Thee. " His blood be upon us." Let the Blood of this Man-God, who is Thy Son, descend upon our souls, and obtain for us Thy mercy. I repent, O infinite Goodness, of having offended Thee, and I love Thee with all my heart. But Thou knowest my weakness; help me ; O Lord, have pity on me. Mary, my hope, pray to Jesus for me.

MEDITATION FOR FRIDAY.

ON THE CONDEMNATION OF JESUS, AND THE JOURNEY TO CALVARY.

1. Pilate at length, through fear of losing the favour of Caesar, after having so many times declared Jesus innocent, condemns Him to die on the Cross. O my most innocent Saviour (laments St. Bernard), and what crime hast Thou committed, that Thou must be condemned to death? ' What bast Thou done, O most innocent Saviour, that Thou shouldst be thus judged?' But I well understand (replies the saint) the sin which Thou hast committed : 'Thy sin is Thy love.' Thy crime is the too great love which Thou hast borne to us. This, rather than Pilate, condemns Thee to death.

The unjust sentence is read ; Jesus hears it, and altogether resigned accepts it, submitting Himself to the will of the Eternal Father, which wills Him to die, and to die on the Cross, for our sins : " He humbled Himself, made obedient unto death, even the death of the cross" (Phil. ii. 8). Ah, my Jesus, if Thou who wert innocent acceptedst death for love of me, I, a sinner, for love of Thee, accept my death in such time and manner as it shall please Thee.

When the sentence had been read, they drag off with fury this innocent Divine Lamb ; they put His own garments on Him again, and taking the Cross, composed of two rough beams, present it to Him. Jesus waits not for them to lay it on Him, but of Himself embraces it, kisses and lays it upon His wounded shoulders, saying, Come, my beloved Cross, three-and-thirty years I have been going about seeking thee ; on thee I desire to die for the love of My little flock. Ah, my Jesus, what more couldst Thou possibly have done to lay on me the necessity of loving Thee ? If one of my servants only had offered himself to die for me, surely he would have won my love; and how then can I have lived so long a time without having loved Thee, knowing that Thou, my sovereign and only Lord, didst die to pardon me ? I love Thee, O my chief Good, and because I love Thee I repent of having offended Thee.

2. Those who had been condemned issue from the tribunal and go on the way to the place of punishment; amongst them goes also the King of Heaven, with His Cross on His shoulders : "And bearing His cross, He went forth to the place which is called Calvary" (St. John xix. 17). Go forth also, ye seraphim, from Paradise, and come to accompany your Lord, who is going to the mount, to be there crucified. What a sight ! A God who goes to be crucified for men! My soul, look, I pray thee, on thy Saviour, who goes to die for thee. Look on Him, how He goes with head bent down, with trembling knees, all torn with wounds and dropping with live blood, with that bundle of thorns on His head, and with that load of wood on His shoulders. O God, He walks with such difficulty, that it seems as if at every step He would breathe forth His soul. O Lamb of God (say thou to Him), whither goest Thou ? I go (He answers) to die for thee. When thou shalt see Me now dead, remember (He says to thee) the love I bore to thee; remember it and love Me. Ah, my Redeemer, how can I have lived for the past so forgetful of Thy love? O my sins, you have caused bitterness to the heart of my Lord, the heart which has loved me so much. My Jesus, I repent of the wrong which I have done Thee ; I thank Thee for the patience which Thou hast shown me, and I love Thee. I love Thee with all my soul, and desire to love Thee alone. Remind me ever, I pray Thee, of the love Thou hast borne me, so that I may never more forget to love Thee.

3. Jesus Christ goes up Calvary, and invites us to follow Him. Yes, my Lord, Thou who art innocent goest before me with Thy Cross. Walk on, for I will not leave Thee. Give me that cross which Thou willest, that I may embrace it, and with it I am willing to follow Thee even unto death. I wish to die together with Thee, who hast died for me. Thou commandest me to love Thee, and I desire nothing else than to love Thee. My Jesus, Thou art, and shalt ever be, my only Love. Assist me to be faithful to Thee. Mary, my hope, pray to Jesus for me.

MEDITATION FOR SATURDAY. ON THE CRUCIFIXION AND DEATH OF JESUS.

1. Lo, we are on Calvary, made the theatre of Divine love, where a God dies for us in a sea of sorrows. When Jesus had arrived there, they violently strip off His garments cleaving to His torn flesh, and cast Him on the Cross. The Divine Lamb stretches Himself out on this bed of death, presents His hands to the executioners, and offers to the Eternal Father the great sacrifice of His life for the salvation of men. Behold, now they nail Him to the Cross and raise Him on it. Look, my soul, on thy Saviour, who, fastened by three hard nails, hangs from the Cross, where He can find neither place nor rest. At one time He leans on His hands, at another on His feet; but where He leans, there the pain is increased. O my Jesus, and what a bitter death is this which Thou diest! I see written over the Cross, " Jesus of Nazareth, King of the Jews" (St. John xix. 19). But except this title of scorn, what token dost Thou show of being a King? Ah, indeed, this throne of tortures, these hands pierced with nails, this head transfixed, this flesh all torn, may well make Thee known for a King, but a King of love. I draw near, then, with tenderness, to kiss these wounded feet. I embrace this Cross, where Thou, made a Victim of love, wouldst die a Sacrifice for me. Ah, my Jesus, what would have become of me if Thou hadst not satisfied the Divine justice? I thank Thee, and I love Thee.

2. Whilst hanging on the Cross, Jesus has no one who can console Him. Among those who stand around Him, some are blaspheming, some are deriding Him : some say, "If Thou art the Son of God, descend from the Cross;" others, " He saved others, Himself He cannot save" (St. Matt, xxvii. 40, 42). And He receives no compassion even from those who are His very companions in punishment ; nay, rather, one of them joins those others in blaspheming Him : " One of the thieves who were hanging with Him, blasphemed Him" (St. Luke xxiii. 39). There stood, it is true, below the Cross, Mary assisting with love her dying Son. But the sight of this Mother in her sorrows, so far from consoling Jesus, afflicted Him so much the more, at seeing the pain which she endured for love of Him. So, then, our Redeemer, finding no comfort here on earth, turned Himself to the Eternal Father in heaven above. But the Father, seeing Him covered with all the sins of mankind, for which He was making satisfaction, said, No, My Son, I cannot console Thee. It is meet that even I too should abandon Thee to Thy pains, and leave Thee to die without comfort. And then it was that Jesus cried out, " My God, My God, why hast Thou forsaken Me?" (St. Matt, xxvii. 46.)

Ah, my Jesus, how do I see Thee in pains and sorrow? Ah, too good reason hast Thou for Thy grief, to think that Thou art suffering in order to be loved by men, and yet that there should be found so few to love Thee. O sweet fames of love, which are consuming the life of a God, consume, I pray you, in me all earthly affections, and make me burn only with love for that Lord who was willing for love of me to lay down His life on an infamous gibbet. But Thou, O Lord, how couldst Thou die for me, foreseeing the injuries which I should afterwards do to Thee? Avenge Thyself, I pray Thee, now on me, but avenge Thyself for my salvation ; grant to me a sorrow, such that it shall always make me sorry for the vexations which I have given Thee. Come, scourges, thorns, nails, and cross, which are so grievously tormenting my Lord, come and wound my heart, and ever remind me of the love which He has borne to me. Save me; my Jesus, and let this saving be to give me the grace of loving Thee,—to love Thee and my own salvation.

3. The Redeemer, now nigh to expiring, with dying breath said, " It is consummated" (St. John xix. 30). As if He had said, O men, all has been completed and done for your redemption. Love Me, then, since I have nothing more that I can do to make you love Me. My soul, look up at thy Jesus who is now going to die. Look at those eyes growing dim, that face grown pale, that Heart which is beating with languid pulse, that Body which is now abandoning itself to death ; and look at that beautiful Soul which is just on the point of forsaking that Sacred Body. The heavens are darkened, the earth trembles, the sepulchres are opened ; signs that now the Maker of the world is about to die. Lo, at last Jesus, after having commended His Blessed Soul to His Father, first giving a deep sigh from His afflicted Heart, and then bowing His head in sign of the offering of His life which at this moment He renewed for our salvation, at length, by the violence of His sorrow, expires and renders up His spirit into the hand of His beloved Father.

Approach up hither, my soul, to this Cross. Embrace the feet of thy dead Saviour, and think that He is dead through the love which He bore to thee. Ah, my Jesus, to what has Thy affection towards me reduced Thee? And who, more than I, has enjoyed the fruits of Thy death? Make me, I beseech Thee, understand what love that must have been that a God should die for me, to the end that from this day forth I may love none other than Thee. I love Thee, O greatest Good ; O true Lover of my soul, into Thy hands I here commend it. I beseech Thee, by the merits of Thy death, make me to die to all earthly loves, in order that I may love Thee alone, who art alone worthy of all my love. Mary, my hope, pray to Jesus for me.

Hail, Jesus, our Love, and Mary, our hope !

"O riven Heart, O Love for me now crucified,
Give to my soul repose within Thy wounded side !"

THE LOVE OF SOULS; OR REFLECTIONS AND AFFECTIONS ON THE PASSION OF JESUS CHRIST. THE CLOCK OF THE PASSION.

HOUR.
1. Having taken leave of Mary, He celebrates his Last Supper.
2. He washes the feet of the Apostles, and institutes the Most Holy Sacrament.
3. He makes His discourse, and goes to the Garden.
4. He prays in the Garden.
5. He begins His agony.
6. He sweats blood.
7. He is betrayed by Judas, and bound.
8. He is led before Annas.
9. He is taken before Caiaphas, and receives a blow on the face.
10. He is blindfolded, struck, and scoffed at.
11. He is led to the council, and declared guilty of death,
12. He is taken to Pilate, and accused.
13. He is mocked by Herod.
14. He is conducted to Pilate, and Barabbas is preferred before Him.
15. He is scourged at the pillar.
16. He is crowned with thorns, and exhibited to the people.
17. He is condemned to death, and goes to Calvary.
18. He is stripped and crucified.
19. He prays for His murderers.
20. He recommends His Spirit to His Father.
21. He dies.
22. He is pierced with the lance.
23. He is taken down from the Cross, and delivered over to His Mother.
24. He is buried, and left in the sepulchre.

INVOCATION OF JESUS AND MARY.

O Saviour of the world, O Love of souls, O Lord most lovely of all beings, Thou by Thy Passion didst come *to* win to Thyself our hearts, by showing us the immense love Thou didst bear to us in accomplishing a redemption which has brought to us a sea of benedictions, and which cost Thee a sea of pains and ignominies. It was principally for this end that Thou didst institute the Most Holy Sacrament of the Altar, in order that we might have a perpetual memorial of Thy Passion : ' That we might have forever a perpetual memorial of so great a benefit,' says St. Thomas, ' He gives His body to be the food of the faithful;' which St Paul had already said : " As often as you shall eat this bread, you shall show the death of the Lord" (1 Cor. xi. 26). Oh, how many holy souls hast Thou persuaded by these prodigies of love, consumed by the flames of Thy love, to renounce all earthly goods, in order to dedicate themselves entirely to loving Thee alone, O most amiable Saviour ! O my Jesus, I pray Thee make me always remember Thy Passion ; and grant that I also, a miserable sinner, overcome at last by so many loving devices, may return to love Thee, and to show Thee, by my poor love, some mark of gratitude for the excessive love which Thou, my God and my Saviour, hast borne to me. Remember, my Jesus, that I am one of those sheep of Thine, to save which Thou didst come down on the earth, and didst sacrifice Thy Divine life. I know that, after having redeemed me by Thy death, Thou hast not ceased to love me, and that Thou dost still bear to me the same love which Thou hadst for me when Thou didst die for my sake. Oh, permit me not any longer to lead a life of ingratitude towards Thee, my God, who dost so much deserve to be loved, and hast done so much to be loved by me.

And thou, O most holy Virgin Mary, who didst take so great a part in the Passion of thy Son, obtain for me, I beseech thee, through the merits of thy sorrows, the grace to experience a taste of that compassion which thou didst so sensibly feel at the death of Jesus ; and obtain for me also a spark of that love which wrought all the martyrdom of thy afflicted heart. Amen.

'Let my mind, O Lord Jesus Christ, I beseech Thee, be absorbed in the fiery and honied sweetness of Thy love, that I may die for love of the love of Thee, who wert pleased to die for love of the love of me' (Prayer of St. Franc. Ass.).

FRUITS OF MEDITATION ON THE PASSION OF JESUS, CHRIST.

1. The Lover of souls, our most loving Redeemer, declared that He had no other motive in coming down upon earth to become man, than to enkindle in the hearts of men the fire of His holy love : "Iam come to cast fire on earth ; and what will I but that it be kindled" (St. Luke xii. 49). And, oh, what beautiful flames of love has He not enkindled in so many souls, especially by the pains that He chose to suffer in His death, in order to prove to us the immeasurable love which He still bears to us ! Oh, how many souls, happy in the Wounds of Jesus, as in burning furnaces of love, have been so inflamed with His love, that they have not refused to consecrate to Him their goods, their lives, and their whole selves, surmounting with great courage all the difficulties which they had to encounter in the observance of the Divine law, for the love of that Lord who, being God, chose to suffer so much for the love of them ! This was just the counsel that the Apostle gave us, in order that we might not fail, but make great advances in the way of salvation : " Think diligently upon Him who endureth such opposition from sinners against Himself, that you be not wearied, fainting in your minds" (Heb. xii. 3).

2. Wherefore St. Augustine, all inflamed with love at the sight of Jesus nailed on the Cross, prayed thus sweetly : Imprint, O Lord, Thy Wounds in my heart, that I may read therein suffering and love : suffering, that I may endure for Thee all suffering ; love, that I may despise for Thee all love. Write, he said, my most loving Saviour, write on my heart Thy Wounds, in order that I may always therein behold Thy sufferings and Thy love. Yes, because, having before my eyes the great sufferings that Thou, my God, didst endure for me, I may bear in silence all the sufferings it may fall to my lot to endure ; and at the sight of the love which Thou didst exhibit for me on the Cross, I may never love or be able to love any other than Thee.

3. And from what source did the saints draw courage and strength to suffer torments, martyrdom, and death, if not from the sufferings of Jesus crucified ? St. Joseph of Leonessa, a Capuchin, on seeing that they were going to bind him with cords for a painful incision that the surgeon was to make in his body, took into his hands his crucifix and said, ' Why these cords ? why these cords? Behold, these are my chains—my Saviour nailed to the Cross for love of me. He through His sufferings constrains me to bear every trial for His sake.' And thus he suffered the amputation without a complaint ; looking upon Jesus, who, "as a lamb before his shearers, was dumb, and did not open His mouth" (Isaias liii. 7). Who, then, can ever complain that he suffers wrongfully, when he considers Jesus, who was " bruised for our sins" ? (Is. liii. 5.) Who can refuse to obey, on account of some inconvenience, when Jesus " became obedient unto death" ? (Phil. ii. 8.) Who can refuse ignominies, when they behold Jesus treated as a fool, as a mock king, as a disorderly person ; struck, spit upon on His face, and suspended upon an infamous gibbet ?

4. Who could love any other object besides Jesus, when they see Him dying in the midst of so many sufferings and insults, in order to captivate our love ? A certain devout solitary prayed to God to teach him what he could do in order to love Him perfectly. Our Lord revealed to him that there was no more efficient way to arrive at the perfect love of Him, than to meditate constantly on His Passion.   St. Teresa lamented and complained of certain books which had taught her to leave off meditating on the Passion of Jesus Christ, because this might be an impediment to the contemplation of His Divinity ; and the saint exclaimed, ' O Lord of my soul, O my Jesus crucified, my Treasure, I never remember this opinion without thinking that I have been guilty of great treachery. And is it possible that Thou, my Lord, couldest be an obstacle to me in the way of a greater good ? Whence, then, do all good things come to me, but from Thee?' And she then added : ' I have seen that, in order to please God, and to induce Him to grant us great graces, He wills that they should all pass through the hands of this most Sacred Humanity, in which His Divine Majesty declared that He took pleasure.'

5. For this reason, Father Balthassar Alvarez said that ignorance of the treasures that we possess in Jesus was the ruin of Christians ; and therefore his most favourite and usual meditation was on the Passion of Jesus Christ. He meditated especially on three of the sufferings of Jesus —Hie poverty, contempt, and pain ; and he exhorted hie penitents to meditate frequently on the Passion of our Redeemer, telling them that they should not consider that they had done anything at all, until they had arrived at retaining Jesus crucified continually present in their hearts.

6. ' He who desires,' says St. Bonaventura, 'to go on advancing from virtue to virtue, from grace to grace, should meditate continually on the Passion of Jesus.' And he adds, ' that there is no practice more profitable for the entire sanctification of the soul than the frequent meditation of the sufferings of Jesus Christ.'

7. St. Augustine also said that a single tear shed at the remembrance of the Passion of Jesus is worth more than a pilgrimage to Jerusalem, or a year of fasting on bread and water. Yes, because it was for this end that our Saviour suffered so much, in order that we should think of His sufferings; because if we think on them, it is impossible not to be inflamed with Divine love: "The charity of Christ presseth us," said St. Paul (2 Cor. r. 14). Jesus is loved by few, because few consider the pains He has suffered for us ; but he that frequently considers them cannot live without loving Jesus. " The charity of Christ presseth us." He will feel himself so constrained by His love, that he will not find it possible to refrain from loving a God so full of love, who has suffered so much to make us love Him.

8. Therefore the Apostle said that he desired to know nothing but Jesus, and Jesus crucified ; that is, the love that He has shown us on the Cross : " I judged not myself to know anything among you but Jesus Christ, and Him crucified" (1 Cor. ii. 2). And, in truth, from what books can we better learn the science of the saints—that is, the science of loving God—than from Jesus crucified? That great servant of God, Brother Bernard of Corlione, the Capuchin, not being able to read, his brother religious wanted to teach him, upon which he went to consult hie crucifix ; but Jesus answered him from the Cross, " What is reading ? what are books ? Behold, I am the Book wherein thou mayest continually read the love I have borne thee." O great subject to be considered during our whole life and during all eternity ! A God dead for the love of us ! a God dead for the love of us ! O wonderful subject !

9. St. Thomas Aquinas was one day paying a visit to St. Bonaventure, and asked him from what book he had drawn all the beautiful lessons he had written. St. Bonaventure showed him the image of the Crucified, which was completely blackened by all the kisses which he had given it, and said,' This is my book, whence I receive everything that I write ; and it has taught me whatever little I know.' In short, all the saints have learned the art of loving God from the study of the crucifix. Brother John of Alvernia, every time

that he beheld Jesus wounded, could not restrain his tears. Brother James of Tuderto, when he heard the Passion of our Redeemer read, not only wept bitterly, but broke out into loud sobs, overcome with the love with which he was inflamed towards his beloved Lord.

10. It was this sweet study of the crucifix which made St. Francis become a great seraph. He wept so continually in meditating on the sufferings of Jesus Christ, that he had almost entirely lost his sight. On one occasion, being found crying out and weeping, he was asked what was the matter with him. ' What ails me ?' replied the saint. 'I weep over the sorrows and insults inflicted on my Lord ; and my sorrow is increased when I think on those ungrateful men who do not love Him, but live without any thought of Him.' Every time that he heard the bleating of a lamb, he felt himself touched with compassion at the thought of the death of Jesus, the Immaculate Lamb, drained of every drop of blood upon the Cross for the sins of the world. And therefore this loving saint could find no subject on which he exhorted his brethren with greater eagerness than the constant remembrance of the Passion of Jesus.

11. This, then, is the Book—Jesus crucified—which, if we constantly read it, will teach us, on the one hand, to have a lively fear of sin, and, on the other hand, will inflame us with love for a God so full of love for us ; while we read in these Wounds the great malice of sin, which reduced a God to suffer such a bitter death in order to satisfy the Divine justice, and the love which our Saviour has shown us in choosing to suffer so much in order to prove to us how much He loved us.

12. Let us beseech the Divine Mother Mary to obtain for us from her Son the grace that we also may enter into these furnaces of love, in which so many loving hearts are consumed, in order that, our earthly affections being there burnt away, we also may burn with those blessed flames, which render souls holy on earth and blessed in heaven. Amen.

CHAPTER I. ON THE LOVE OF JESUS CHRIST IN BEING WILLING TO SATISFY THE DIVINE JUSTICE FOR OUR SINS.

1. We read in history of a proof of love so prodigious, that it will be the admiration of all ages. There was once a king, lord of many kingdoms, who had one only son, go beautiful, so holy, so amiable, that he was the delight of his father, who loved him as much as himself. This young prince had a great affection for one of his slaves ; so much so, that the slave having committed a crime, lor which he had been condemned to death, the prince offered himself to die for the slave ; the father, being jealous of justice, was satisfied to condemn his beloved son to death, in order that the slave might remain free from the punishment he deserved : and thus the son died a malefactor's death, and the slave was freed from punishment.

2. This fact, the like of which has never, happened in this world, and never will happen, is related in the Gospels, where we read that the Son of God, the Lord of the universe, seeing that man was condemned to eternal death in punishment of his sins, chose to take upon Himself human flesh, and thus to pay by His death the penalty due to man: "He was offered because it was His own will" (Is. liii. 7). And His Eternal Father caused Him to die upon the Cross to have us miserable sinners : " He spared not His own Son, but delivered Him up for us all" (Rom. viii. 32). What dost thou think, O devout soul, of this love of the Son and of the Father ?

3. Thou didst, then, O my beloved Redeemer, choose by Thy death to sacrifice Thyself in order to obtain the pardon of my sins. And what return of gratitude shall I then make to Thee ? Thou hast done too much to oblige me to love Thee ; I should indeed be most ungrateful to Thee if I did not love Thee with my whole heart. Thou hast given for me Thy Divine life ; I, miserable sinner that I am, give Thee my own life. Yes, I will at least spend that period of life that remains to me only in loving Thee, obeying Thee, and pleasing Thee.

4. O men, men, let us love this our Redeemer, who, being God, has not disdained to take upon Himself our sins, in order to satisfy by His sufferings for the chastisement which we have deserved : " Surely He hath borne our infirmities, and carried our sorrows" (Isaias liii. 4). St. Augustine says, that our Lord in creating us formed us by virtue of His power, but in redeeming us He has saved us from death by means of His sufferings : ' He created us in His strength ; He sought us hack in His weakness.' How much do I not owe Thee, O Jesus my Saviour ! Oh, if I were to give my blood a thousand times over,—if I were to spend a thousand lives for Thee,—it would yet be nothing. Oh, how could anyone that meditated much on the love which Thou hast shown him in Thy Passion, love anything else but Thee ? Through the love with which Thou didst love us on the Cross, grant me the grace to love Thee with my whole heart. I love Thee, infinite Goodness; I love Thee above every other good ; and I ask nothing more of Thee but Thy holy love.

5. 'But how is this?' continues St. Augustine. How is it possible, O Saviour of the world, that Thy love has arrived at such a height, that when I had committed the crime, Thou shouldst have to pay the penalty ? 'Whither has Thy love reached ? I have sinned; Thou art punished.' And what could it then signify to Thee, adds St. Bernard, that we should lose ourselves and be chastised, as we well deserved to be ; that Thou shouldst choose to satisfy with Thy innocent flesh for our Bins, and to die in order to deliver us from death? 'O good Jesus, what doest Thou? We ought to have died, and it is Thou who diest. We have sinned, and Thou sufferest. A deed without precedent, grace without merit, charity without measure !' O deed, which never has had and never will have its match ! O grace which we could never merit ! O love which can never be understood !

6. Isaias had already foretold that our blessed Redeemer should be condemned to death, and as an innocent lamb brought to the sacrifice : " He shall be led as a sheep to the slaughter" (Is. liii. 7). What a cause of wonder it must have been to the Angels, O my God, to behold their innocent Lord led as a victim to be sacrificed on the Altar of the Cross for the love of man ! And what a cause of horror to heaven and to hell, the sight of a God extended as an infamous criminal on a shameful gibbet for the sins of His creatures!

7. " Christ hath redeemed us from the curse of the law, being made a curse for us (for it is written, Cursed is every one that hangeth on a tree) : that the blessing of Abraham might come to the Gentiles through Jesus Christ" (Gal. iii. 13). ' He was made a curse upon the Cross,' says St. Ambrose, ' that thou mightest be blessed in the kingdom of God.' O my dearest Saviour, Thou wert, then, content, in order to obtain for me the blessing of God, to embrace the dishonour of appearing upon the Cross accursed in the sight of the whole world, and even forsaken in Thy sufferings by Thy Eternal Father,—a suffering which made Thee cry out with a loud voice, " My God, My God, why hast Thou forsaken Me ?" Yes, observes Simon of Cassia, it was for this end that Jesus was abandoned in His Passion in order that we might not remain abandoned in the sins which we have committed : ' Therefore Christ was abandoned in His sufferings that we might not be abandoned in our guilt.' O prodigy of compassion ! O excess of love of God towards men ! And how can there be a soul who believes this, O my Jesus, and yet loves Thee not ?

8. " He hath loved us, and washed us from our sins in His own blood" (Apoc. i. 5). Behold, O men, how far the love of Jesus for us has carried Him, in order to cleanse us from the filthiness of our sins. He has even shed every drop of His Blood that He might prepare for us in this His own Blood a bath of salvation : ' He offers His own Blood,' says a learned writer, ' speaking better than the blood of Abel : for that cried for justice ; the Blood of Christ, for mercy.' Whereupon St. Bonaventure exclaims, 'O good Jesus, what hast Thou done?' O my Saviour, what indeed hast Thou done ? How far hath Thy love carried Thee ? What hast Thou seen in me which hath made Thee love me so much? 'Wherefore hast Thou loved me so much? Why, Lord, why? What am I?' Wherefore didst Thou choose to suffer so much for me ? Who am I that Thou wouldest win to Thyself my love at so dear a price ? Oh, it was entirely the work of Thy infinite love ! Be Thou eternally praised and blessed for it.

9. " O all ye that pass by the way, attend and see if there be any sorrow like to My sorrow" (Lament, i. 12). The same seraphic

doctor, considering these words of Jeremias as spoken of our blessed Redeemer while He was hanging on the Cross dying for the love of us, says, ' Yes, Lord, I will attend and see if there be any love like unto Thy love.' By which he means, I do indeed see and understand, O my most loving Redeemer, how much Thou didst suffer upon that infamous tree ; but what most constrains me to love Thee is the thought of the affection which Thou hast shown me in suffering so much, in order that I might love Thee.

10. That which most inflamed St. Paul with the love of Jesus was the thought that He chose to die, not only for all men, but for him in particular: "He loved me, and delivered Himself up for me" (Gal. ii. 20). Yes, He has loved me, said he, and for my sake He gave Himself up to die. And thus ought every one of us to say; for St. John Chrysostom asserts that God has loved every individual man with the same love with which He has loved the world : ' He loves each man separately with the same measure of charity with which He loves the whole world.' So that each one of us is under as great obligation to Jesus Christ for having suffered for everyone, as if He had suffered for him alone. For supposing Jesus Christ had died, my brother, to save you alone, leaving all others to their original ruin, what a debt of gratitude you would owe to Him ! But you ought to feel that you owe Him a greater obligation still for having died for the salvation of all. For if He had died for you alone, what sorrow would it not have caused you to think that your neighbours, parents, brothers, and friends would be damned, and that you would, when this life was over, be forever separated from them? If you and your family had been slaves, and someone came to rescue you alone, how would you not entreat of him to save your parents and brothers together with yourself ! And how much would you thank him if he did this to please you ! Say, therefore, to Jesus: O my sweetest Redeemer, Thou hast done this for me without my having asked Thee ; Thou hast not only saved me from death at the price of Thy Blood, but also my parents and friends, so that I may have a good hope that we may all together enjoy Thy Presence for ever in Paradise. O Lord, I thank Thee, and I love Thee, and I hope to thank Thee for it, and to love Thee forever in that blessed country.

11. Who could ever, says St. Laurence Justinian, explain the love which the Divine Word bears to each one of us, since it surpasses the love of every son towards his mother, and of every mother for her son. 'The intense charity of the Word of God surpasses all maternal and filial love ; neither can human words express how great His love is to each one of us !' So much so, that our Lord revealed to St. Gertrude, that He would be ready to die as many times as there were souls damned, if they were yet capable of redemption : ' I would die as many deaths as there are souls in hell.' O Jesus, O Treasure more worthy of love than all others, why is it that men love Thee so little ? Oh, do Thou make known what Thou hast suffered for each of them, the love that Thou bearest them, the desire Thou hast to be loved by them, and how worthy Thou art of being loved. Make Thyself known, O my Jesus, make Thyself loved.

12. "I am the Good Shepherd," said our Redeemer ; "the good shepherd gives his life for his sheep" (St. John x. 11). But, O my Lord, where are there in the world shepherds like unto Thee? Other shepherds will slay their sheep in order to preserve their own life. Thou, O too loving Shepherd, didst give Thy Divine life in order to save the life of Thy beloved sheep. And of these sheep, I, O most amiable Shepherd, have the happiness to be one. What obligation, then, am I not under to love Thee, and to spend my life for Thee, since Thou hast died for the love of me in particular ! And what confidence ought I not to have in Thy Blood, knowing that it has been shed to pay the debt of my sins ! " And thou shalt say in that day, I will give thanks to Thee, O Lord. Behold, God is my Saviour ; I will deal confidently, and will not fear" (Is. xii. 1, 2). And how can I any longer mistrust Thy mercy, O my Lord, when I behold Thy Wounds ? Come, then, O sinners, and let us have recourse to Jesus, who hangs upon that Cross as it were upon a throne of mercy. He has appeased the Divine justice, which we had insulted. If we have offended God, He has done penance for us; all that is required for us is contrition for our sins.

13. O my dearest Saviour, to what have Thy pity and love for me reduced Thee ? The slave sins, and Thou, Lord, payest the penalty for him. If, therefore, I think of my sins, the thought of the punishment I deserve must make me tremble ; but when I think of Thy death, I find I have more reason to hope than to fear. O Blood of Jesus, thou art all my hope.

14. But this Blood, as it inspires us with confidence, also obliges us to give ourselves entirely to our Blessed Redeemer. The Apostle exclaims, " Know you not, that you are not your own? For you are bought with a great price" (1 Cor. vi. 19, 20). Therefore, O my Jesus, I cannot any longer, without injustice, dispose of myself, or of my own concerns, since Thou hast made me Thine by purchasing me through Thy death. My body, my soul, my life are no longer mine ; they are Thine, and entirely Thine. In Thee alone, therefore, will I hope. O my God, crucified and dead for me, I have nothing else to offer Thee but this soul, which Thou hast bought with Thy Blood ; to Thee do I offer it. Accept of my love, for I desire nothing but Thee, my Saviour, my God, my Love, my All. Hitherto I have shown much gratitude towards men ; to Thee alone have I, alas, been most ungrateful. But now I love Thee, and I have no greater cause of sorrow than my having offended Thee. O my Jesus, give me confidence in Thy Passion ; root out of my heart every affection that belongs not to Thee. I will love Thee alone, who dost deserve all my love, and who hast given me so much reason to love Thee.

15. And who, indeed, could refuse to love Thee, when they see Thee, who art the Beloved of the Eternal Father, dying such a bitter and cruel death for our sakes? O Mary, O Mother of fair love, I pray thee, through the merits of thy burning heart, obtain for me the grace to live only in order to love thy Son, who, being in Himself worthy of an infinite love, has chosen at so great a cost to acquire to Himself the love of a miserable sinner like me. O Love of souls, O my Jesus, I love Thee, I love Thee, I love Thee ; but still I love Thee too little. Oh, give me more love, give me flames that may make me live always burning with Thy love. I do not myself deserve it ; but Thou dost well deserve it, O infinite Goodness. Amen, This I hope, so may it be.

CHAPTER II. JESUS CHOSE TO SUPPER SO MUCH FOR US, IN ORDER THAT WE MAY UNDERSTAND THE GREAT LOVE HE HAS FOR US. '

1. ' Two things,' says Cicero, ' make us know a lover— his doing good to his beloved, and suffering torments for him ; and the latter is the greatest sign of true love.' God has indeed already shown His love to man by many benefits bestowed upon him; but His love would not have been satisfied by only doing good to man, as says St. Peter Chrysologus, if He had not found the means to prove to him how much He loved him by also suffering and dying for him, as He did by taking upon Him human flesh : ' But He held it to be little if He showed His love without suffering ;' and what greater means could God have discovered to prove to us the immense love which He bears us than by making Himself man and suffering for us ? 'In no other way could the love of God towards us be shown,' writes St. Gregory Nazianzen. My beloved Jesus, how much hast Thou laboured to show me Thy love, and to make me enamoured of Thy goodness. Great indeed, then, would be the injury I should do Thee, if I were to love Thee but little, or to love anything else but Thee.

2. Ah, when He showed Himself to us, a God, wounded, crucified, and dying, did He not indeed (says Cornelius à Lapide) give us the greatest proofs of the love that He bears us ? ' God showed His utmost love on the Cross.' And before him St. Bernard said that Jesus, in His Passion, showed us that His love towards us could not be greater than it was: 'In the shame of the Passion is shown the greatest and incomparable love.' The Apostle writes, that when Jesus Christ chose to die for our salvation, then appeared how far the love of God extended towards us miserable creatures: "The goodness and kindness of God our Saviour appeared" (Tit. iii. 4). O my most loving Saviour, I feel indeed that all Thy Wounds speak to me of the love that Thou bearest me. And who that had so many proofs of Thy love could resist loving Thee in return. St. Teresa was indeed right, O most amiable Jesus, when she said that he who loves Thee not gives a proof that he does not know Thee.

3. Jesus Christ could easily have obtained for us salvation without suffering, and in leading a life of ease and delight; but no, St. Paul says, "having joy set before Him, He endured the Cross" (Heb. xii. 2). He refused the riches, the delights, the honours of the world, and chose for Himself a fife of poverty, and a death full of suffering and ignominy. And wherefore ? Would it not have sufficed for Him to have offered to His Eternal Father one single prayer for the pardon of man? for this prayer being of infinite value, would have been sufficient to save the world, and infinite worlds besides. Why, then, did He choose for Himself so much suffering, and a death so cruel, that an author has said very truly, that through mere pain the Soul of Jesus separated itself from His Body ? To what purpose so much cost in order to save man ? St. John Chrysostom answers, a single prayer of Jesus would indeed have sufficed to redeem us ; but it was not sufficient to show us the love that our God has borne us : 'That which sufficed to redeem us was not sufficient for love.' And St. Thomas confirms this when he says, ' Christ, in suffering from love, offered to God more than the expiation of the offence of the human race demanded.' Because Jesus loved us so much, He desired to be loved very much by us; and therefore He did everything that He could, even unto suffering for us, in order to conciliate our love, and to show that there was nothing more that He could do to make us love Him : 'He endured much weariness,' says St. Bernard, ' that He might bind man to love Him much.'

4. And what greater proof of love, says our Saviour Himself, can a friend show towards the person he loves than to give his life for his sake ? " Greater love than this no man hath, that a man lay down his life for his friends" (St. John xv. 13). But Thou, O most loving Jesus, says St. Bernard, hast done more than this, since Thou hast given Thy life for us, who were not Thy friends, but Thy enemies, and rebels against Thee : 'Thou hast a greater charity, Lord, in giving Thy life for Thy enemies.' And this is what the Apostle observes when he writes, " He commendeth His charity towards us, because when as yet we were sinners, according to the time Christ died for us" (Rom. v. 8, 9). Thou wouldest then die for me, Thy enemy, O my Jesus ; and yet can I resist so much love ? Behold, here I am ; since Thou dost so anxiously desire that I should love Thee, I will drive away every other love from my breast, and will love Thee alone.

5. St. John Chrysostom says, that the principal end Jesus had in His Passion was to discover to us His love, and thus to draw our hearts to Himself by the remembrance of the pains He has endured for us : ' This was the principal cause of the Passion of our Lord; He wished it to be known how great was the love of God for man, of God, who would rather be loved than feared.' St. Thomas adds, that we may, through the Passion of Jesus, know the greatness of the love that God bears to man : ' By this man understands the greatness of the love of God to man;' and St. John had said before, " In this we have known the charity of God, because He hath laid down His life for us" (1 St. John iii. 16). O my Jesus, Immaculate Lamb sacrificed on the Cross for me, ' *tardus labor non sit cossus;*' let not all that Thou hast suffered for me be lost, but accomplish in me the object of Thy great sufferings ! Oh, bind me entirely with the sweet chains of Thy love, in order that I may not leave Thee, and that I may never more be separated from Thee : 'Most sweet Jesus, suffer me not to be separated from Thee; suffer me not to be separated from Thee.'

6. St. Luke relates that Moses and Elias on Mount Tabor, speaking of the Passion of Jesus Christ, called it an excess: "and they spoke of His *excess* that He should accomplish in Jerusalem" (St. Luke ix. 31). 'Yes,' says St. Bonaventure, and rightly was the Passion of Jesus called an excess ; for ' it was an excess of suffering, and an excess of love.' And a devout author adds, ' What more could He suffer, that He has not endured ? The excess of His love reached the highest point.' Yes, indeed; for the Divine law imposes on men no other obligation than that of loving their neighbours as themselves ; but Jesus has loved man more than Himself : 'He loved these more than Himself,' says St. Cyril. Thou didst, then, O my beloved Redeemer, —I will say to Thee with St. Augustine,—love me more than Thyself, since to save me Thou wouldest lose Thy Divine life,—a life infinitely more precious than the lives of all men and angels put together. Thou didst love me more than Thyself, because Thou wert willing to die for me.

7. O infinite God, exclaims the Abbot Guerric, Thou hast for the love of men (if it is lawful to say so) become prodigal of Thyself. 'Yes, indeed,' he adds, ' since Thou hast not been satisfied with bestowing Thy gifts, but Thou hast also given Thyself to recover lost man.' O prodigy, O excess of love, worthy only of infinite goodness! ' And who,' says St. Thomas of Villanova, ' will ever be able, Lord, to understand even in the slightest degree the immensity of Thy love in having loved us miserable worms so much, that Thou didst choose to die, even upon a cross, for us?' ' Oh, how this love,' continues the same saint, ' exceeds all measure, all understanding!'

8. It is a pleasing thing to see a person beloved by some great man, and more so if the latter has the power of raising him to some great fortune ; but how much more sweet and pleasing must it be to us to see ourselves beloved by God, who can raise us up to an eternity of happiness ? Under the old law men might have doubted whether God loved them with a tender love ; but after having seen Him shed His Blood on an infamous gibbet and die for us, how can we doubt His loving us with infinite tenderness and affection ? O my soul, behold now thy Jesus, hanging from the Cross all covered with wounds ! behold how, by these wounds, He proves to thee the love of His enamoured Heart : ' The secrets of His Heart are revealed through the wounds of His Body,' says St. Bernard. My dearest Jesus, it does indeed afflict me to see Thee dying with such dreadful sufferings upon an ignominious tree ; but at the same time I am greatly consoled and inflamed with love for Thee, when I see by means of these Wounds the love that Thou bearest me. O heavenly Seraphs, what do you think of the love of my God, " who loved me and delivered Himself for me"? (Gal. ii. 20.)

9. St. Paul says, that when the Gentiles heard it preached that Jesus was crucified for the love of men, they thought it such nonsense that they could not believe it. " But we preach Christ crucified, unto the Jews, indeed, a stumbling-block, and unto the Gentiles foolishness" (1 Cor. i. 22). And how is it possible, said they, to believe that an omnipotent God, who wants nothing in order to be perfectly happy as He is, would choose to become man and die on a cross to save men ? This would be the same, said they, as to believe that a God had become mad for love of men. " But unto the Gentiles foolishness." And thus they refused to believe it. But faith teaches us that Jesus has really undertaken and accomplished this great work of redemption which the Gentiles esteemed and called folly. 'We have seen,' says St. Laurence Justinian, ' Eternal Wisdom, the Only-begotten of God, become as it were a fool through the excessive love He bears man.' Yes, adds Cardinal Hugo, for it seemed nothing but a folly that a God should choose to die for men : 'It seemed a folly that God should die for the salvation of men.'

10. The Blessed Giacopone, who in this world had been a man of letters, and afterwards became a Franciscan, seemed to have become mad through the love that he bore to Jesus Christ. One clay Jesus appeared to him and said, Giacopone, why do you commit these follies ? ' Why ?' he answered, ' because You have taught them me. If I am mad,' said he, ' You have been more mad than I, in that You have died for me. I am a fool, for Thou hast been a greater fool.' Thus also St. Mary Magdalen of Pazzi, being in an ecstasy, exclaimed, ' O God of love ! O God of love ! The love that Thou bearest to creatures, O my Jesus, is too great indeed.' And one day, when rapt out of herself, she took an image of the Crucified One, and began running about the monastery, crying, ' O Love ! Love ! I shall never rest, my God, from calling Thee Love.' Then turning to the religious, she said, ' Do you not know, my dear sisters, that Jesus Christ is nothing but love ? He is even mad with love, and I will go on saying it continually.'

And she added, that she wished she could be heard by the whole universe when she called Jesus 'Love,' in order that the love of Jesus might be known and loved by all. And she sometimes even began to ring the bell, in order that all the people in the world should come (as she desired, if it had been possible) to love her Jesus.

11. Yes, my sweetest Redeemer, permit me to say so, this Thy spouse was indeed right when she called Thee mad with love. And does it not indeed seem a folly that Thou shouldest choose to die for love of me, for such an ungrateful worm as I am, and whose offences Thou didst foresee, as well as the infidelities of which I should be guilty? But if Thou, my God, art thus become mad, as it were, for the love of me, how is it that I do not become mad for the love of a God ? When I "have seen Thee crucified and dead for me, how is it that I can think of any other than Thee ? Yes, O my Lord, my sovereign Good, more worthy of love than every other good, I love Thee more than myself. I promise for the future to love none other but Thee, and to think constantly on the love Thou hast shown me by dying in the midst of so many sufferings for me.

12. O Scourges, O Thorns, O Nails, O Cross, O Wounds, O sufferings, O death of my Saviour, you irresistibly constrain me to love Him who has so much loved me ! O Incarnate Word, O loving God, my soul is enamoured with Thee! I would fain love Thee so much, that I should find no pleasure but in pleasing Thee, my most sweet Lord ; and since Thou dost so earnestly desire my love, I protest that I will only live for Thee. I desire to do whatever Thou willest of me. O my Jesus, I pray Thee, help me, and grant that I may please Thee entirely and continually in time and in eternity. Mary, my Mother, entreat Jesus for me, in order that He may grant me His holy love ; for I desire nothing else in this world and in the next but to love Jesus. Amen.

CHAPTER III. JESUS, FOR LOVE OF US, CHOSE TO SUFFER THE PAINS OF HIS PASSION EVEN FROM THE BEGINNING OF HIS LIFE.

1. The Divine Word came into the world and took upon Him human flesh in order to make Himself loved of man, and therefore He came with such a longing to suffer for our sakes, that He would not lose a moment in begins ning-to torment Himself, at least by apprehension. Hardly was He conceived in the womb of Mary, when He represented to His Mind all the sufferings of His Passion; and in order to obtain for us pardon and Divine grace, He offered Himself to His Eternal Father to satisfy for us through His dolours all the chastisements due to our sins ; and from that moment He began to suffer everything that He afterwards endured in His most bitter death. O my most loving Redeemer, what have I hitherto done or suffered for Thee ? If I could for a thousand years endure for Thy sake all the torments that all the martyrs have suffered, they would yet be nothing compared with that one first moment in which Thou didst offer Thyself and begin to suffer for me.

2. The martyrs did indeed suffer great pains and ignominy; but they only endured them at the time of their martyrdom. Jesus even from the first instant of His life continually suffered all the torments of His Passion; for, from the first moment, He had before His eyes all the horrid scene of torments and insults which He was to receive from men. Wherefore He said by the mouth of the Prophet : " My sorrow is continually before Me" (Ps. xxxvii. 18). O my Jesus, Thou hast been so greedy to suffer for my sake, that Thou wouldest even endure Thy sufferings before the time ; and yet I am so greedy after the pleasures of this world. How many times have I offended Thee in order to please my body ! O my Lord, through the merits of Thy sufferings, take away from me, I beseech Thee, all affection for earthly pleasures. For Thy love I desire to abstain from this satisfaction *[mention someone in particular]*.

3. God in His compassion for us does not generally reveal to us the trials that await us before the time when we are destined to endure them. If a criminal who is executed on a gibbet had had revealed to him from the first use of his reason the torture that awaited him, could he even have been capable of joy? If Saul from the beginning of his reign had had present to his mind the sword that was to pierce him, if Judas had foreseen the cord that was to suffocate him,—how bitter would their life have been. Our kind Redeemer, even from the first instant of His life, had always present before Him the scourges, the thorns, the Cross, the outrages of His Passion, the desolate death that awaited Him. When He beheld the victims which were sacrificed in the temple, He well knew that they were figures of the sacrifice which He, the Immaculate Lamb, would one day consummate on the Altar of the Cross. When He beheld the city of Jerusalem, He well knew that He was there to lose His life in a sea of sorrows and reproaches. When He saw His dear Mother, He already imagined He saw her in an agony of suffering at the foot of the Cross, near to His dying Self. So that, O my Jesus, the horrible sight of all these evils kept Thee during the whole of Thy life continually tormented and afflicted before the time of Thy death. And Thou didst accept and suffer everything for my sake.

4. O my agonising Lord, the sight alone of all the sins of the world, especially of mine, by which Thou didst already foresee I should offend Thee, rendered Thy life more afflicted and painful than all the lives that ever have been or ever will be. But, O my God, in what barbarous law is it written that a God should have such great love for a creature, and yet that creature should live without loving his God, or rather should offend and displease Him ? O my Lord, make me know the greatness of Thy love, in order that I may no longer be ungrateful to Thee. Oh, if I but loved Thee, my Jesus,—if I really loved Thee,—how sweet it would be to me to suffer for Thee !

5. Jesus appeared one day on the cross to Sister Magdalen Orsini, who had been suffering for some time from some great affliction, and animated her to suffer it in peace.
The servant of God answered, ' But, Lord, Thou didst only hang on the Cross for three hours, whereas I have gone on suffering this pain for several years.' Jesus Christ then said to her reproachingly, ' O ignorant that thou art, what dost thou mean? From the first moment that I was in My Mother's womb, I suffered in My Heart all that I afterwards endured on the Cross.' And I, my dear Redeemer, how can I, at the sight of such great sufferings which Thou didst endure for my sake, during Thy whole life, complain of those crosses which Thou dost send me for my good. I thank Thee for having redeemed me with so much love and such sufferings. In order to animate me to suffer with patience the pains of this life, Thou didst take upon Thyself all our evils. O my Lord, grant that Thy sorrows may be ever present to my mind, in order that I may always accept and desire to suffer for Thy love.

6. "Great as the sea is Thy destruction" (Lament, ii. 13). As the waters of the sea are all salt and bitter, so the life of Jesus Christ was full of bitterness and void of all consolation, as He Himself declared to St. Margaret of Cortona. Moreover, as all the waters of the earth unite in the sea, so did all the sufferings of men unite in Jesus Christ ; wherefore He said by the mouth of the Psalmist, "Save Me, O God, for the waters are come in even unto My soul. I am come into the depth of the sea, and a tempest hath overwhelmed Me" (Ps. lxviii. 2, 3). Save Me, O God, for sorrows have entered in even to the in most parts of My soul, and I am left submerged in a tempest of ignominy and of sufferings, both interior and exterior. '

O my dearest Jesus, my Love, my Life, my All, if I behold from without Thy Sacred Body, I see nothing else but wounds. But if I enter into Thy desolate Heart, I find nothing but bitterness and sorrows, which made Thee suffer the agonies of death. O my Lord, and who but Thee, who art infinite Goodness, would ever suffer so much, and die for one of Thy creatures ? But because Thou art God, Thou dost love as a God alone can love, with a love which cannot be equalled by any other love.

7. St. Bernard says, ' In order to redeem the slave, the Father did not spare His own Son, nor did the Son spare Himself.' O infinite love of God ! On the one band the Eternal Father required of Jesus Christ to satisfy for, all the sins of men : " The Lord hath laid on

Him the iniquity of us all" (Is. liii. 6). On the other hand, Jesus, in order to save men in the most loving way that He could, chose to take upon Himself the utmost penalty due to Divine justice for our sins. Wherefore, as St. Thomas asserts, He took upon Himself in the highest degree all the sufferings and outrages that ever were borne. It was on this account that Isaias called Him " a man of sorrows, despised, and the most abject of men" (Is. liii. 3). And with reason ; for Jesus was tormented in all the members and senses of His Body, and was still more bitterly afflicted in all the powers of His Soul ; so that the internal pains which He endured infinitely surpassed Hb external sufferings. Behold Him, then, torn, bloodless ; treated as an impostor, as a sorcerer, a madman ; abandoned even by His friends, and finally persecuted by all, until He finished His life upon an infamous gibbet.

8. " Know you what I have done to you ?" (St. John xiii. 12.) O my Lord, I do indeed know how much Thou hast done and suffered for my sake ; but Thou knowest, alas, that I have hitherto done nothing for Thee. My Jesus, help me to suffer something for Thy love before death overtakes me. I am ashamed of appearing before Thee ; but I will no longer be ungrateful, as I have been so many years towards Thee. Thou hast deprived Thyself of every pleasure for me; I will for the love of Thee renounce all the pleasures of the senses. Thou hast suffered so many pains for me ; I will for Thy sake suffer all the pains of my life and of my death as it shall best please Thee. Thou hast been forsaken ; I will be content that all should forsake me, provided Thou dost not forsake me, O my only and sovereign Good. Thou hast been persecuted ; I accept whatever persecution may befall me. Finally, Thou hast died for me; I will die for Thee. O my Jesus, my Treasure, my Love, my AU, I love Thee. Oh, give me more love ! Amen.

CHAPTER IV. OF THE GREAT DESKS WHICH JESUS HAD TO SUFFER AND TO DIE FOR LOVE OF US.

1. Oh, how exceedingly tender, loving, and constraining was that declaration of our Blessed Redeemer concerning His coming into the world, when He said that He had come to kindle in souls the fire of Divine love, and that His only desire was that this holy flame should be enkindled in the hearts of men : "Iam come to cast fire upon the earth ; and what will I but that it should be kindled?" (St. Luke xii. 49.) He continued immediately to say that He was expecting to be baptised with the baptism of His own Blood—not, indeed, to wash out His own sins, since He was incapable of sinning, but to wash out our sins, which He had come to satisfy by His sufferings : ' The Passion of Christ is called baptism, because we are purified in His Blood.' And therefore our loving Jesus, in order to make us understand how ardent was His desire to die for us, added, with sweetest expression of His love, that He felt an immense longing for the time of His Passion, so great was His desire to suffer for our sakes. These are His loving words : "I have a baptism wherewith I am to be baptised ; and how am I straitened until it be accomplished ?" (St. Luke xii. 50.)

2. O God, the Lover of men, what more couldst Thou have said or done in order to put me under the necessity of loving Thee ? And what good could my love ever do Thee, that Thou didst choose to die, and didst so much desire death in order to obtain it ? If a servant of mine had only desired to die for me, he would have attracted my love ; and can I then live without loving Thee with all my heart, my King and God, who didst die for me, and who hadst such a longing for death in order to acquire to Thyself my love ?

3. " Jesus, knowing that His hour was come that He should pass out of the world to the Father, having loved His own, ... He loved them unto the end" (John xiii. 1). St. John says that Jesus called the hour of His Passion *His* hour ; because, as a devout commentator writes, this was the time for which our Redeemer had most sighed during His whole life; because by suffering and dying for men, He desired to make them understand the immense love that He bore to them : ' That is the hour of the lover, in which he suffers for the object beloved ;' because suffering for the beloved is the most fit way of discovering the love of the lover, and of captivating to ourself the love of the beloved. O my dearest Jesus, in order to show me the great love Thou bearest me, Thou wouldst not commit the work of my redemption to any other than Thyself. Was my love, then, of such consequence to Thee, that Thou wouldst suffer so much in order to gain it ? Oh, what more couldst Thou have done if Thou hadst had to gain to Thyself the love of Thy Divine Father ? What more could a servant endure to acquire to himself the affections of his master than what Thou hast suffered in order that Thou mayest be loved by me, a vile, ungrateful slave?

4. But behold our loving Jesus already on the point of being sacrificed on the Altar of the Cross for our salvation, in that blessed night which preceded His Passion. Let us hear Him saying to His disciples, in the last supper that He makes with them, u With desire have I desired to eat this pasch with you" (St. Luke xxii. 15). St. Laurence Justinian, considering these words, asserts that they were all words of love : ' With desire have I desired ; this is the voice of love.' As if our loving Redeemer had said, O men, know that this night, in which My Passion will begin, has been the time most longed after by Me during the whole of My life ; because I shall now make known to you, through My sufferings and My bitter death, how much I love you, and shall thereby oblige you to love Me in the strongest way it is possible for Me to do. A certain author says, that in the Passion of Jesus Christ the Divine Omnipotence united itself to Love,—Love sought to love man to the utmost extent that Omnipotence could arrive at ; and Omnipotence sought to satisfy Love as far as its desire could reach.

O sovereign God ! Thou hast given Thyself entirely to me ; and how, then, shall I not love Thee with my whole self? I believe,—yes, I believe Thou hast died for me ; and how can I, then, love Thee so little as constantly to forget Thee, and all that Thou hast suffered for me ? And why, Lord, when I think on Thy Passion, am I not quite inflamed with Thy love, and do I not become entirely Thine, like so many holy souls who, after meditating on Thy sufferings, have remained the happy prey of Thy love, and have given themselves entirely to Thee ?

5. The spouse in the Canticles said, that whenever her Spouse introduced her into the sacred cellar of His Passion, she saw herself so assaulted on all sides by Divine love, that, all languishing with love, she was constrained to seek for relief to her wounded heart : " The king brought me into the cellar of wine, he set in order charity in me. Stay me up with flowers, compass me about with apples ; because I languish with love" (Quit. ii. 4,5). And how is it possible for a soul to enter upon the meditation of the Passion of Jesus Christ without being wounded, as by so many darts of love, by those sufferings and agonies which so greatly afflicted the Body and Soul of our loving Lord, and without being sweetly constrained to love Him who loved her so much ? O Immaculate Lamb, thus lacerated, covered with blood, and disfigured, as I behold Thee on this Cross, how beautiful and how worthy of love dost Thou yet appear to me ! Yes, because all these wounds that I behold in Thee are to me signs and proofs of the great love that Thou bearest to me. Oh, if all men did but contemplate Thee often in that state in which Thou wert one day made a spectacle to all Jerusalem, who could help being seized with Thy love ? O my beloved Lord, accept me to love Thee, since I give Thee all my senses and all my will. And how can I refuse Thee anything, if Thou hast not refused me Thy Blood, Thy life, and all Thyself?

6. So great was the desire of Jesus to suffer for us, that in the night preceding His death, He not only went of His own will into the Garden, where He knew that the Jews would come and take Him, but knowing that Judas the traitor was already near at hand with the company of soldiers, He said to His disciples, " Arise, let us go ; behold he that will betray Me is at hand" (St. Mark xiv. 42). He would even go Himself to meet them, as if they came to conduct Him, not to the punishment of death, but to the crown of a great kingdom. O my sweet Saviour, Thou dost, then, go to meet Thy death with such a longing to die, through the desire that Thou hast to be loved by me I And shall not I have a desire to die for Thee, my God, in order to prove to Thee the love that I bear Thee ? Yes, my Jesus, who hast died for me, I do also desire to die for Thee. Behold, my blood, my life, I offer all to Thee. I am ready to die for Thee as Thou wilt, and when Thou wilt. Accept this miserable sacrifice which a miserable sinner offers to Thee, who once offended Thee, but now loves Thee more than himself.

7. St. Laurence Justinian, in considering this word *"Sitio"* (I thirst), which Jesus pronounced on the Cross when He was expiring,

says that this thirst was not a thirst which proceeded from dryness, but one that arose from the ardour of the love that Jesus had for us : ' This thirst springs from the fever of His love.' Because by this word our Redeemer intended to declare to us, more than the thirst of the body, the desire He had of suffering for us, by showing us His love ; and the immense desire He had of being loved by us, by the many sufferings He endured for us : ' This thirst proceeds from the fever of His love.' And St. Thomas says, ' By this *"Sitio"* is shown the ardent desire for the salvation of the human race.'

O God, enamoured of souls, is it possible that such an excess of goodness can remain without being corresponded to ? It is said that love must be repaid by love ; but by what love can Thy love ever be repaid ? It would be necessary for another God to die for Thee, in order to compensate for the love that Thou hast borne us in dying for us. And how, then, couldst Thou, O my Lord, say that Thy delight was to dwell with men, if Thou dost receive from them nothing but injuries and ill-treatment ? Love made Thee, then, change into delights the sufferings and the insults Thou hast endured for us.

8. O my Redeemer, most worthy of love, I will no longer resist the stratagems of Thy love; I give Thee from henceforth my whole love. Thou art and shall be always the only-beloved One of my soul. Thou didst become man in order that Thou mayest have a life to devote to me; I would fain have a thousand lives, in order that I may sacrifice them all for Thee. I love Thee, O infinite Goodness, and I will love Thee with all my strength. I will do all that lies in my power to please Thee. Thou, being innocent, hast suffered for me; I, a sinner, who have deserved hell, desire to suffer for Thee as much as Thou willest. O my Jesus, assist, I pray Thee, by Thy merits, this desire which Thou dost Thyself give me. O infinite God, I believe in Thee, I hope in Thee, I love Thee. Mary, my Mother, intercede for me. Amen.

CHAPTER V. ON THE LOVE OF JESUS IN LEAVING HIMSELF FOR OUR FOOD BEFORE HIS DEATH.

1. "Jesus, knowing that His hour was come that He should pass out of this world to the Father, having loved His own who were in the world, He loved them to the end" (St. John xiii. 1). Our most loving Redeemer, on the last night of His life, knowing that the much-longed for time had arrived on which He should die for the love of man, had not the heart to leave us alone in this valley of tears ; but in order that He might not be separated from us even by death, He would leave us His whole Self as food in the Sacrament of the Altar ; giving us to understand by this, that, having given us this gift of infinite worth, He could give us nothing further to prove to us His love : " He loved them unto the end." Cornelius à Lapide, with St. Chrysostom and Theophylact, interpret the words ' unto the end' according to the Greek text, and write thus : " He loved them with an excessive and supreme love." Jesus in this Sacrament made His last effort of love towards men, as the Abbot Guerric says : ' He poured out the whole power of His love upon His friends.'

This was still better expressed by the Holy Council of Trent, which, in speaking of the Sacrament of the Altar, said that our Blessed Saviour ' poured out of Himself in it, as it were, all the riches of His love towards us.' The angelical St. Thomas was therefore right in calling this Sacrament ' a Sacrament of love, and a token of the greatest love that a God could give us.' And St. Bernard called it ' The Love of loves.' And St. Mary Magdalen of Pazzi said that a soul, after having communicated, might say, ' It is consummated ;' that is to say, My God, having given Thyself to me in this Holy Communion, has nothing more to give me. This saint, one day, asked one of her novices what she had been thinking of after Communion ; she answered, ' Of the *love of Jesus.*' 'Yes,' replied the saint ; ' when we think of this love, we cannot pass on to other thoughts, but must stop upon love.'

O Saviour of the world, what dost Thou expect from men, that Thou hast been induced even to give them Thyself in food ? And what can there be left to Thee to give us after this Sacrament, in order to oblige us to love Thee? Ah, my most loving God, enlighten me that I may know what an excess of goodness this has been of Thine, to reduce Thyself unto becoming my food in Holy Communion ! If Thou hast, therefore, given Thyself entirely to me, it is just that I also should give myself wholly to Thee. Yes, my Jesus, I give myself entirely to Thee. I love Thee above every good, and I desire to receive Thee in order to love Thee more. Come, therefore, and come often, into my soul, and make it entirely Thine. Oh, that I could truly say to Thee, as the loving St. Philip Neri said to Thee when he received Thee in the Viaticum, ' Behold my Love, behold my Love; give me my Love.'

2. " He that eateth My Flesh, and drinketh My Blood, abideth in Me, and I in Him" (St. John vi. 57). St. Denis, the Areopagite, says that love always tends towards union with the object beloved. And because food becomes one thing with him who eats it, therefore our Lord would reduce Himself into food, in order that receiving Him in Holy Communion, we might become of one substance with Him : " Take ye and eat," said Jesus ; " this is My Body." As if He had said, remarks St. John Chrysostom, ' Eat Me, that the highest union may take place.' O man, feed thyself on Me, in order that thou and I may become one substance. In the same way, says St. Cyril of Alexandria, as two pieces of melted wax unite together, so a soul that communicates is so thoroughly united to Jesus, that Jesus remains in her and she in Jesus. O my beloved Redeemer, exclaims, therefore, St. Laurence Justinian, how couldst Thou ever come to love us so much that Thou wouldst unite Thyself to us in such a way that Thy heart and ours should become but one heart ? ' Oh, how admirable is Thy love, O Lord Jesus, who wouldst incorporate us in such a manner with Thy Body, that we should have but one heart with Thee.'

Well did St. Francis of Sales say, in speaking of Holy Communion : ' In no action does our Saviour show Himself more loving or more tender than in this one, in which, as it were, He annihilates Himself and reduces Himself into food in order to penetrate our souls, and unite Himself to the hearts of His faithful ones.' So that, says St. John Chrysostom, 'To that Lord on whom the angels even dare not fix their eyes, to Him we unite ourselves, and we are made one body, one flesh. But what shepherd,' adds the saint, 'feeds the sheep with his own blood ? Even mothers give their children to nurses to feed them ; but Jesus in the Blessed Sacrament feeds us with His own Blood, and unites us to Himself. What shepherd feeds his sheep with his own blood ? And why do I say shepherd ? There are many mothers who give their children to others to nurse ; but this He has not done, but feeds us with His own Blood.' In short, says the saint, because He loved us so ardently, He chose to make Himself one with us by becoming our food. 'He mixed Himself with us, that we might be one ; this they do whose love is ardent.'

O infinite Love, worthy of infinite love, when shall I love Thee, my Jesus, as Thou hast loved me ? O Divine Food, Sacrament of love, when wilt Thou draw me entirely to Thyself? Thou hast nothing left to do in order to make Thyself loved by me. I am constantly intending to begin to love Thee, I constantly promise Thee to do so ; but I never begin. I will from this day begin to love Thee in earnest. Oh, do Thou enable me to do so. Enlighten me, inflame me, detach me from earth, and permit me not any longer to resist so many enticements of Thy love. I love Thee with my whole heart, and I will therefore leave everything in order to please Thee, my Life, my Love, my All. I will constantly unite myself to Thee in this Holy Sacrament, in order to detach myself from everything, and to love Thee only, my God. I hope, through Thy gracious assistance, to be enabled to do so.

3. St. Laurence Justinian says : 'We have seen the All-wise made foolish by excess of love.' We have seen a God who is Wisdom itself become a fool through the love He has borne to man. And is it not so ? Does it not seem, exclaims St. Augustine, a folly of love, that a God should give Himself as food to His creatures? 'Does it not seem madness to say, Eat my Flesh, drink my Blood ?' And what more could a creature have said to his Creator ? 'Shall I make bold to say, that the Creator of all things was beside Himself through the excess of His loving goodness?' Thus St. Denis speaks, and says, that God through the greatness of His love has almost gone out of Himself ; for, being God, He has gone so far as to become man, and even to make Himself the food of men. But, O Lord, such an excess was not becoming Thy Majesty. No, but love, answers St. John Chrysostom for Jesus, does not go about looking for reasons when it desires to do good and to make itself known to the object beloved ; it goes, not where it is

becoming, but where it is carried by its desire. ' Love is unreasoning, and goes as it is led, and not as it ought.'

O my Jesus, how ought I not to be covered with shame when I consider that, having Thee before me, who art the infinite Good and lovely above every good, and so full of love for my soul, I have yet turned back to love vile and contemptible things, and for their sake have forsaken Thee. O my God, I beseech Thee, discover to me every day more and more the greatness of Thy goodness, in order that I may every day be more and more enamoured of Thee, and may labour more and more to please Thee. Ah, my Lord, what object more beautiful, more good, more holy, more amiable can I love beside Thee ? I love Thee, infinite Goodness, I love Thee more than myself, and I desire to live only that I may love Thee, who dost deserve all my love.

4. St. Paul remarks also on the time which Jesus chooses to make us this gift of the most Holy Sacrament ; a gift which surpasses all the other gifts which an Almighty God could make ; as St. Clement says, 'A gift surpassing all fullness.' And St. Augustine says, 'Although omnipotent, He could give no more.' The Apostle remarks that "The Lord Jesus, the same night in which He was betrayed, took bread and, giving thanks, broke and said : Take ye and eat ; this is my Body which shall be delivered for you" (1 Cor. xi. 23, 24). In that same night, then, that men were thinking of preparing torments and death for Jesus, our beloved Redeemer thought of leaving them Himself in the Blessed Sacrament ; giving us thereby to understand that His love was so great, that, instead of being cooled by so many injuries, it was then more than ever yearning towards us. O most loving Saviour, how couldest Thou have so great love for men as to choose to remain with them on this earth to be their food, after their having driven Thee away from it with so much ingratitude !

Let us also remark the immense desire which Jesus had during all His life for the arrival of that night, in which He had determined to leave us this great pledge of His love. For at the moment of His instituting this most sweet Sacrament, He said, " With desire I have desired to eat this pasch with you" (St. Luke xxii. 15) ; words which discover to us the ardent desire which He had to unite Himself with us in Communion through the love which He bore us : ' This is the voice of most burning charity,' says St. Laurence Justinian. And Jesus still retains at the present time the same desire towards all the souls that love Him. There is not a bee, said He one day to St. Matilda, that throws itself with such eagerness upon the flowers in order to suck out the honey, as I, through the violence of my love, hasten to the soul that desires Me.

O Lover, too full of love, there are no greater proofs left for Thee to give me in order to persuade me that Thou dost love me. I bless Thy goodness for it. O my Jesus, I beseech Thee, draw me entirely to Thyself. Make me love Thee henceforth with all the affections and tenderness of which I am capable. Let it suffice to others to love Thee with a love only appreciative and predominant, for I know that Thou wilt be satisfied with it ; but I shall not be satisfied until I see that I love Thee also with all the tenderness of my heart, more than friend, more than brother, more than father, and more than spouse. And where indeed shall I find a friend, a brother, a father, a spouse, who will love me as much as Thou hast loved me, my Creator, my Redeemer, and my God, who for the love of me hast spent Thy Blood and Thy life ; and, not content with that, dost give Thyself entirely to me in this Sacrament of love. I love Thee, then, O my Jesus, with all the affections of my soul ; I love Thee more than myself. Oh, help me to love Thee ; I ask nothing more of Thee.

5. St. Bernard says that God loves us for no other reason than that He may be loved by us: ' God only loved that He might be loved.' And therefore our Saviour protested that He had come upon earth in order to make Himself loved : " I am come to send a fire upon the earth." And oh, what flames of holy love does Jesus kindle in souls in this most Divine Sacrament ! The venerable Father Francis Olimpio, a Theatine, said that nothing was so fit to excite our hearts to love the Sovereign Good as the most Holy Communion. Hesychius called Jesus in the Sacrament a ' Divine fire.' And St. Catherine of Sienna, one day perceiving in the hands of a priest Jesus in the Sacrament under the appearance of a furnace of love, was full of astonishment that the whole world was not consumed by the fire. The Abbot Rupert, and St. Gregory of Nyssa, said that the altar itself was the wine-cellar where the espoused soul is inebriated with the love of her Lord ; so much so, that, forgetful of earth, she burns and languishes with holy love : " The king brought me," says the spouse in the Canticles, " into the cellar of wine ; he set in order charity in me. Stay me up with flowers, compass me about with apples ; because I languish with love" (Cant. ii. 4, 5).

O Love of my soul, most Holy Sacrament ; oh, that I could always remember Thee, to forget everything else, and that I could love Thee alone without interruption and without reserve ! Ah, my Jesus, Thou hast knocked sa frequently at the door of my heart, that Thou hast at last, I hope, entered therein. But since Thou hast entered there, drive away, I pray Thee, all its affections that do not tend towards Thyself. Possess Thyself so entirely of me, that I may be able with truth to say to Thee from this day forth, with the Prophet, "What have I in heaven ? and besides Thee what do I desire on earth ? The God of my heart, and my portion forever" (Ps. lxxii. 20). Yes, O my God, what else do I desire but Thee upon earth or in heaven ? Thou alone art and shalt always be the only Lord of my heart and my will ; and Thou alone shalt be all my portion, all my riches, in this life and in the next.

6. Go, said the Prophet Isaias, go, publish everywhere the loving inventions of our God, in order to make Himself loved of men : " You shall draw waters with joy out of the Saviour's fountains ; and you shall say in that day, Praise ye the Lord, and call upon His name, make His inventions known among the people" (Is. xii. 3, 4). And ' what inventions has not the love of Jesus made in order to make Himself loved by us ? Even on the Cross He has opened in His wounds so many fountains of grace, that to receive them it is sufficient to ask for them in faith. And not satisfied with this, He has given us His whole Self in the most Holy Sacrament.

O man, says St. John Chrysostom, wherefore art thou so niggardly, and dost use so much reserve in thy love for that God who hath given His whole Self to thee without any reserve ? ' He gave Himself wholly to thee, reserving nothing for Himself.' This is just, says the angelic doctor, what Jesus has done in the Sacrament of the Altar, wherein 'He has given us all that He is and all that He has.' Behold, adds St. Bonaventure, that immense God, 'whom the world cannot contain, become our prisoner and captive' when we receive Him into our breast in Holy Communion.

Wherefore St. Bernard, transported with love when he considered this, exclaimed, My Jesus would make Himself ' the inseparable guest of my heart.' And since my God, he concludes, has chosen to ' spend Himself entirely for my sake,' it is reasonable that I should employ all that I am in serving and loving Him.

Ah, my beloved Jesus, tell me, what more is there left for Thee to invent in order to make Thyself loved ? And shall I, then, continue to live so ungrateful to Thee as I have hitherto done ? My Lord, permit it not. Thou hast said, that he who feeds on Thy Flesh in Communion shall live through the virtue of Thy grace : " He that eateth Me, the same also shall live by Me" (St. John vi. 58). Since, then, Thou dost not disdain that I should receive Thee in Holy Communion, grant that my soul may always live the true life of Thy grace. I repent, O Sovereign Good, of having despised it in times past ; but I bless Thee that Thou dost give me time to weep over the offences that I have committed against Thee, and to love Thee in this world. During the life that remains to me, I will place all my affections in Thee, and endeavour to please Thee as much as I possibly can. Help me, O my Jesus ; forsake me not, I beseech Thee. Save me by Thy merits, and let my salvation be to love Thee always in this life and in eternity. Mary, my Mother, do thou also assist me.

CHAPTER VI. ON THE BLOODY SWEAT AND AGONY SUFFERED BY JESUS IN THE GARDEN.

1. Behold how our most loving Saviour, having come to the Garden of Gethsemani, did of His own accord make a beginning of His bitter Passion by giving full liberty to the passions of fear, of weariness, and of sorrow to come and afflict Him with all their torments : " He began to fear, and to be heavy, to grow sorrowful, and to be sad" (St. Mark xiv., St. Matt. xxvi.). He began, then, first to feel a great fear of death, and of the sufferings He would have soon to endure. "He began to fear;" but how? Was it not He Himself that had offered Himself spontaneously to endure all these torments? " He was offered because He willed it." Was it not He who had so much ' desired this hour of His Passion, and who had said shortly before, " With desire have I desired to eat this pasch with you" ? And yet how is it that He was seized with such a fear of death, that He even prayed His Father to deliver Him from it? " My Father, if it be possible, let this chalice pass from Me" (St. Matt xxvi. 39). The Venerable Bede answers this, and says, ' He prays that the chalice may pass from Him, in order to show that He was truly man.' He, our loving Saviour, chose indeed to die for us in order by His death to prove to us the love that He bore us ; but in order that men might not suppose that He had assumed a fantastic body (as some heretics have blasphemously asserted), or that in virtue of His Divinity He had died without suffering any pain, He therefore made this prayer to His heavenly Father, not indeed with a view of being heard, but to give us to understand that He died as man, and afflicted with a great fear of death and of the sufferings which should accompany His Death. O most amiable Jesus, Thou wouldst, then, take upon Thee our fearfulness in order to give us Thy courage in suffering the trials of this life. Oh, be Thou forever blessed for Thy great mercy and love ! Oh, may all our hearts love Thee as much as Thou desirest, and as much as Thou deservest !

2. " He began to be heavy." He began to feel a great weariness on account of the torments that were prepared for Him. When one is weary, even pleasures are painful. Oh, what anguish united to this weariness must Jesus Christ have felt at the horrible representation which then came before His mind, of all the torments both exterior and interior which, during the short remainder of His life, were so cruelly to afflict His Body and His blessed Soul! Then did all the sufferings He was to endure pass-distinctly before His eyes, as well as all the insults He should endure from the Jews and from the Romans; all the injustice of which the judges of His cause would be guilty towards Him ; and, above all, He had before Him the vision of that Death of desolation which He should have to endure, forsaken by all, by men and by God, in the midst of a sea of sufferings and contempt. And this it was that caused Him such heavy grief that He was obliged to pray for consolation to His Eternal Father. O my Jesus, I compassionate Thee, I thank Thee, and I love Thee.

3. " And there appeared to Him an angel. . . . strengthening Him" (St. Luke xxii. 43). Strength came, but, says the Venerable Bede, this rather increased than lightened His sufferings : 'Strength did not diminish, but increased His sorrow.' Yes, for the angel strengthened Him that He might suffer still more for the love of men, and the glory of His Father. Oh, what sufferings did not this first combat bring Thee, my beloved Lord ! During the progress of Thy Passion, the scourges, the thorns, the nails came one after the other to torment Thee. But in the Garden all the sufferings of Thy whole Passion assaulted Thee altogether and tormented Thee. And Thou didst accept all for my sake and my good. O my God, how much I regret not having loved Thee in times past, and having preferred my own accursed pleasures to Thy will. I detest them now above every evil, and repent of them with my whole heart. O my Jesus, forgive me.

4. " He began to grow sorrowful and to be sad." Together with this fear and weariness, Jesus began to feel a great melancholy and affliction of soul. But, my Lord, art Thou not He who didst give to Thy martyrs such a delight in suffering that they even despised their torments and death? St. Augustine said of St. Vincent, that he spoke with such joy during his martyrdom, that it seemed as if it were not the same person who suffered and who spoke. It is related of St. Laurence, that whilst he was burning on the gridiron, such was the consolation he enjoyed in his soul, that he insulted the tyrant, saying, ' Turn, and eat.' How, then, my Jesus, didst Thou, who gavest each great joy to Thy servants in dying, choose for Thyself such extreme sorrowfulness in Thy Death ?

5. O Delight of Paradise, Thou dost rejoice heaven and earth with Thy gladness; why, then, do I behold Thee so afflicted and sorrowful? Why do I hear Thee say that the sorrow that afflicts Thee is enough to take away Thy life ? " My soul is sorrowful even unto death" (St. Mark xiv. 34). O my Redeemer, why is this ? Ah, I understand it all ! It was less the thought of Thy sufferings in Thy bitter Passion, than of the sins of men that afflicted Thee ; and amongst these, alas, were my sins, which caused Thee this great dread of death.

6. He, the Eternal Word, as much as He loved Hie Father, so much did He hate sin, of which He well knew the malice ; wherefore, in order to deliver the world from sin, and that He might no longer behold His beloved Father offended, He had come upon earth, and had made Himself Man, and had undertaken to suffer such a painful Death and Passion. But when He saw that, notwithstanding all His sufferings, there would yet be so many sine committed in the world, His sorrow for this, says St. Thomas, exceeded the sorrow that any penitent has ever felt for his own sins : ' It surpassed the sorrow of all ' contrite souls ;' and, indeed, it surpassed every sorrow that ever could afflict a human heart. The reason is, that all the sorrows that men feel are always mixed with some relief ; but the sorrow of Jesus was pure sorrow without any relief : 'He suffered pure pain without any admixture of consolation .'

Oh, if I loved Thee, my Jesus, if I loved Thee, the consideration of all that Thou hast suffered for me would render all sufferings, all contempt, and all vexations sweet to me. Oh, grant me, I beseech Thee, Thy love, in order that I may endure with pleasure, or at least with patience; the little Thou givest me to suffer. Oh, let me not die so ungrateful to all Thy loving-kindnesses. I desire, in alt the tribulations that shall happen to me, to say constantly, My Jesus, I embrace this trial for Thy love ; I will suffer it in order to please Thee.

7. We read in history, that several penitents being enlightened by Divine light to see the malice of their sins, have died of pure sorrow for them. Oh, what torment, then, must not the Heart of Jesus endure at the sight of all the sins of the world, of all the

blasphemies, sacrileges, acts of impurity, and all the other crimes which should be committed by men after His Death, every one of which, like a wild-beast, tore His heart separately by its own malice ? Wherefore our afflicted Lord, during His Agony in the Garden, exclaimed, Is this, therefore, O men, the reward that you render Me for My immeasurable love? Oh, if I could only see that, grateful for My affection, you gave up sin and began to love Me, with what delight should I not hasten to die for you ! But to behold, after all My sufferings, so many sins ; after so much love, such ingratitude;— this is what afflicts Me the most, makes Me sorrowful even unto death, and makes Me sweat pure Blood : " And His sweat became as drops of blood trickling down upon the ground" (St. Luke xxii. 44). So that, according to the Evangelist, this Bloody Sweat was so copious, that it first bathed all the vestments of our Blessed Redeemer, and then came forth in quantity and bathed the ground.

8. Ah, my loving Jesus, I do not behold in this Garden either scourges or thorns or nails that pierce Thee ; how, then, is it that I see Thee all bathed in Blood from Thy head to Thy feet ? Alas, my sins were the cruel press which, by dint of affliction and sorrow, drew so much Blood from Thy Heart. I was, then, one of Thy most cruel executioners, who contributed the most to crucify Thee with my sins. It is certain that, if I had sinned less, Thou, my Jesus, wouldst have suffered less. As much pleasure, therefore, as I have taken in offending Thee, so much the more did I increase the sorrow of Thy Heart, already full of anguish. How, then, does not this thought make me die of grief, when I see that I have repaid the love Thou hast shown me in Thy Passion by adding to Thy sorrow and suffering ! I, then, have tormented this Heart, so Loving and so worthy of love, which has shown so much love to me. My Lord, since I have now no other means left of consoling Thee than to weep over my offences towards Thee, I will now, my Jesus, sorrow for them and lament over them with my whole heart. Oh, give me, I pray Thee, so great sorrow for them as may make me to my last breath weep over the displeasure I have caused Thee, my God, my Love, my All.

9. "He fell upon His face" (St. Matt. xxvi. 39). Jesus, beholding Himself charged with the burden of satisfying for all the sins of the world, prostrated Himself, with His Face on the ground, to pray for men, as if He were ashamed to raise His eyes towards heaven, loaded as He was with such iniquities. O my Redeemer, I behold Thee pale and worn out with sorrow ; Thou art in the agony of death, and Thou dost pray : " And being in an agony, He prayed the longer" (St. Luke xxii. 43). Tell me, my Saviour, for whom dost Thou pray? Ah, Thou didst not pray so much for Thyself at that hour as for me ; Thou didst offer to Thy Eternal Father Thy all-powerful prayers, united to Thy sufferings, to obtain for me, a wretched sinner, the pardon of my sins : " Who, in the days of His flesh, with a strong cry and tears, offering up prayers and supplications to Him that was able to save Him from death, was heard for His reverence" (Heb. v. 7). O my beloved Redeemer, how is it possible that Thou couldst love so much one who has so grievously offended Thee ? How couldst Thou embrace such sufferings for me, foreseeing, as Thou didst, all the ingratitude of which I should be guilty towards Thee.

10. O my afflicted Lord, make me share in that sorrow which Thou didst then have for my sins. I abhor them at this present moment ; and I unite this my hatred to the horror that Thou didst feel for them in the Garden. O my Saviour, look not upon my sins, for hell itself would not be sufficient to expiate them, but look upon the sufferings that Thou hast endured for me ! O love of my Jesus, Thou art my Love and my Hope. O my Lord, I love Thee with my whole soul, and will always love Thee. I beseech Thee, through the merits of that weariness and sadness which Thou didst endure in the Garden, give me fervour and courage in all works that may contribute to Thy glory. Through the merits of Thy Agony, grant me Thy assistance to resist all the temptations of the flesh and of hell. My God, grant me the grace always to commend myself to Thee, and always to repeat to Thee, with Jesus Christ : " Not as I will, but as Thou willest." May Thy Divine will, not mine, be ever done. Amen.

CHAPTER VII. ON THE LOVE OF JESUS IN SUFFERING SUCH GREAT CONTEMPT IN HIS PASSION.

1. Bellarmine says, that to noble spirits affronts cause greater pain than sufferings of body : 'Noble spirits think more of ignominy than of pains of body.' Because, if the former afflict the flesh, the latter afflict the soul, which, in proportion as it is more noble than the body, so much the more does it feel pain. But who ever could have imagined that the most noble Personage in heaven and earth, the Son of God, by coming into the world to make Himself Man for love of men, would have had to be treated by them with such reproaches and injuries, as if He had been the lowest and most vile of all men ? " We have seen Him despised and the most abject of men" (Is. liii. 2). St. Anselm asserts that Jesus Christ was willing to suffer such and so great dishonours, that it could not be possible for Him to be more humbled than He was in His Passion : ' He humbled Himself so much, that He could not go beyond it.'

O Lord of the world, Thou art the greatest of all kings ; but Thou hast willed to be despised more than all men, in order to teach me the love of contempt. Because, then, Thou hast sacrificed Thine honour for love of me, I am willing to suffer for love of Thee every affront which shall be offered to me.

2. And what kind of affronts did not the Redeemer suffer in His Passion ? He saw Himself affronted by His own disciples. One of them betrays Him, and sells Him for thirty pieces. Another denies Him many times, protesting publicly that he knows Him not ; and thus attesting that he was ashamed to have known Him in the past. The other disciples, then, at seeing Him taken and bound, all fly and abandon Him : " Then His disciples leaving Him, all fled away" (St. Mark xiv. 50).

O my Jesus, thus abandoned, who will ever undertake Thy defence, if, when Thou art first taken, those most dear to Thee depart from and forsake Thee ? But, my God, to think that this dishonour did not end with Thy Passion ! How many souls, after having devoted themselves to follow Thee, and after having been favoured by Thee with many graces and special signs of love, being then driven by some passion of vile interest, or human respect, or sordid pleasure, have ungratefully forsaken Thee ! Which of these ungrateful ones is found to turn and lament, saying, Ah, my dear Jesus, pardon me ; for I will not leave Thee again. I will rather lose my life a thousand times than lose Thy grace, O my God, my Love, my All.

3. Behold how Judas, arriving in the Garden together with the soldiers, advances, embraces his Master, and kisses Him. Jesus suffers him to kiss Him ; but, knowing already his evil intent, could not refrain from complaining of this most unjust treachery, saying, "Judas, betrayest Thou the Son of man with a kiss ?" (St. Luke xxii. 48.) Then those insolent servants crowd around Jesus, lay hand upon Him, and bind Him as a villain : " The servants of the Jews apprehended Jesus, and bound Him" (St. John xviii. 12).

Ah, me ! what do I see ? A God bound ! By whom ? By men ; by worms created by Himself. Angels of Paradise, what say ye to it ? And Thou, my Jesus, why dost Thou allow Thyself to be bound ? What, says St. Bernard, have the bonds of slaves and of the guilty to do with Thee, who art the Holy of Holies, the King of kings, and the Lord of lords? ' O King of kings and Lord of lords, what hast Thou to do with chains ?'

But if men bind Thee, wherefore dost Thou not loosen and free Thyself from the torments and death which they are preparing for Thee? But I understand it. They are not, O my Lord, these ropes which bind Thee. It is only love which keeps Thee bound, and constrains Thee to suffer and die for us : 'O Charity,' exclaims St. Laurence Justinian, ' how strong is Thy chain, by which God was able to be bound !' O Divine Love, thou only wast able to bind a God, and conduct Him to death for the love of men.

4. 'Look, O man,' says St. Bonaventure, 'at these dogs dragging Him along, and the Lamb, like a victim meekly following without resistance. One seizes, another binds Him ; another drives, another strikes Him.' They carry our sweet Saviour, thus bound, first to the house of Annas, then to that of Caiaphas ; where Jesus, being asked by that wicked one about His disciples and His doctrine, replied that He had not spoken in private, but in public, and that they who were standing roundabout well knew what He had taught : " I spoke openly ; lo, these know what I said" (St. John xviii. 21). But at this answer one of those servants, treating Him as if too bold, gave Him a blow on the cheek : " One of the officers standing by gave Jesus a blow, saying, Answerest Thou the high-priest thus ?" (St. John xviii. 22.) Here exclaims St. Jerome : ' Ye angels, how is it that ye are silent ? How long can such patience withhold you in your astonishment ?'

Ah, my Jesus, how could an answer so just and modest deserve such an affront in the presence of so many people ? The worthless high-priest, instead of reproving the insolence of this audacious fellow, praises him, or at least by signs approves. And Thou, my Lord, sufferest all this to compensate for the affronts which I, a wretch, have offered to the Divine Majesty by my sins. My Jesus, I thank Thee for it. Eternal Father, pardon me by the merits of Jesus.

5. Then the iniquitous high-priest asked Him if He were verily the Son of God : " I adjure Thee by the living God, that Thou tell us if Thou be the Christ, the Son of God" (St. Matt. xxvi. 63). Jesus, out of respect for the name of God, affirmed that He was so indeed ; whereupon Caiaphas rent his garments, saying that He had blasphemed ; and all cried out that He deserved death : "But they answering said, He is guilty of death" (St. Matt. xxvi. 65). Yes, O my Jesus, with truth do they declare Thee guilty of death, since Thou hast willed to take upon Thee to make satisfaction for me, who deserved eternal death. But if by Thy death Thou hast acquired for me life, it is just that I should spend my life wholly, yea, and if need be lose it, for Thee. Yes, my Jesus, I will no longer live for myself; but only for Thee, and for Thy love. Succour me by Thy grace.

6. "Then they spat in His face and buffeted Him" (St. Matt. xxvi. 67). After having proclaimed Him guilty of death, as a man already given over to punishment, and declared infamous, the rabble set themselves to ill-treat Him all the night through with blows, and buffets, and kicks, with plucking out His beard, and even spitting in His face, by mocking Him as a false prophet and saying, " Prophesy to us, O Christ, who it is that struck Thee" (St. Matt. xxvi. 68). All this our Redeemer foretold by Isaias : " I have given My Body to the strikers, and My cheeks to them that plucked them; I have not turned away My face from them that rebuked and spit upon Me" (Is. 1. 6). The devout Thauler relates that it is an opinion of St. Jerome, that all the pains and infirmities which

Jesus suffered on that night shall be made known only on the day of the last judgment. St. Augustine, speaking of the ignominies suffered by Jesus Christ, says, ' If this medicine cannot cure our pride, I know not what can.' Ah, my Jesus, how is it that Thou art so humble and I so proud ? O Lord, give me light; make me know who Thou art, and who I am.

"Then they spat in His face." "Spat!" O God, what greater affront can there be than to be defiled by spitting : ' To be spit upon is to suffer the extreme of insult,' says Origen. Where are we wont to spit, except in the most filthy place ? And didst Thou, my Jesus, suffer Thyself to be spit upon in the face 7 Behold how these wretches outrage Thee with blows and kicks, insult Thee, spit on Thy face, do with Thee just what they will ; and dost Thou not threaten nor reprove them ? " When He was reviled, He reviled not ; when He suffered, He threatened not ; but delivered Himself to him that judged Him unjustly" (1 St. Pet. ii. 23). No, but like an innocent lamb, humble and meek, Thou didst suffer all without so much as complaining, offering all to the Father to obtain the pardon of our sins : " Like a lamb before the shearer, He shall be dumb and shall not open His mouth" (Is. liii.7). St. Gertrude one day, when meditating on the injuries done to Jesus in His Passion, began to praise and bless Him ; this was so pleasing to our Lord, that He lovingly thanked her.

Ah, my reviled Lord, Thou art the King of heaven, the Son of the Most High ; Thou surely deservest not to be ill-treated and despised, but to be adored and loved by all creatures. I adore Thee, I bless Thee, I thank Thee, I love Thee with all my heart. I repent of having offended Thee. Help me, have pity upon me.

7. When it was day, the Jews conduct Jesus to Pilate, to make him condemn Him to death ; but Pilate declares Him to be innocent : " I find no cause in this Man" (St. Luke xxiii. 4). And to free himself from the importunities of the Jews who pressed on him, seeking the death of the Saviour, he sends Him to Herod. It greatly pleased Herod to see Jesus Christ brought before him, hoping that in his presence, in order to deliver Himself from death, He would have worked one of those miracles of which he had heard tell ; wherefore he asked Him many questions. But Jesus, because He did not wish to be delivered from death, and because that wicked one was not worthy of His answers, was silent, and answered him not. Then the proud king, with his court, offered Him many insults, and making them cover Him with a white robe, as if declaring Him to be an ignorant and stupid fellow, sent Him back to Pilate : " But Herod with his soldiers despised Him, and mocked Him, putting on Him a white robe, and sent Him back to Pilate" (St. Luke xxiii. 11). Cardinal Hugo in his Commentary says, ' Mocking Him as if a fool, he clothed Him with a white robe.' And St. Bonaventure, ' He despised Him as if impotent, because He worked no miracle ; as if ignorant, because He answered him not a word ; as if idiotic, because He did not defend Himself.'

O Eternal Wisdom, O Divine Word ! This one other ignominy was wanting to Thee, that Thou shouldest be treated as a fool bereft of sense. So greatly does our salvation weigh on Thee, that through love of us Thou willest not only to be reviled, but to be satiated with revilings ; as Jeremias had already prophesied of Thee : " He shall give His cheek to him that striketh Him ; He shall be filled with reproaches" (Lament, iii. 30). And how couldest Thou bear such love to men, from whom Thou hast received nothing but ingratitude and slights ? Alas, that I should be one of these, who have outraged Thee worse than Herod. Ah, my Jesus, chastise me not, like Herod, by depriving me of Thy voice. Herod did not recognise Thee for what Thou art ; I confess Thee to be my God : Herod loved Thee not ; I love Thee more than myself. Deny me not, I beseech Thee, deny me not the voice of Thy inspiration, as I have deserved by the offences I have committed against Thee. Tell me what Thou wilt have of me, for, by Thy grace, I am ready to do all that Thou wilt.

8. When Jesus had been led back to Pilate, the governor inquired of the people whom they wished to have released at that Passover, Jesus or Barabbas, a murderer. But the people cried out, " Not this Man, but Barabbas." Then said Pilate, "What, then, shall I do with Jesus?" They answered, "Let Him be crucified." But what evil hath this innocent One done ? replied Pilate : " What evil hath He done ?" They repeated, " Let Him be crucified." And even up to this time, O God, the greater part of mankind continue to say, " Not this Man, but Barabbas preferring to Jesus Christ some pleasure of sense, some point of honour, some outbreak of wounded pride.

Ah, my Lord, well knowest Thou that at one time I did Thee the same injury when I preferred my accursed tastes to Thee. My Jesus, pardon me, for I repent of the past, end from henceforth I prefer Thee before everything. I esteem Thee, I love Thee more than any good ; and am willing a thousand times to die rather than forsake Thee. Give me holy perseverance ; give me Thy love.

9. Presently we will speak of the other reproaches which Jesus Christ endured, until He finally died on the Cross : "He endured the Cross, despising the shame" (Heb. xii. 2). In the mean while let us consider how truly in our Redeemer was fulfilled what the Psalmist had foretold, that in His Passion He should become the reproach of men, and the outcast of the people : "But I am a worm, and no man ; the reproach of men, and the abject of the people" (Ps. xxi. 7) ; even to a death of ignominy, suffered at the hands of the executioner on a Cross, as a malefactor between two malefactors : " And He was reputed with the wicked" (Is. liii. 12). O Lord, the most high, exclaims St. Bernard, become the lowest among men ! O lofty one become vile ! O glory of Angels become the reproach of men : ' O lowest and highest ! O humble and sublime ! O reproach of men and glory of Angels !'

10. O grace, O strength of the love of God, continues St. Bernard ! Thus did the Lord most high over all become the most lightly esteemed of all ! 'O grace, O power of love, did the highest of all thus become the lowest of all?' And who was it (adds the saint) that did this ? 'Who hath done this ? Love.' All this hath the love which God bears towards men done, to prove how He loves us, and to teach us by His example how to suffer with peace contempt and injuries : " Christ suffered for us (writes St. Peter), leaving you an example, that you may follow His steps" (1 St. Pet. ii. 21). St. Eleazar, when asked by his wife how he came to endure with such peace the great injuries that were done him, answered : I turn to look on Jesus enduring contempt, and say that my affronts are as nothing in respect to those which He my God was willing to bear for me.

Ah, my Jesus, and how is it that, at the sight of a God thus dishonoured for love of me, I know not how to suffer the least contempt for love of Thee? A sinner, and proud! And whence, my Lord, can come this pride? I pray Thee, by the merits of the contempt Thou sufferedst, give me grace to suffer with patience and gladness all affronts and injuries. From this day forth I propose by Thy help never more to resent them, but to receive with joy all the reproaches which shall be offered me. Truly have I deserved greater contempt for having despised Thy Divine Majesty, and deserved the contempt of hell. Exceeding sweet and pleasant to me hast Thou rendered affronts, my beloved Redeemer, by having embraced such great contempt for love of me. Henceforth I propose, in order to please Thee, to benefit as much as possible whoever despises me ; at least to speak well of and pray for him. And even now I pray Thee to heap up Thy graces on all these from whom I have received any injury. I love Thee, O infinite Good, and will ever love Thee as much as I can. Amen.

CHAPTER VIII. ON THE SCOURGING OF JESUS CHRIST.

1. Let us enter into the pretorium of Pilate, one day made the horrible scene of the ignominies and pains of Jesus; let us see how unjust, how shameful, how cruel was the punishment there inflicted on the Saviour of the world. Pilate, seeing that the Jews continued to make a tumult against Jesus, as a most unjust judge condemned Him to be scourged : " Then Pilate took Jesus and scourged Him" (St. John xix. 1). The iniquitous judge thought by means of this barbarity to win for Him the compassion of His enemies, and thus to deliver Him from death : " I will chastise Him" (he said) " and let Him go" (St. Luke xxiii. 16). Scourging was the chastisement inflicted on slaves only. Therefore, says St. Bernard, our loving Redeemer willed to take the form, not only of a slave, in order to subject Himself to the will of others, but even of a bad slave, in order to be chastised with scourges, and so to pay the penalty due from man, who had made himself the slave of sin.' Taking not only the form of a slave, that He might submit, but even of a bad slave, that he might be beaten and suffer the punishment of the slave of sin.'

O Son of God, O Thou great Lover of my soul, how couldst Thou, the Lord of infinite Majesty, thus love an object so vile and ungrateful as I am, as to subject Thyself to so much punishment, to deliver me from the punishment which was my due. A God scourged ! It were a greater marvel that God should receive the lightest blow, than that all men and all Angels should be destroyed. Ah, my Jesus, pardon me the offences I have committed against Thee, and then chastise me as shall please Thee. This alone is enough, — that I love Thee, and that Thou love me ; and then I am content to suffer all the pains Thou willest.

2. As soon as He had arrived at the pretorium (as was revealed to St. Bridget), our loving Saviour, at the command of the servants, stripped Himself of His garments, embraced the column, and then laid on it His hands to have them bound. O God, already is begun the cruel torture ! O Angels of heaven, come and look on this sorrowful spectacle ; and if it be not permitted you to deliver your King from this barbarous slaughter which men have prepared for Him, at least come and weep for compassion. And thou, my soul, imagine thyself to be present at this horrible tearing of the Flesh of Thy beloved Redeemer. Look on Him, how He stands,—thy afflicted Jesus,—with His head bowed, looking on the ground, blushing all over for shame, He awaits this great torture. Behold these barbarians, like so many ravening dogs, are already with the scourges attacking this innocent Lamb. See how one beats Him on the breast, another strikes His shoulders, another smites His loins and His legs ; even His Sacred Head and His beautiful Face cannot escape the blows. Ah, me! already flows that Divine Blood from every part; already with that Blood are saturated the scourges, the hands of the executioners, the column, and the ground. 'He is wounded' (mourns St. Peter Damian) 'over His whole Body, torn with the scourges ; now they twine round His shoulders, now round His legs—weals upon weals, wounds added to fresh wounds.' Ah, cruel men, with whom are you dealing thus? Stay—stay; know that you are mistaken. This Man whom you are torturing is innocent and holy ; it is myself who am the culprit ; to me, to me, who have sinned, are these stripes and torments due. But you regard not what I say. And how canst Thou, O Eternal Father, bear with this great injustice ? How canst Thou behold Thy beloved Son suffering thus, and not interfere in His behalf? What is the crime that He has ever committed, to deserve so shameful and so severe a punishment ?

3. " For the wickedness of My people have I struck Him" (Is. liii. 8). I well know, says the Eternal Father, that this My Son is innocent; but inasmuch as He has offered Himself as a satisfaction to My justice for all the sins of mankind, it is fitting that I should so abandon Him to the rage of His enemies. Hast Thou, then, my adorable Saviour, in compensation for our sins, and especially for those of impurity,—that most prevalent vice of mankind,— been willing to have Thy most pure Flesh torn in pieces ? And who, then, will not exclaim, with St. Bernard, ' How unspeakable is the love of the Sou of God towards sinners !'

Ah, my Lord, smitten with the scourge, I return Thee thanks for such great love, and I grieve that I am myself, by reason of my sins, one of those who scourge Thee. O my Jesus, I detest all those wicked pleasures which have cost Thee so much pain. Oh, how many years ought I not already to have been in the flames of hell ! And why hast Thou so patiently awaited me until now ? Thou hast borne with me, in order that at length, overcome by so many wiles of love, I might give myself up to love Thee, abandoning sin. O my beloved Redeemer, I will offer no further resistance to Thy loving affection ; I desire to love Thee henceforth to the uttermost of my power. But Thou already knowest my weakness ; Thou knowest how often I have betrayed Thee. Do Thou detach me from all earthly affections which hinder me from being all Thine own. Put me frequently in mind of the love which Thou hast borne me, and of the obligation which I am under of loving Thee. In Thee I place all my hopes, my God, my Love, my All.

4. St. Bonaventure sorrowfully exclaims, ' The royal Blood is flowing; bruise is superadded to bruise, and gash to gash.' That Divine Blood was already issuing from every pore ; that Sacred Body was already become but one perfect Wound ; yet those infuriated brutes did not forbear from adding blow to blow, as the Prophet had foretold : "And they have added to the grief of my wounds" (Ps. lxviii. 27). So that the thongs not only made the whole Body one Wound, but even bore away pieces of it into the air, until at length the gashes in that Sacred Flesh were such that the bones might have been counted : ' The Flesh was so torn away, that the bones could be numbered.' Cornelius à Lapide says that in this torment Jesus Christ ought, naturally speaking, to have died; but He willed, by His Divine power, to keep Himself in life, in order to suffer yet greater pains for love of us ; and St. Laurence Justinian: had observed the same thing before : ' He evidently ought to have died. Yet He reserved Himself unto life, it being His will to endure heavier sufferings.'

Ah, my most loving Lord, Thou art worthy of an infinite love ; Thou hast suffered so much in order that I might love Thee. Oh, never permit me, instead of loving Thee, to offend or displease Thee more ! Oh, what place in hell should there not be set apart for me, if, after having known the love that Thou hast borne towards such a wretch, I should damn myself, despising a God who had suffered scorn, smitings, and scourgings for me ; and who had, moreover, after my having so often offended Him, so mercifully pardoned me! Ah, my Jesus, let it not, oh, let it not be thus ! O my God, how would the love and the patience which Thou hast shown towards me be there for me in hell, another hell even yet more full of torments.

5. Cruel in excess to our Redeemer was this torture of His scourging in the first place, because of the great number of those by whom it was inflicted ; who, as was revealed to St. Mary Magdalen of Pazzi, were not fewer than sixty. And these, at the instigation of the devils, and even more so of the priests, who were afraid lest Pilate should, after this punishment, be minded to release the

Lord, as he had already protested to them, saying, " I will therefore scourge Him, and let Him go," aimed at taking away His life by means of this scourging. Again, all theologians agree with St. Bonaventura, that, for this purpose, the sharpest implements were selected, so that, as St. Anselm declares, every stroke produced a wound ; and that the number of the strokes amounted to several thousand, the flagellation being administered (as Father Crasset says), not after the manner of the Jews, for whom the Lord had forbidden that the. number of strokes should ever exceed forty : " Yet so, that they exceed not the number of forty ; lest thy brother depart shamefully torn" (Deut. xxv. 3); but after the manner of the Romans, with whom there -was no measure. And so it is related by Josephus, the Jew (who lived shortly after our Lord), that Jesus was torn in His scourging to such a degree, that the bones of His ribs were laid bare ; as it was also revealed by the most Holy Virgin to St. Bridget, in these words : ' I, who was standing by, saw His Body scourged to the very ribs, so that His ribs themselves might be seen. And what was even yet more bitter still, when the scourges were drawn back, His Flesh was furrowed by them.' To St. Teresa Jesus revealed Himself in His scourging ; so that the saint wished to have Him painted exactly as she had seen Him, and told the painter to represent a large piece of flesh torn off, and hanging down from the left elbow ; but when the painter inquired as to the shape in which he ought to paint it, he found, on turning round again to his picture, the piece of flesh already drawn. Ah, my beloved and adored Jesus, how much hast Thou suffered for love of me! Oh, let not so many pangs, and so much Blood, be lost for me !

6. But from the Scriptures alone it clearly appears how barbarous and inhuman was the scourging of Jesus Christ. For why was it that Pilate should, after the scourging, ever have shown Him to the people, saying, " Behold the Man !" were it not that our Saviour was reduced to so pitiable a condition, that Pilate believed the very sight of Him would have moved His enemies themselves to compassion, and hindered them from any longer demanding His death ? Why was it that in the journey which Jesus, after this, made to Calvary, the Jewish women followed Him with tears and lamentations? " But there followed Him a great multitude of the people, and women, who bewailed and lamented Him" (St. Luke xxiii. 27). Was it, perhaps, because those women loved Him and believed Him to be innocent ? No, the women, for the most part, agree with their husbands in opinion; so that they, too, esteemed Him guilty ; but the appearance of Jesus after His scourging was so shocking and pitiable, as to move even those who hated Him to tears ; and therefore it was that the women gave vent to their tears and sighs. Why, again, was it that in this journey the Jews took the Cross from off His shoulders, and gave it the Cyrenean to carry. According to the most probable opinion, and as the words of St. Matthew clearly show : " They compelled him to bear His Cross" (St. Matt, xxvii. 42) ; or as St. Luke says : " And on him they laid the Cross, that he might carry it after Jesus" (St. Luke xxiii. 26). Was it, perhaps, that they felt pity for Him and wished to lessen His pains. No, those guilty men hated Him, and sought to afflict Him to their uttermost. But, as the blessed Denis, the Carthusian, says, 'They feared lest He should die upon the way;' seeing that our Lord after the scourging was so drained of Blood and so exhausted in strength as to be scarcely able any longer to stand, falling down as He did on His road under the Cross, and faltering as He went (so to speak) at every step, as if at the point of death ; therefore, in order to take Him alive to Calvary and see Him dead upon the Cross, according to their desire, that His name might ever after be one of infamy : " Let us cut Him off," said they (as the Prophet had foretold), "from the land of the living, and let his name be remembered no more" (Jer. xi. 19),— this was the end for which they constrained the Cyrenean to bear the Cross.

Ah, my Lord, great is my happiness in understanding how much Thou hast loved me, and that Thou dost even now preserve for me the same love which Thou didst bear me then, in the time of Thy Passion ! But how great is my sorrow at the thought of having offended so good a God! By the merit of Thy scourging, O my Jesus, I ask Thy pardon. I repent, above every other evil, of having offended Thee ; and I purpose rather to die than to offend Thee again. Pardon me all the wrongs that I have done Thee, and give me the grace ever to love Thee for the time to come.

7. The Prophet Isaias has described more clearly than all the pitiable state to which he foresaw our Redeemer reduced. He said that His most holy Flesh would have to be not merely wounded, but altogether bruised and crushed to pieces : " But He was wounded for our iniquities, He was bruised for our transgressions" (Is. liii.). For (as the Prophet goes on to say) the Eternal Father, the more perfectly to satisfy His justice, and to make mankind understand the deformity of sin, was not contented without beholding His Son pounded piecemeal, as it were, and torn to shreds by the scourges : " And the Lord willed to bruise Him in infirmity" (Is. liii.); so that the Blessed Body of Jesus had to become like the body of a leper, all wounds from head to foot : " And we esteemed Him as a leper, and one smitten of God" (Is. liii.).

Behold, then, O my lacerated Lord, the condition to which our iniquities have reduced Thee : ' O good Jesus, it is ourselves who sinned ; and dost Thou bear the penalty of it?' Blessed for evermore be Thy exceeding charity ; and mayest Thou be beloved as Thou dost deserve by all sinners ; and, above all, by me, who have done Thee more despite than others.

8. Jesus one day manifested Himself under His scourging to Sister Victoria Angelini ; and, showing her His Body one mass of wounds, said to her, ' These Wounds, Victoria, every one of them ask thee for love.' 'Let us love the Bridegroom, ' said the loving St. Augustine, 'and the more He is presented to us veiled under deformity, the more precious and sweet is He made to the bride.' Yes, my sweet Saviour, I see Thee all covered with wounds ; I look into Thy beautiful Face ; but, O my God, it no longer wears its beautiful appearance, but disfigured and blackened with blood, and bruises, and shameful spittings : " There is no beauty in Him, nor comeliness : and we beheld Him, and esteemed Him not" (Is. liii.). But the more I see Thee so disfigured, O my Lord, the more beautiful and lovely dost Thou appear to me. And what are these disfigurements that I behold but signs of the tenderness of that love which Thou dost bear towards me?

I love Thee, my Jesus, thus wounded and torn to pieces for me ; would that I could see myself too torn to pieces for Thee, like so many martyrs whose portion this has been. But if I cannot offer Thee wounds and blood, I offer Thee at least all the pains which it will be my lot to suffer. I offer Thee my heart ; with this I desire to love Thee more tenderly even than I am able. And whom is there that ray soul should love more tenderly than a God, who has endured scourging and been drained of His Blood for me ?' I love Thee, O God of love ! I love Thee, O infinite Goodness ! I love Thee, O my Love, my All ! I love Thee, and I would never cease from saying, both in this life and in the other : I love Thee, I love Thee, I love Thee. Amen.

CHAPTER IX. ON THE CROWNING OF THORNS.

1. As the soldiers, however, perseveringly continued their cruel scourging of the innocent Lamb, it is related that one of those who were standing by came forward, and, taking courage, said to them : You have no orders to kill this Man, as you are trying to do. And, saying this, he cut the cords wherewith the Lord was standing bound. This was revealed to St. Bridget : ' Then a certain man, his spirit being moved within him, demanded: Are you going to kill Him in this manner, uncondemned? and forthwith he cut His bonds.' But hardly was the scourging ended, when those barbarous men, urged on and bribed by the Jews with money (as St. John Chrysostom avers), inflict upon the Redeemer a fresh kind of torture : " Then the soldiers of the governor taking Jesus into the pretorium, gathered together the whole band, and stripped Him, clothed Him in a purple robe, and plaiting a crown of thorns, they put it upon His head, and a reed in His right hand" (St. Matt, xxvii. 27-30). Behold how the soldiers strip Him again ; and, treating Him as a mock king, place upon Him a purple garment, which was nothing else but a ragged cloak, one of those that were worn by the Roman soldiers, and called a chlamys ; in His hand they place a reed to represent a sceptre, and upon His head a bundle of thorns to represent a crown.

Ah, my Jesus, and art not Thou, then, true King of the universe ? And how is it that Thou art now become King of sorrow and reproach ? See whither love has brought Thee! O my most lovely God, when will that day arrive whereon I may so unite myself to Thee, that nothing may ever more have power to separate me from Thee, and I may no longer be able to cease from loving Thee ! O Lord, as long as I live in this world, I always stand in danger of turning my back upon Thee, and of refusing to Thee my love, as I have unhappily done in time past. O my Jesus, if Thou foreseest that by continuing in life I should have to suffer this greatest of all misfortunes, let me die at this moment, while I hope that I am in Thy grace ! I pray Thee, by Thy Passion, not to abandon me to so great an evil. I should indeed deserve it for my sins ; but Thou dost deserve it not. Choose out any punishment for me rather than this. No, my Jesus, my Jesus, I would not see myself ever again separated from Thee.

2. " And plaiting a crown of thorns, they put it upon His head" (St. Matt, xxvii. 29). It was a good reflection of the devout Lanspergius, that this torture of the crown of thorns was one most full of pain ; inasmuch as they everywhere pierced into the Sacred Head of the Lord, the most sensitive part, it being from the head that all the nerves and sensations of the body diverge ; while it was also that torture of His Passion which lasted the longest, as Jesus suffered from the thorns up to His Death, remaining, as they did, fixed in His Head. Every time that the thorns on His Head were touched, the anguish was renewed afresh. And the common opinion of authors agrees with that of St. Vincent Ferrer, that the crown was intertwined with several branches of thorns, and fashioned like a helmet or hat, so that it fitted upon the whole of the head, down to the middle of the forehead ; according to the revelation made to St. Bridget : 'The crown of thorns embraced His Head most tightly, and came down as low as the middle of the forehead.'

And, as St. Laurence Justinian says, with St. Peter Damian, the thorns were so long that they penetrated even to the brain : 'The thorns perforating the brain.' While, the gentle Lamb let Himself be tormented according to their will, without speaking a word, without crying out, but compressing His eyes together through the anguish, He frequently breathed forth, at that time, bitter sighs, as is the wont of one undergoing a torture which has brought him to the point of death, according as was revealed to the Blessed Agatha of the Cross : ' He very often closed His eyes, and uttered piercing sighs, like those of one about to die.' So great was the quantity of the Blood which flowed from the Wounds upon His Sacred Head, that upon His Face there was no appearance of any other colour save that of Blood, according to the revelation of St. Bridget : ' So many streams of Blood rushing down over His Face, and filling His hair, and eyes, and beard, He seemed to be nothing but one mass of Blood.' And St. Bonaventure adds, that the beautiful Face of the Lord was no longer seen, but it appeared rather the face of a man who had been scarified : ' Then might be seen no longer the face of the Lord Jesus, but that of a man who had undergone excoriation.'

O Divine Love, exclaims Salvian, I know not how to call Thee, whether sweet or cruel ; seeming, as Thou dost, to have been at one and the same time both sweet and cruel too : ' O Love, what to call Thee I know not, sweet or cruel ! Thou seemest to be both.' Ah, my Jesus, true, indeed, it is that love makes Thee sweet, as regards us, showing Thee forth to us as so passionate a lover of our souls ; but it makes Thee pitiless towards Thyself, causing Thee to suffer such bitter torments. Thou wast willing to be crowned with thorns to obtain for us a crown of glory in heaven : ' He was crowned with thorns, that we may be crowned with the crown that is to be given to the elect in heaven.' O my sweetest Saviour, I hope to be Thy crown in Paradise, obtaining my salvation through the merits of Thy sufferings ; there will I forever praise Thy love and Thy mercies : 'The mercies of the Lord will I forever sing ; yea, I will sing them forever.'

3. Ah, cruel Thorns, ungrateful creatures, wherefore do ye torment your Creator thus? But to what purpose, asks St. Augustine, dost thou find fault with the thorns ? They were but innocent instruments—our sins, our evil thoughts, were the wicked thorns which afflicted the Head of Jesus Christ : ' What are the thorns but sinners?' Jesus having one day appeared to St. Teresa crowned with thorns, the saint began to compassionate Him ; but the Lord made answer to her : ' Teresa, compassionate me not on account of the wounds which the thorns of the Jews produced ; but commiserate Me on account of the wounds which the sins of Christians occasion Me.'

Thou, too, therefore, O my soul, didst then inflict torture upon the venerable Head of thy Redeemer by thy many consentings to evil r "Know thou and behold how grievous and bitter it is for thee to have left the Lord thy God"
(Jer. ii. 19). Open now thine eyes, and see, and bitterly bewail all thy lifelong the evil that thou hast done in so ungratefully turning thy back upon thy Lord and God. Ah, my Jesus ! no, Thou hast not deserved that I should have treated Thee as I have done. I have done evil ; I have been in the wrong : I am sorry for it with all my heart. Oh, pardon me, and give me a sorrow which may make me bewail all my life long the wrongs that I have done Thee. My Jesus, my Jesus, pardon me, wishing, as I do, to love Thee forever.

4. "And bowing the knee before Him, they derided Him, saying, Hail, King of the Jews : and spitting upon Him, they took a reed, and smote Him upon the head" (St. Matt, xxvii. 29, 30). St. John adds, "And they gave Him blows" (St. John xix. 3). When those barbarians had placed upon the head of Jesus that crown of torture, it was not enough for them to press it down as forcibly as they could with their hands, but they took a reed to answer the purpose of a hammer, that so they might make the thorns penetrate the

more deeply. They then began to turn Him into derision, as if He had been a mock king ; first of all saluting Him on their bended knee as King of the Jews ; and then, rising up, they spit into His Face, and buffeted Him with shouts and jests of scorn. Ah, my Jesus, to what art Thou reduced ! Had any one happened by chance to pass that place and seen Jesus Christ so drained of Blood, clad in that ragged purple garment, with that sceptre in His hand, with that crown upon His Head, and so derided and ill-treated by that low rabble, what would he *ever* have taken Him to be but the vilest and most wicked man in the world ! Behold the Son of God become at that time the disgrace of Jerusalem ! O men (hereupon exclaims the Blessed Denis, the Carthusian), if we will not love Jesus Christ because He is good, because He is God, let us love Him at least for the many pains which He had suffered for us : 'If we love Him not because He is good, because He is God, let us at least love Him because He has suffered so many things for our salvation.'

    Ah, my dear Redeemer, take back a rebellious servant who has run away from Thee, but who now returns to Thee in penitence. While I was fleeing from Thee and despising Thy love, Thou didst not cease from following after me to draw me back to Thyself ; and therefore I cannot fear that Thou wilt drive me away now that I seek Thee, value Thee, and love Thee above everything. Make known to me what I have to do to please Thee ; wishing, as I do, to do it all. O my most lovely God, I wish to love Thee in earnest; and I desire to give Thee no displeasure more. Aid me with Thy grace. Let me not leave Thee more. Mary, my hope, pray to Jesus for me. Amen.

CHAPTER X. ON THE " ECCE HOMO."

1. Pilate, seeing the Redeemer reduced to that condition, so moving, as it was, to compassion, thought that the mere sight of Him would have softened the Jews. He therefore led Him forth into the balcony ; he raised up the purple garment, and exhibiting to the people the Body of Jesus all covered with wounds and gashes, he said to them, Behold the man : ᵘ Pilate went forth again to them, and saith to them : Behold, I am bringing Him out to you, that you may know that I find no fault in Him. Jesus, therefore, went forth, wearing the crown of thorns and the purple garment ; and he saith unto them, Behold the Man" (St. John xix. 4, 5). "Behold the Man!" as though he would have said, Behold the Man against whom you have laid an accusation before me, and who wanted to make Himself a King. I, to please you, have sentenced Him, innocent although He be, to be scourged : ' Behold the Man, not honoured as a king, but covered with disgrace.' Behold Him now, reduced to such a state that He wears the appearance of a man that has been flayed alive ; and He can have but little life left in Him. If, with all this, you want me to condemn Him to death, I tell you that I cannot do so, as I find not any reason for condemning Him. But the Jews, on beholding Jesus thus ill-treated, waxed more fierce : " When, therefore, the chief priests and the officers saw Him, they cried out, saying, Crucify Him ! crucify Him !" (St. John xix. 6.) Pilate, seeing that they could not be pacified, washed his hands in the presence of the people, saying, " I am innocent of the Blood of this just Man ; look you to it." And they made answer, " His Blood be upon us, and upon our children" (St. Matt, xxvii. 24, 25).

O my beloved Saviour, Thou art the greatest of all kings ; yet now I behold Thee the most reviled of all mankind. If this ungrateful people knows Thee not, I know Thee ; and I adore Thee as my true King and Lord. I thank Thee, O my Redeemer, for all the outrages Thou hast suffered for me ; and I pray Thee to give me a love for contempt and pains, since Thou hast so lovingly embraced them. I blush at having in time past loved honours and pleasures so much, that for their sake I have often gone so far as to renounce Thy grace and Thy love. I repent of this above every other evil. I embrace, O Lord, all the pains and ignominies which will come to me from Thy hands. Do Thou bestow upon me that resignation which I need. I love Thee, my Jesus, my Love, my All.

2. But while Pilate from the balcony was exhibiting Jesus to that populace, at the selfsame time the Eternal Father from heaven was presenting to us His beloved Son, saying, in like manner, " Behold the Man." Behold this Man, who is my only-begotten Son, whom I love with the same love wherewith I love Myself : " This is My Beloved Son, in whom I am well pleased." Behold the Man, your Saviour, Him whom I promised, and for whom you were anxiously waiting. 'Behold the Man, who is nobler than all other men, become the Man of sorrows. Behold Him, and see to what a pitiable condition He has reduced Himself through the love which He has borne towards you, and in order to be, at least out of compassion, beloved by you again. Oh, look at Him, and love Him ; and if His great worth move you not, at least let these sorrows and ignominies which He suffers for you move you to love Him.

Ah, my God and Father of my Redeemer, I love Thy Son, who suffers for love of me ; and I love Thee, who with so much love hast abandoned Him to so many pains for me. Oh, look not on my sins, by which I have so often offended Thee and Thy Son : "Look upon the Face of Thy Christ." Behold Thine Only-begotten, all covered with wounds and shame in satisfaction for my faults ; and for His merits pardon me, and never let me again offend Thee. " His blood be upon us." The Blood of this Man, so dear unto Thee, who prays to Thee for us, and impetrates Thy mercy, let this descend upon our souls, and obtain for us Thy grace. O my Lord, I hate and abhor all that I have done that displeases Thee ; and I love Thee, O infinite Goodness, more than I love myself. For love of this Thy Son give me Thy love, to enable me to conquer every passion, and to undergo every suffering in order to please Thee.

3. " Go forth, ye daughters of Sion, and behold King Solomon in his crown, wherewith his mother crowned him on the day of his espousals, and on the day of the joy of his heart" (Cant. iii. 11). Go forth, ye souls redeemed, ye daughters of grace, go forth to see your gentle King, on the day of His Death (the day of His joy, for thereon He made you His spouses, giving up His life upon the Cross), crowned by the ungrateful synagogue, His mother, with a crown ; not indeed one of honour, but one of suffering and shame: ' Go forth,' says St. Bern aid, 'and behold your King in a crown of poverty and misery.' O most beautiful of all mankind ! O greatest of all monarchs ! O most lovely of all Spouses ! to what a state do I see Thee reduced, covered with wounds and contempt I Thou art a Spouse, but a Spouse of Blood : ' To me Thou art a Spouse of Blood it being by means of Thy Blood that Thou hast willed to espouse Thyself to our souls. Thou art a King, but a King of suffering and a King of love ; it being by sufferings that Thou hast willed to gain our affections.

O most beloved Spouse of my soul ! would that I were continually recalling to my mind how much Thou hast suffered for me, that so I might never cease from loving and pleasing Thee! Have compassion upon me, who have tost Thee so much. In requital for so many sufferings endured by Thee, Thou art content if I love Thee. Yes, I do love Thee, infinite Loveliness, I love Thee above everything ; yet it is but little that I love Thee. O my beloved Jesus, give me more love, if Thou wouldst that I should love Thee more. I desire to have a very great love for Thee. Such a wretched sinner as I ought to have been burning in hell ever since the moment in which I first gravely offended Thee ; but Thou hast borne with me even until this hour, because Thou dost not wish me to burn with that miserable fire, but with the blessed fire of Thy love. This thought, O God of my soul, sets me all in flame with the desire of doing all that I can to please Thee. Help me, O my Jesus ; and since Thou hast done so much, complete the work, and make me wholly Thine.

4. But the Jews going on to insult the governor, crying out, " Away with Him ! away with Him ! crucify Him !" Pilate said to them, "Shall I crucify your King ?" and they made answer, " We have no king but Caesar" (St. John xix. 15). The worldly-minded, who love the riches, the honours, and the pleasures of earth, refuse to have Jesus Christ for their King ; because, as far as this earth is concerned, Jesus was but a King of poverty, shame, and sufferings. But if such as these refuse Thee, O my Jesus, we choose Thee for our only King, and we make our protestation that 'we have no King but Jesus.' Yes, most lovely Saviour, ' Thou art my King;' Thou art and hast for ever to be my only Lord.

True King, indeed, art Thou of our souls; for Thou hast created them, and redeemed them from the slavery of Satan : " Thy kingdom come." Exercise, then, Thy dominion, and reign forever in our poor hearts ; may they ever serve and obey Thee ! Be it for others to serve the monarchs of earth, in hope of the good things of this world. Our desire it is to serve only Thee, our afflicted and despised King, in hope only of pleasing Thee, without any earthly consolations. Dear to us, from this day forth, shall shame and sufferings be, since Thou hast been willing to endure so much of them for love of us. Oh, grant us the grace to be faithful unto Thee;

and to this end bestow upon us the great gift of Thy love. If we love Thee, we shall also love the contempt and the sufferings which were so much beloved by Thee ; and we shall ask Thee for nothing but that which Thy faithful and loving servant St. John of the Cross asked of Thee : 'Lord, to suffer and be despised for Thee; Lord, to suffer and be despised for Thee !'   O Mary, my Mother, intercede for me. Amen.

CHAPTER XI. ON THE CONDEMNATION OF JESUS CHRIST, AND HIS JOURNEY TO CALVARY.

1. Pilate was going on making excuses to the Jews, to the effect that he could not condemn that innocent One to death, when they worked upon his fears by telling him: "If thou lettest this Man go, thou art no friend of Caesar's" (St. John xix. 12). And hence the miserable judge, blinded by the fear of losing Caesar's favour, after having so often recognised and declared the innocence of Jesus Christ, at last condemned Him to die by crucifixion : " Then he delivered Him up to them, that He might be crucified" (St. John xix. 16). O my beloved Redeemer (St. Bernard hereupon bewails), what crime hast Thou committed that Thou shouldst have to be condemned to death, and that death the death of the Cross? ' What hast Thou done, O most innocent Saviour, that the judgment upon Thee should be such? Of what crime hast Thou been guilty?' Ah, I well understand, replies the saint, the reason for Thy death; I understand what has been Thy crime : ' Thy crime is Thy love.' Thy crime is the too great love which Thou hast borne to men ; it is this, not Pilate, that condemns Thee to die. No, adds St. Bonaventure, I see no just reason for Thy death, O my Jesus, save the excess of the affection which Thou bearest to us : ' I see no cause for death but the superabundance of love.' Ah, so great an excess of love, goes on St. Bernard, how strongly does it constrain us, O loving Saviour, to consecrate all the affections of our hearts unto Thee ! 'Such love wholly claims for itself our love.' O my dear Saviour, the mere knowledge that Thou dost love me should be sufficient to make me live detached from everything, in order to study only how to love Thee and please Thee in all things: ' Love is strong as death.' If love is as strong as death, oh, by Thy merits, my Saviour, grant me such a love for Thee as shall make me hold all earthly affections in abhorrence. Give me thoroughly to understand that all my good consists in pleasing Thee, O God, all Goodness and all Love ! I curse that time in which I loved Thee not. I thank Thee for that Thou dost give me time in which to love Thee. I love Thee, O my Jesus, infinite in loveliness, and infinitely loving. With my whole self do I love Thee, and I assure Thee that I would wish to die a thousand deaths rather than ever again cease from loving Thee.

2. The unjust sentence of death is read over to Jesus, who stands condemned ; He listens to it, and humbly accepts it. No complaint does He make of the injustice of the judge ; no appeal does He make to Caesar, as did St. Paul, but, all gentle and resigned, He submits Himself to the decree of the Eternal Father, who condemns Him to the Cross for our sins : " He humbled Himself, being made obedient even unto death, and that the death of the Cross" (Phil. ii. 8). And, for the love which He bears to man, He is content to die for us : " He loved us, and gave Himself up for us" (Gal. ii. 20).

O my merciful Saviour, how much do I thank Thee ! How deeply am I obliged to Thee ! I desire, O my Jesus, to die for Thee, since Thou hast so lovingly accepted of death for me. But if it is not granted me to give Thee my blood and life at the hands of the executioner, as the Martyrs have done, I, at least, accept with resignation the death which awaits me ; and I accept of it in the manner, and at the time, which shall please Thee. Henceforth do I offer it up to Thee in honour of Thy Majesty, and in satisfaction for my sins. I pray Thee, by the merits of Thy Death, to grant me the happiness to die in Thy grace and love.

3. Pilate delivers over the innocent Lamb into the hands of those wolves, to do with Him what they will : "But he delivered Jesus up to their will" (Luke xxiii. 25). These ministers of Satan seize hold of Him fiercely ; they strip Him of the purple garment, as is suggested to them by the Jews, and put His own raiment again upon Him : " They stripped Him of the purple garment, and clothed Him in His own raiment, and led Him away to crucify Him" (Matt, xxvii. 31). And this they did, says St. Ambrose, in order that Jesus might be recognised, at least, by His apparel ; His beautiful Face being so much disfigured with Blood and Wounds, that in other apparel it would have been difficult for Him to have been recognised as the Person He was : ' They put on Him His own raiment, that He might the better be recognised by all ; since, as His Face was all bloody and disfigured, it would not have been an easy matter for all to have recognised Him.' They then take two rough beams, and of them they quickly construct the Cross, the length of which was fifteen feet, as St. Bonaventure says, with St. Anselm, and they lay it upon the shoulders of the Redeemer.

But Jesus did not wait, says St. Thomas of Villanova, for the executioner to lay the Cross upon Him ; of His own accord He stretched forth His hands, and eagerly laid hold of it, and placed it upon His own wounded shoulders : 'He waited not till the soldier should lay it upon Him, but He grasped hold of it joyfully.' Come, He then said, come, My beloved Cross ; it is now three-and-thirty years that I am sighing and searching for thee. I embrace thee, I clasp thee to My Heart, for thou art the Altar upon which it is My will to sacrifice My Life out of love for My flock.

Ah, my Lord, how couldst Thou do so much good to one who has done Thee so much evil ? O God, when I think of Thy having gone so far as to die under torments to obtain for me the Divine friendship, and that I have so often voluntarily lost it afterwards through my own fault, I would that I could die of grief ! How often hast Thou forgiven me, and I have gone back and offended Thee again ! How could I ever have hoped for pardon, were it not that I knew that Thou hast died in order to pardon me ? By this Thy Death, then, I hope for pardon, and for perseverance in loving Thee. I repent, O my Redeemer, of having offended Thee. By Thy merits, pardon me, who promise never to displease Thee more. I prize and love Thy friendship more than all the good things of this world. Oh, let it not be my lot to go back and lose it ! Inflict me, O Lord, with any punishment rather than with this. O my Jesus, I am not willing to lose Thee anymore ; no, I would sooner be willing to lose my life : I wish to love Thee always.

4. The officers of justice come forth with the criminals condemned ; and in the midst of these also moves forward unto death the King of heaven, the only-begotten Son of God, laden with His Cross : " And bearing His own Cross, He went forth to that place which is called Calvary" (St. John xix. 17). Do ye too, O blessed Seraphim, sally forth from heaven, and come and accompany your Lord, who is going to Calvary, there to be executed, together with the malefactors, upon a gibbet of infamy.

O horrifying sight ! A God executed ! Behold that Messias who but a few days before had been proclaimed the Saviour of the world, and received with acclamations and benedictions by the people, who cried out, " Hosanna to the Son of David ; blessed be He that cometh in the name of the Lord" (St. Mark xi. 10) ; and, after all, to see ,Him as, bound, ridiculed, and execrated by all, He moves along, laden with a Cross, to die the death of a villain ! A God executed for men ! And shall we find any man who loves not this God? O my Eternal Lover, late is it that I begin to love Thee : grant that during the remainder of my life, I may make amends for the time that I have lost. I know, indeed, that all that I can do is but little in comparison of the love which Thou hast borne me ; but it is at least my wish to love Thee with my whole heart. Too great a wrong should I be doing Thee if, after so many kindnesses, I were to divide my heart in twain, and give a part of it to some object other than Thyself! From this day forth I consecrate unto Thee all my life, my will, my liberty : dispose of me as Thou pleasest. I beg Paradise of Thee, that there I may love Thee with all my strength. I wish to love Thee exceedingly in this life, that I may love Thee exceedingly for all eternity. Aid me by Thy grace : this I beg of Thee, and hope for, through Thy merits.

5. Imagine to thyself, O my soul, that you meet Jesus as He passes along in this sorrowful journey. As a lamb borne along to the slaughter-house, so is the loving Redeemer conducted unto death : "As a lamb He is led to the slaughter" (Is. liii. 7). So drained of Blood is He and wearied out with His torments, that for very weakness He can scarcely stand. Behold Him, all torn with wounds, with that bundle of thorns upon His head, with that heavy Cross upon His shoulders, and with one of those soldiers dragging Him along by a rope. Look at Him as He goes along, with Body bent double, with knees all of a tremble, dripping with Blood ; and so painful is it to Him to walk, that at every step He seems ready to die.

Put the question to Him : O Divine Lamb, hast Thou not yet had Thy fill of sufferings? If it is by them that Thou dost aim at gaining my love, oh, let Thy sufferings end here, for I wish to love Thee as Thou dost desire. No, He replies, I am not yet content : then shall I be content when I see myself die for love of you. And whither, O my Jesus, art Thou going now ? I am going, He replies, to die for you. Hinder Me not : this only do I ask of, and recommend to, you, that, when you shall see Me actually dead upon the Cross for you, you will keep in mind the love which I have borne you ; bear it in mind, and love Me.

O my afflicted Lord, how dear did it cost Thee to make me comprehend the love which Thou hast had for me ! But what benefit could ever have resulted to Thee from my love, that Thou hast been willing to expend Thy Blood and Thy life to gain it ? And how could I, after having been bound by so great love, have been able so long to live without loving Thee, and unmindful of Thy affection? I thank Thee, for that now Thou dost give me light to make me know how much Thou hast loved me. O infinite Goodness, I love Thee above every good. Would, too, that I had the power of offering a thousand lives in sacrifice unto Thee, willing as Thou hast been to sacrifice Thine own Divine life for me. O grant me those aids to love Thee which Thou hast merited for me by so many sufferings ! Bestow upon me that sacred fire which Thou didst come to enkindle upon earth by dying for us. Be ever reminding me of Thy Death, that I may never forget to love Thee.

6. " His government was upon His shoulder" (Is. ix. 6). The Cross, says Tertullian, was precisely the noble instrument whereby Jesus Christ made acquisition of so many souls ; since, by dying thereon, He paid the penalty due to our sins, and thus rescued us from hell, and made us His own. " Who His own Self bore our sins in His Body upon the tree" (1 Peter ii. 23). If God, then, O my Jesus, burdened Thee with all the sins of men,—" The Lord laid upon Him the iniquities of us all" (Is. liii. 6), —I, with my own sins, added to the weight of the Cross that Thou barest to Calvary.

Ah, my sweetest Saviour, Thou didst even then foresee all the wrongs that I should do Thee; yet, notwithstanding, Thou didst not cease from loving me, or from preparing for me all the mercies which Thou hast since employed towards me. If, then, to Thee I have been dear, most vile and ungrateful sinner as I am, who have so much offended Thee, good reason is there why Thou shouldst be dear to me, Thou, my God, infinite in beauty and goodness, who hast loved me so much. Ah, would that I had never displeased Thee. Now, my Jesus, do I know the wrong that I have done Thee. O ye accursed sins of mine, what have you done ? You have caused me to sadden the loving Heart of my Redeemer, that Heart which has loved me so much. O my Jesus, forgive me, repenting, as I do, of having done despite unto Thee. From henceforth it is Thou who art to be the only object of my love. I love Thee, O infinite Loveliness, with all my heart; and I resolve to love none else but Thee. Pardon me, O Lord, and give me Thy love ; I ask Thee for nothing more: ' Give me Thy love only together with Thy grace' (I say unto Thee with St. Ignatius), 'and I am rich enough.'

7. " If any man will come after Me, let him deny himself, and follow Me" (St. Matt. xvi. 24). Since, then, O my Redeemer, Thou dost go before me with Thy Cross, innocent as Thou art, and dost invite me to follow Thee with mine, go forward, for I will not abandon Thee. If, in time past, I have abandoned Thee, I confess that I have done wrong. Give me now what Thou wilt, embracing it, as I do, whatsoever it be, and willing, as I am, to accompany Thee with it even unto death : " Let us go forth from the camp, bearing His reproach" (Heb. xiii. 13). And how, O Lord, can it be possible for us not, for Thy love, to love sufferings and shame, loving them so much, as Thou hast done, for our salvation ?

But since Thou dost invite us to follow Thee, yea, it is our wish to follow Thee and to die with Thee : give us only the strength to carry it out. This strength we ask of Thee, and hope for, by Thy merits. I love Thee, O my most lovely Jesus, I love Thee with all my soul, and I will never abandon Thee more ; enough for me has been the time that I have gone astray from Thee. Bind me now to Thy Cross. If I have despised Thy love, I repent of it with all ,my heart ; and I now prize it above every good.

8. Ah, my Jesus, and who am I that Thou wishest to have me for a follower of Thine, and commandest me to love Thee, and if I will not love Thee, threatenest me with hell ? And why, I will say to Thee with St. Augustine, shouldst Thou hold out to me the threat of eternal miseries ? For what greater misery could befall me than that of not loving Thee, O most lovely God, my Creator, my Redeemer, my Paradise, my All ? I see that, as a just chastisement of my offences against Thee, I should have deserved to be condemned to the inability of ever loving Thee more; but because Thou dost still love me, Thou dost continue to command me to love Thee, evermore repeating to my heart, " Thou shalt love the Lord thy God with all thy heart, with all thy soul, and with all thy mind." I thank Thee, O my Love, for this sweet precept; and in order to obey Thee, I do love Thee with all my heart, with all my soul, and with all my mind. I repent of not having loved Thee in time past. At this moment I would rather choose to undergo every suffering than live without loving Thee, and I purpose evermore to seek Thy love. Help me, O my Jesus, to be ever making acts of love towards Thee, and to depart out of this life while making an act of love, that so I may come to love Thee, face to face, in Paradise, where I shall ever after love Thee without imperfection and without interruption, with all my powers, for all eternity. O Mother of God, pray for me. Amen.

CHAPTER XII. ON THE CRUCIFIXION OF JESUS.

1. Behold, here we are at the Crucifixion, at that last torture, which brought death to Jesus Christ ; here we are at Calvary, converted into a theatre for the display of Divine love, where a God departs this life in an ocean of sufferings : "And when they had come to the place which is called Calvary, they crucified Him there" (St. Luke xxiii. 33). The Lord having, with great difficulty, at length reached the top of the Mount alive, they violently, for the third time, tear His clothes from off Him, sticking, as they did, to the sores upon His wounded Flesh, and they throw Him down upon the Cross. The Divine Lamb stretches Himself out upon that bed of torment; He reaches forth to the executioners His hands and His feet to be nailed ; and raising His eyes to heaven, He offers up to His Eternal Father the great sacrifice of His life for the salvation of men. After the nailing of one of His hands, the nerves shrink, so that they had need of main force and ropes, as was revealed to St. Bridget, to draw the other hand and the feet up to the places where they were to be nailed ; and this occasioned so great a tension of the nerves and veins, that they broke asunder with a violent convulsion : ' They drew My hands and My feet with a rope to the places of the nails, so that the nerves and veins were stretched out to the full and broke asunder ;' inasmuch that all His bones might have been numbered, as David had already predicted : " They pierced My hands and My feet, they numbered all My bones" (Ps. xxi. 17, 18). Ah, my Jesus, by what power was it that Thy hands and Thy feet were nailed to this wood, but by the love Thou didst bear to men ? Thou, by the pain of Thy pierced hands, wert willing to pay the penalty due to all the sins of touch that men have committed ; and, by the pain of Thy feet, Thou wert willing to pay for all the steps by which we have gone our way to offend Thee. O my crucified Love, with these pierced hands give me Thy benediction ! Oh, nail this ungrateful heart of mine to Thy feet, that so I may no more depart from Thee, and that this will of mine, which has so often rebelled against Thee, may remain ever steadily fixed in Thy love. Grant that nothing else but Thy love, and the desire of pleasing Thee, may move me. Although I behold Thee suspended upon this gibbet, I believe Thee to be the Lord of the world, the true Son of God, and the Saviour of mankind. For pity's sake, O my Jesus, never abandon me again at any period of my life ; and more especially at the hour of my death, in those last agonies and struggles with hell, do Thou assist me, and strengthen me to die in Thy love. I love Thee, my crucified Love, I love Thee with all my heart.

2. St. Augustine says, there is no death more bitter than that of the Cross : ' Among all the different kinds of death, there was none worse.' Because, as St. Thomas observes, those who are crucified have their hands and their feet pierced through, parts which, being entirely composed of nerves, muscles, and veins, are the most sensitive to pain ; and the very weight of the body itself, which is suspended from them, causes the pain to be continuous and ever increasing in its intensity up to the moment of death. But the pains of Jesus were far beyond all other pains ; for, as the angelic Doctor says, the Body of Jesus Christ, being perfectly constituted, was more quick and sensitive to pain —that Body which was fashioned for Him by the Holy Spirit, expressly with a view to His suffering as He had foretold ; as the Apostle testifies, "A body thou hast fitted to Me" (Heb. x. 5). Moreover, St. Thomas says, that Jesus Christ took upon Himself an amount of suffering so great, as to be sufficient to satisfy for the temporal punishment merited by the sins of all mankind. Tiepoli tells us that, in the Crucifixion, there were dealt twenty-eight strokes of the hammer upon His hands, and thirty-six upon His feet.

O my soul, behold thy Lord, behold thy Life, hanging upon that tree : "And thy life shall be, as it were, hanging before thee" (Deut. xxviii. 66). Behold how, upon that gibbet of pain, fastened by those cruel nails, He finds no place of rest. Now He leans His weight upon His hands, now upon His feet ; but on what part soever He leans, the anguish increases. He turns His afflicted Head, now on one side, now on the other : if He lets it fall towards His breast, the hands, by the additional weight, are rent the more ; if He lowers it towards His shoulders, the shoulders are pierced with the thorns ; if He leans it back upon the Cross, the thorns enter the more deeply into the Head. Ah, my Jesus, what a death of bitterness is this that Thou art enduring! O my crucified Redeemer, I adore Thee on this throne of ignominy and pain. Upon this Cross I read it written that Thou art a King : " Jesus of Nazareth, King of the Jews." But apart from this title of scorn, what is the evidence that Thou dost give of being a King ? Ah, these hands transfixed with nails, this Head pierced with thorns, this throne of sorrow, this lacerated Flesh, make me well know that Thou art King, but King of love ! With humility, then, and tenderness do I draw near to kiss Thy sacred feet, transfixed for love of me ; I clasp in my arms this Cross, on which Thou, being made a victim of love, wast willing to offer Thyself in sacrifice for me to the Divine justice : " being made obedient unto death, the death of the Cross." O blessed obedience which obtained for us the pardon of our sins ! And what would have become of me, O my Saviour, hadst Thou not paid the penalty for me? I thank Thee, O my Love, and by the merits of this sublime obedience do I pray Thee to grant me the grace of obedience in everything to the Divine will. All that I desire Paradise for is, that I may love Thee forever, and with all my strength.

3. Behold the King of heaven, who, hanging on that gibbet, is now on the point of giving up the ghost. Let us, too, ask of Him, with the Prophet : " What are those wounds in the middle of Thy hands ?" (Zach. xiii. 6.) Tell me, O my Jesus, what are these wounds in the middle of Thy hands? The Abbot Rupert makes answer for Jesus :
' They are the memorials of charity, the price of redemption.' They are tokens, says the Redeemer, of the great love which I bear towards you ; they are the payment by which I set you free from the hands of your enemies, and from eternal death. Do thou, then, O faithful soul, love thy God, who hath had such love for thee ; and if thou dost at any time feel doubtful of His love, turn thine eyes (says St. Thomas of Villanova)—turn thine eyes to behold that Cross, those pains, and that bitter Death which He has suffered for thee ; for such proofs will assuredly make thee know how much thy Redeemer loves thee : ' The Cross testifies, the pains testify, the bitter Death which He had endured for thee testifies this.' And St. Bernard adds, that the Cross cries out, every wound of Jesus cries out, that He loves us with a true love : ' The Cross proclaims, the Wounds proclaim, that He truly loves.'

O my Jesus, how do I behold Thee weighed down with sorrow and sadness! Ah, too much reason hast Thou to think that while Thou dost suffer even to die of anguish upon this wood, there are yet so few souls that have the heart to love Thee ! O my God, how many hearts are there at the present moment, even among those that are consecrated to Thee, who either love Thee not, or love Thee not enough ! O beautiful flame of love, thou that didst consume the life of a God upon the Cross, oh, consume me too, consume all the disorderly affections which live in my heart, and make me live burning and sighing only for that loving Lord of mine, who, for love of me, was willing to end His life, consumed by torments, upon a gibbet of ignominy ! O my beloved Jesus, I wish ever to love Thee, and Thee alone, alone ; my only wish is to love my Love, my God, my All.

4. "Thine eyes shall behold thy teacher" (Is. xxx. 20). It was promised to men that with their own eyes they should see their Divine Master. The whole life of Jesus was one continuous example and school of perfection; but never did He better inculcate His own most excellent virtues than from the pulpit of His Cross. There what an admirable instruction does He give us on patience, more especially in time of infirmity; for with what constancy does Jesus upon the Cross endure with most perfect patience the pains of His most bitter Death. There, by His own example, He teaches us an exact obedience to the Divine precepts, a perfect resignation to God's will; and, above all, He teaches us how we ought to love. Father Paul Segneri, the younger, wrote to one of his penitents, that she ought to keep these words written at the foot of the Crucifix : " See what it is to love."

It seems as though our Redeemer from the Cross said to us all, " See what it is to love," whenever, in order to avoid something that is troublesome, we abandon works that are pleasing in His sight, or at times even go so far as to renounce His grace and His love. He has loved us even unto death, and came not down from the Cross till after having left His life thereon. Ah, my Jesus, Thou hast loved me even unto dying for me ; and I too wish to love Thee even unto dying for Thee. How often have I offended and betrayed Thee in time past! O my Lord, revenge Thyself upon me ; but let it be the revenge of pity and love. Bestow upon me such a sorrow for my sins as may make me live in continual grief and affliction through pain at having offended Thee. I protest my willingness to suffer every evil for the time to come, rather than displease Thee. And what greater evil could befall me than that of displeasing Thee, my God, my Redeemer, my Hope, my Treasure, my All?

5. "And I, if I be lifted up from the earth, will draw all things to Myself. But this He said, signifying what death He should die" (St. John xii. 32). Jesus Christ said, that when He should have been lifted up upon the Cross, He would, by His merits, by His example, and by the power of His love, have drawn towards Himself the affection of all souls : ' He drew all the nations of the world to His love, by the merit of His Blood, by His example, and by His love.' Such is the commentary of Cornelius à Lapide. St. Peter Damian tells us the same : ' The Lord, as soon as He was suspended upon the Cross, drew all men to Himself through a loving desire.' And who is there, Cornelius goes on to say, that will not love Jesus, who dies for love of us? 'For who will not reciprocate the love of Christ, who dies out of love for us?' Behold, O redeemed souls (as Holy Church exhorts us), behold your Redeemer upon that Cross, where His whole Form breathes love, and invites you to love Him : His head bent downwards to give us the kiss of peace, His arms stretched out to embrace us, His heart open to love us : ' His whole figure (as St. Augustine says) breathes love, and challenges us to love Him in return : His head bent downwards to kiss us, His hands stretched out to embrace us, His bosom open to love us.'

Ah, my beloved Jesus, how could my soul have been so dear in Thy sight, beholding, as Thou didst, the wrongs that Thou wouldst have to receive at my hands I Thou, in order to captivate my affections, wert willing to give me the extremest proofs of love. Come, ye Scourges, ye Thorns, Nails and Cross, which tortured the Sacred Flesh of my Lord, come ye, and wound my heart ; be ever reminding me that all the good that I have received, and all that I hope for, comes to me through the merits of His Passion. O Thou Master of love, others teach by word of mouth, but Thou upon this bed of death dost teach by suffering; others teach from interested motives, Thou from affection, asking no recompense excepting my salvation. Save me, O my Love, and let my salvation be the bestowal of the grace ever to love and please Thee ; the love of Thee is my salvation.

6. While Jesus was dying upon the Cross, the men who were around Him never ceased to torment Him with reproaches and insults. Some said to Him : " He saved others, Himself He cannot save." Others : " If He be the King of Israel, let Him now come down from the Cross." And Jesus, while these are outraging Him, what is He doing upon the Cross ? He is, perhaps, praying the Eternal Father to punish them ? No ; He is praying Him to pardon them: " Father, forgive them, for they know not what they do" (St. Luke xxiii. 34). Yes, says St. Thomas ; to show forth the immense love which He had for men, the Redeemer asked pardon of God for His very crucifiers : 'To show forth the abundance of His charity, He asked pardon for His persecutors.' He asked it, and obtained it ; for, when they had seen Him dead, they repented of their sin : "They returned smiting their breasts."

Ah, my dear Saviour, behold me at Thy feet : I have been one of the most ungrateful of Thy persecutors ; do Thou for me likewise pray Thy Father to pardon me. True, indeed, it is that the Jews and the executioners knew not what they were doing when they crucified Thee ; but I well knew that, in sinning, I was offending a God who had been crucified, and had died for me. But Thy Blood and Thy Death have merited, even for me, the Divine mercy. I cannot feel doubtful of being pardoned, after I see Thee die to obtain pardon for me. Ah, my sweet Redeemer, turn towards me one of those looks of love wherewith Thou didst look upon me, when dying for me upon the Cross ! Look upon me and pardon me all the ungratefulness which I have shown to Thy love. I repent, O my Jesus, of having despised Thee. I love Thee with all my heart ; and, at the sight of Thy example, because I love Thee, I love all those likewise who have offended me. I wish them all possible good, and I purpose to serve them, and to assist them to the utmost of my power, for love of Thee, O my Lord, who hast been willing to die for me, who have so much offended Thee.

7. " Remember me," said the good thief to Thee, O my Jesus ; and he had the consolation of hearing these words from Thee : "This day Thou shalt be with Me in Paradise" (St. Luke xxiii. 43). Be mindful of me, say I likewise unto Thee ; be mindful, O Lord, that I am one of those sheep for whom Thou didst give Thy Life. Give me, too, the consolation of making me feel that Thou dost forgive me, vouchsafing me a great sorrow for my sins. Do Thou, O great Priest, who dost sacrifice Thyself for love of Thy creatures, have compassion upon me. From this day forth do I sacrifice to Thee my will, my senses, my satisfactions, and all my desires. I believe that Thou, my God, didst die, crucified, for me. Let Thy Divine Blood, I pray Thee, flow also upon me ; let it wash me from my sins. Let it inflame me with holy love, and make me all Thine own. I love Thee, O my Jesus, and I wish that I could die, crucified, for Thee, who didst die, crucified, for me.

O Eternal Father, I have offended Thee ; but behold Thy Son, who, hanging upon this Tree, makes satisfaction to Thee for me with the sacrifice which He offers Thee of His Divine Life. I offer Thee His merits, which are all mine, for He has made them over to me ; and, for love of this Thy Son, I pray Thee to have mercy upon me. The greatest mercy which I ask of Thee is, that Thou wouldst give me Thy grace, which, miserable wretch that I am, I have so often willfully despised. I repent of having outraged Thee, and I love Thee, I love Thee, my God, my All ; and, to please Thee, I am ready to endure every shame, every pain, every sorrow, and every death.

CHAPTER XIII. ON THE LAST WORDS OF JESUS UPON HIS CROSS, AND ON HIS DEATH.

1. St. Laurence Justinian says, that the Death of Jesus was the most bitter and painful of all the deaths that men have ever died; since the Redeemer died upon the Cross without any, even the slightest, alleviation : ' He was crucified wholly without any alleviation of suffering.' In the case of other sufferers, the pain is always mitigated, at all events, by some consoling thought ; but the pain and sorrow of Jesus in His sufferings was pure pain, pure sorrow, without mitigation : 'The extent of the suffering of Christ appears to us from the purity of its pain and sorrow,' says the angelic Doctor.' And hence St. Bernard, when contemplating Jesus dying upon the Cross, utters this lamentation: O my Jesus, when I behold Thee upon this Tree, I find nothing in Thee from Head to foot but gain and sorrow. 'From the sole of Thy foot to the crown of Thy Head I find nothing but pain and grief.'

O my sweet Redeemer, O Love of my soul, wherefore wouldst Thou shed all Thy Blood ? wherefore sacrifice Thy Divine Life for an ungrateful worm like me? O my Jesus, when shall I so unite myself to Thee, as never more to be able to separate myself from Thee, or to cease from loving Thee ? Ah, Lord, as long as I live in this world I stand in danger of denying to Thee my love, and of losing Thy friendship, as I have done in times past. O my dearest Saviour, if, by continuing in life, I shall have to suffer this great evil, by Thy Passion, I pray, Thee, let me die at this moment, while, as I hope, I am in Thy grace. I love Thee, and I wish to love Thee always.

2. Jesus, by the mouth of the Prophet, made lamentation that, when dying upon the Cross, He went in search of someone to console Him, but found none : " And I looked for one that would comfort Me, and I found none" (Ps. lxviii. 21). The Jews and the Romans, even while He was dying, uttered against Him their execrations and blasphemies. The Most Holy Mary—yes, she stood beneath the Cross, in order to afford Him some relief, had it been in her power to do so ; but this afflicted and loving Mother, by the sorrow which she suffered through sympathy with His pains, only added to the affliction of this her Son, who loved her so dearly. St. Bernard says, that the pains of Mary all went towards increasing the torments of the Heart of Jesus : ' The Mother being filled with it, the ocean of her sorrow poured itself back upon the Son.' So that the Redeemer, in beholding Mary sorrowing thus, felt His Soul pierced more by the sorrows of Mary than by His own ; as was revealed to St. Bridget by the Blessed Virgin herself : ' He, on beholding me, grieved more for me than for Himself. Whence St. Bernard says, ' O good Jesus, great as are Thy bodily sufferings, much more dost Thou suffer in Thy Heart through compassion for Thy Mother.'

What pangs, too, must not those loving Hearts of Jesus and Mary have felt when the moment arrived in which the Son, before breathing His last, had to take His leave of the Mother ! Behold what the last words were with which Jesus took His leave in this world of Mary : " Mother, behold Thy Son assigning to her John, whom, in His own place, He left her for a son.

O Queen of Sorrows, things given as memorials by. a beloved son at the hour of his death, how very dear they are, and never do they slip away from the memory of a mother ! Oh, bear it in mind, that thy Son, who loved thee so dearly, has, in the person of John, left me, a sinner, to thee for a son. For the love which thou didst bear to Jesus, have compassion on me. I ask thee not the good things of earth : I behold thy Son dying in such great pains for me ; I behold thee, my innocent Mother, enduring also for me such great sufferings ; and I see that I, a miserable being, who deserve hell on account of my sins, have not suffered anything for love of thee—I wish to suffer something for thee before I die. This is the grace that I ask of thee; and, with St. Bonaventure, I say to thee, that if I have offended thee, justice requires that I should have suffering as a chastisement ; and if I have been serving thee, it is but reason that I should have suffering as a reward : ' O Lady, if I have offended thee, wound my heart for justice' sake; if I have served thee, I ask thee for wounds as my recompense.' Obtain for me, O Mary, a great devotion and a continual remembrance of the Passion of thy Son; and, by that pang which thou didst suffer on beholding Him breathe His last upon, the Cross, obtain for me a good death. Come to my assistance, O my Queen, in that last moment ; make me die, loving and pronouncing the sacred names of Jesus and of Mary.

3. Jesus, seeing that He found no one to console Him upon this earth, raised His eyes and His Heart to His Father, craving relief from Him. But the Eternal Father, beholding the Son clad in the garment of a sinner, replied : No, my Son, I cannot give Thee consolation, now that Thou art making satisfaction to My justice for all the sins of men ; it is fitting that I too should abandon Thee to Thy pains, and let Thee die without solace. And then it was that our Saviour, crying out with a loud voice, said, My God, My God, and why hast Thou too abandoned Me ?

Jesus cried out with a loud voice, saying, My God, My God, why hast Thou forsaken Me ?" (St. Matt, xxvii. 46.) In his explanation of this passage, the blessed Denis, the Carthusian, says, that Jesus uttered these words with a loud cry, to make all men understand the greatness of the pain and sorrow in which He died. And it was the will of the loving Redeemer, adds St. Cyprian, to die bereft of every Consolation, to give proof to us of His love, and to draw to Himself all our love : 'He was left in dereliction, that He might show forth His love towards us, and might attract our love towards Himself.'

Ah, my beloved Jesus, Thou art in the wrong to make Thy lamentation, saying, My God, why hast Thou abandoned Me? "Why," dost Thou say? And why, I will say to Thee, hast Thou been willing to undertake to pay our penalty? Didst Thou not know that for our sins we had already deserved to be abandoned by God? With good reason, then, is it that Thy Father hath abandoned Thee, and leaves Thee to die in an ocean of sufferings and griefs. Ah, my Redeemer, Thy dereliction gives me both affliction and consolation : it is afflicting to me to see Thee die in such great pain ; but it is consoling, in that it encourages me to hope that, by Thy merits, I shall not remain abandoned by the Divine mercy, according as I should deserve, for having myself so often abandoned Thee in order to follow my own, humours. Make me understand that, if to Thee it was so hard to be deprived, even for a brief interval, of the sensible Presence of God, what my pain would be if I were to be deprived of God for ever. Oh, by this dereliction of Thine, suffered with so much pain, forsake me not, O my Jesus, especially at the hour of my death ! Then, when all shall have abandoned me, do not Thou abandon me, my Saviour. Ah, my Lord, who wert so left in desolation, be Thou my comfort in my desolations ! Already do I understand that, if I shall love Thee without consolation, I shall content Thy heart the more. But Thou knowest my weakness ; help me by Thy grace, and then grant me perseverance, patience, and resignation.

4. Jesus, drawing nigh unto death, said, "Sitio," I thirst. Tell me, Lord, says Leo of Ostia, for what dost Thou thirst ? Thou makest no mention of those immense pains which Thou dost suffer upon the Cross ; but Thou complainest only of thirst : ' Lord, what dost Thou thirst for ? Thou art silent about the Cross, and criest out about the thirst.' ' My thirst is for your salvation,' is the reply which St. Augustine makes for Him. O soul, says Jesus, this thirst of Mine is nothing but the desire which I have for thy salvation. He, the loving Redeemer, with extremest ardour, desires our souls ; and therefore He panted to give Himself wholly to us by His Death. This was His thirst, wrote St. Laurence Justinian : ' He thirsted for us, and desired to give Himself to us.' St. Basil of Seleucia says, moreover, that Jesus Christ, in saying that He thirsted, would give us to understand that He, for the love which He bore us, was dying with the desire of suffering for us even more than what He had suffered : ' Oh, that desire, greater than the Passion!'

O most lovely God, because Thou lovest us, Thou dost desire that we should desire Thee : ' God thirsts to be thirsted for,' as St. Gregory teaches us. Ah, my Lord, dost Thou thirst for me, a most vile worm as I am ? and shall I not thirst for Thee, my infinite God? Oh, by the merits of this thirst endured upon the Cross, give me a great thirst to love Thee, and to please Thee in all things. Thou hast promised to grant us whatever we seek from Thee : " Ask, and ye shall receive." I ask of Thee but this one gift—the gift of loving Thee. I am, indeed, unworthy of it ; but in this has to be the glory of Thy Blood,—the turning of a heart into a great lover of Thee, which has, at one time, so greatly despised Thee ; to make a perfect flame of charity of a sinner who is altogether full of mire and of sins. Much more than this hast Thou done in dying for me. Would that I could love Thee, O Lord infinitely good, as much as Thou dost deserve. I delight in the love which is borne Thee by the souls that are enamoured of Thee, and still more in the love Thou bearest towards Thyself. With this I unite my own wretched love. I love Thee, O Eternal God ; I love Thee, O infinite Loveliness ! Make me ever to increase in Thy love ; reiterating to Thee frequent acts of love, and studying to please Thee in everything, without intermission and without reserve,. Make me, wretched and insignificant as I may be, make me at least to be all Thine own.

5. Our Jesus, now on the point of expiring, in dying accents said, "It is finished." He, while uttering the aforesaid word, ran over in His mind the whole course of His life. He beheld all the fatigues He had gone through, —the poverty, the pains, the ignominies He had suffered ; and He offered them all anew to His Eternal Father for the salvation of the world. Then, turning Himself back again to us, it seems as if He repeated, "It is finished;" as though He had said, O men, all is consummated ; all is fulfilled; your redemption is accomplished; the Divine justice is satisfied ; Paradise is opened ; " and behold your time, the time of lovers" (Ezech. xvi. 8). It is time at last, O men, that you should surrender yourselves to My love. Love Me, then ; oh, love Me ; for there is nothing more that I can do in order to be loved by you. You see what I have done in order to gain your love. For you I have led a life which has been but one series of tribulations. At its close, before I died, I have been content to let Myself be drained of Blood, have My Face spit upon, My Flesh torn to pieces, My Head crowned with thorns ; until I agonised upon this Cross, as you see Me now. What is there that remains ? It only remains for Me to die for you. Yes, it is My will to die. Come, O Death ; I give thee leave to take away My life for the salvation of My flock. And do you, My flock, love Me, love Me ; for I can do no more in order to make Myself beloved by you. 'It is consummated' (says the Blessed Tauler) : 'all that justice exacted, all that charity demanded, all that could have been done to give proof of love.'

Oh, would that I too, my beloved Jesus, could say in dying : Lord, I have fulfilled all ; I have accomplished all that Thou hast given me to do; I have borne my cross with patience ; I have pleased Thee in all things. Ah, my God, were I now to die, I should not die content ; for nothing of this could I say with truth. But am I always to live thus ungrateful to Thy love? Oh, grant me the grace to please Thee during the remainder of my life, that, when death shall come, I may be able to say to Thee, that from this time at least I have fulfilled Thy will. If in time past I have offended Thee, Thy Death is my hope. For the future it is my wish not to betray Thee more ; but from Thee it is that I hope for my perseverance. By' Thy merits, O my Jesus, I ask and hope it from Thee.

6. Behold Jesus at length actually dying. Behold Him, my soul, how He is agonising amid the last respirations of His life. Behold those dying eyes, that Face so pale, that feebly palpitating Heart, that Body already wrapt in the arms of death, and that beautiful Soul now on the point of leaving that wounded Body. The sky shrouds itself in darkness ; the earth quakes; the graves open. Alas, what portentous signs are these ! They are signs that the Maker of the world is now dying.

Behold, in the last place, how our Redeemer, after having commended His blessed Soul to His Eternal Father, first breathing forth from His afflicted Heart a deep sigh, and then bowing down His Head in token of His obedience, and offering up His Death for the salvation of men, at length, through the violence of the pain, expires, and delivers up His Spirit into the hands of His beloved Father : " And crying out with a loud voice, He said, Father, into Thy hands I commend My Spirit ; and saying this, He gave up the ghost."

Draw near, O my soul, to the foot of that holy Altar whereon the Lamb of God is now lying dead, sacrificed for thy salvation. Draw near, and reflect that He is dead for the love which He has borne thee. Ask your dead Lord for what you wish, and hope for all. O Saviour of the world, O my Jesus, behold to what Thy love for men has at length reduced Thee! I thank Thee that Thou hast been willing, Thou, our God, to lose Thy life that we might not lose our souls. I thank Thee for all men, but especially for myself. And who is there more than I that has reaped the fruits of Thy Death ? I, through Thy merits, without even so much as knowing it, was, in the outset, by baptism, made a child of the Church; through Thy love I have been forgiven so often since, and have received so many special graces ; through Thee I have the hope of dying in the grace of God, and of coming to love Thee in Paradise.

O my beloved Redeemer, how greatly am I obliged to Thee ! Into Thy pierced Hands I commend my poor soul. Make me well understand what love there must have been in a God who died for me : would that I could, O Lord, die for Thee ! But what would the death of a wicked slave weigh against the death of his Lord and God ?
Would that I could, at least, love Thee as much as I am able ; but without Thy help, O my Jesus, I can do nothing. Oh, help me ! and, through the merits of Thy Death, make me die to all earthly affections, that so I may love Thee only, who dost deserve all my love. I love Thee, O infinite Goodness, I love Thee, my chief Good ; and, with St. Francis, I pray Thee : ' May I die for the love of Thy love, who didst vouchsafe to die for the love of my love.' May I die to everything, out of gratitude, at least, for Thy great love, who hast vouchsafed to die, through Thy love for me, and in order to be beloved by me. O Mary, my Mother, intercede for me. Amen.

CHAPTER XIV. ON THE HOPE WHICH WE HAVE IN THE DEATH OF JESUS CHRIST.

1. Jesus is the only Hope of our salvation : " There is no salvation in any other but Him" (Acts iv. 12). I am the only door, says He ; and he that shall enter in through Me shall assuredly find life eternal : "I am the door ; if any one enter by Me, he shall be saved" (St. John x. 9). And what sinner would ever have been able to hope for pardon, if Jesus had not, by His Blood and by His Death, made satisfaction to the Divine justice for us ? "He shall bear their iniquities" (Is. liii.). It is by this that the Apostle encourages us, saying : "If the blood of goats and of oxen sanctify such as are defiled to the cleansing of the flesh, how much more shall the Blood of Christ, who, through the Holy Ghost, offered Himself up to God, cleanse our conscience from dead works to serve the living God!" (Heb. ix. 13.) If the blood of goats and of bulls offered up in sacrifice removed from the Jews the outward defilements of the body, that so they could be admitted to the worship of the Sanctuary, how much more shall the Blood of Jesus Christ, who for love offered Himself up as a satisfaction for us, remove the sins from our souls to enable us to serve our God Most High!

Our loving Redeemer, having come into the world for so other end but that of saving sinners, and beholding the sentence of condemnation already recorded against us for our sins, what was it that He did? He, by His own Death, paid the penalty that was due to ourselves ; and with His own Blood cancelling the sentence of the condemnation, in order that the Divine justice might no more seek from us the satisfaction due, He nailed it to the same Cross whereon He died : " Blotting out the handwriting of the decree that was against us, which was contrary to us. And the same He took out of the way, fastening it to the Cross" (Col. ii. 14).

" Christ entered once into the holy place, having found for us eternal redemption" (Heb. vi. 12). Ah, my Jesus, hadst Thou not found this mode of obtaining pardon for us, who would ever have been able to find it ? It was with reason that David cried out, "Declare His ways" (Ps. ix. 12). Make known, O ye blessed, the loving contrivances which our God has employed in order to save us. Since, then, O my sweet Saviour, Thou hast had such a love for me, cease not from exercising mercy towards me. Thou, by Thy Death, hast rescued me from the hands of Lucifer : into Thy hands do I consign my soul; it is for Thee to save it : " Into Thy hands I commend my spirit ; Thou hast redeemed me, O God of truth."

2. "Little children, these things I write to you, that you may not sin : but if any man sin, we have an Advocate with the Father, Jesus Christ the Just, and He is the propitiation for our sins" (1 John ii. 1). Jesus Christ did not, with His Death, bring to an end His intercession for us with the Eternal Father : even at the present moment He is acting as our Advocate ; and it seems as if He knew not what else to do in heaven, as St. Paul writes, but be moving the Father to exercise mercy towards us : " ever living to make intercession for us" (Heb. vii. *25)*. And the Apostle adds, that this is the end for which our Saviour is ascended into heaven : " that He may now appear in the Presence of God for us" (Heb. ix. 24). As rebels are driven away from the presence of their king, so should we sinners have never more been deemed worthy of admission into the Presence of our God, even so much as to ask His pardon ; but Jesus, as our Redeemer, makes appearance for us in the Divine Presence, and, through His merits, obtains for us the grace that we had lost : " You are come to Jesus the Mediator, and to the sprinkling of blood, which speaketh better than Abel" (Heb. xii. 24). Oh, with how much greater effect does the Blood of the Redeemer implore for us the Divine mercy, than did the blood of Abel plead for chastisement on Cain ! My justice (said God to St. Mary Magdalen of Pazzi) is transformed into mercy by the vengeance taken on the innocent Flesh of Jesus Christ. The Blood of this My Son pleads not with Me for vengeance, like the blood of Abel, but pleads only for mercy and pity ; and at the sound of this voice My justice cannot but rest appeased. This Blood so binds its hands, that (so to speak) it cannot stir to take that vengeance upon sins which it used to take before.

"Be not unmindful of the kindness of thy Surety? (Eccl. xxix. 20). Ah, my Jesus, I was already incapable, after my sins, of making satisfaction to the Divine justice, when Thou, by Thy Death, wert willing to make satisfaction for me. Oh, what ingratitude would mine be now; were I to be unmindful of this Thy so great mercy ! No, my Redeemer, never will I be unmindful of it ; I desire to be ever thanking Thee for it, and to show forth my thankfulness by loving Thee, and doing all that I can to please Thee. Do Thou aid me by that grace which Thou hast, by so many sufferings, merited for me. I love Thee, my Jesus, my Love, my Hope !

3. " Come, O my dove, into the clefts of the rock" (Cant. ii. 13). Oh, what a safe place of refuge shall we ever find in the sacred clefts of the rock, in the Wounds, that is to say, of Jesus Christ : ' The clefts of the rock,' says St. Peter Damian, 'are the Redeemer's Wounds ; in these has our soul placed its hope.' There shall we be set free from that feeling of distrust which the sight of the sins we have committed may produce ; there shall we find weapons wherewith to defend ourselves when we shall be tempted to sin anew : "Have confidence, my children; I have overcome the world" (St. John xvi. 33). If you have not sufficient strength (our Saviour exhorts us) to resist the assaults of the world, that offers you its pleasures, place your confidence in Me, for I have overcome it ; and thus shall you likewise overcome. Pray the Eternal Father, said He, for the sake of My merits, to give you strength, and I promise you that He will grant you whatever you ask of Him in My Name : "Amen, amen, I say unto you, if you ask anything of the Father in My Name, He will give it you" (St. John xvi. 23). And elsewhere He confirms to us the promise, saying, that whatsoever grace we shall, for His love, ask of God, He Himself, who is one with the Father, will give it us : " Whatsoever you shall ask of the Father in My Name, that I will do : that the Father may be glorified in the Son" (St. John xiv. 13). Ah, Father Eternal, trusting to the merits and to these promises of Jesus Christ, I ask not of Thee the good things of earth, but Thy grace alone. True *it* is that, after the wrongs I have done Thee, I should not deserve either pardon or grace ; yet, if I deserve them not, Thy Son hath merited them for me, by offering up His Blood and His life for me. For the love, then, of this Thy Son, grant me Thy pardon. Give me a great sorrow for my sins, and a great love towards Thee. Enlighten me to know how lovely is Thy goodness, and how great is the love which Thou hast borne me from all eternity. Make known to me Thy will, and give me strength to fulfil it perfectly. O Lord, I love Thee, and desire to do all that Thou dost desire of me.

4. Oh, how great is the hope of salvation which the Death of Jesus Christ imparts to us : " Who is He that shall condemn? Christ Jesus who died, who also maketh intercession for us" (Romans viii. 34). Who is it, asks the Apostle, that has to condemn us? It is

that same Redeemer who, in order not to condemn us to eternal death, condemned Himself to a cruel death upon a Cross. From this St. Thomas of Villanova encourages us, saying, What dost thou fear, sinner, if thou art willing to leave off thy sin ? How should that Lord condemn thee, who died in order not to condemn thee? How should He drive thee away when thou returnest to His feet, He who came from heaven to seek thee when thou wert fleeing from Him ?

'What art thou afraid of, sinner ? How shall He condemn thee penitent, who dies that you may not be condemned? How shall He cast thee off returning, who came from heaven seeking thee?' But greater still is the encouragement given us by this same Saviour of ours, when, speaking by Isaias, He says, " Behold, I have graven thee upon My hands ; thy walls are always before My eyes" (Is. xlix, 16). Be not distrustful, My sheep ; see how much thou didst cost Me. I keep thee engraven upon My hands, in these Wounds which I have suffered for thee ; these are ever reminding Me to help thee, and to defend thee from thine enemies : love Me, and have confidence.

Yes, my Jesus, I love Thee, and feel confidence in Thee. To rescue me, yea, this has cost Thee dear ; to save me will cost Thee nothing. It is Thy will that all should be saved, and that none should perish. If my sins cause me to dread, Thy goodness reassures me, more desirous as Thou art to do me good than I am to receive it. Ah, my beloved Redeemer, I will say to Thee with Job : " Even though Thou shouldest kill me, yet will I hope in Thee, and Thou wilt be my Saviour" (Job xiii. 15). Wert Thon even to drive me away from Thy Presence, O my Love, yet would not I leave off from hoping in Thee, who art my Saviour. Too much do these Wounds of Thine and this Blood encourage me to hope for every good from Thy mercy. I love Thee, O dear Jesus ; I love Thee, and I hope.

The glorious St. Bernard one day in sickness saw himself before the judgment-seat of God, where the devil was accusing him of his sins, and telling him that he diet not deserve Paradise : ' It is true that I deserve not Paradise,' the saint replied ; 'but Jesus has a twofold title to this kingdom,—in the first place, as being by nature Son of God ; in the next place, as having purchased it by His Death. He contents Himself with the first of these, and the second He makes over to me ; and therefore it is that I ask and hope for Paradise.' We, too, can say the same y for St. Paul tells us that the will of Jesus Christ to die, consumed by sufferings, had for its end the obtaining of Paradise for all sinners that are penitent, and resolved to amend : " And, being perfected, He was made the cause of eternal salvation to all that obey Him" (Heb. viii. 9). And hence the Apostle subjoins : " Let us run to the fight proposed unto us, looking on Jesus, the Author and Finisher of faith, who, having joy proposed unto Him, underwent the Cross, despising the shame" (Heb. xii. 1, 2). Let us go forth with courage to fight against our enemies, fixing our eyes on Jesus Christ, who, together with the merits of His Passion, offers us the victory and the crown.

He has told us that He is gone to heaven to prepare a place for us : " Let not your heart be troubled . . . . for I go to prepare a place for you" (St. John xiv. 12). He has told, and is continually telling, His Father, that since He has consigned us to Him, He wishes us to be with Him in Paradise : " Father, those whom Thou hast given Me, I will that where I am they also may be with Me" (St. John xvii. 24). And what greater mercy could we have hoped for from the Lord, says St. Anselm, than for the Eternal Father to have said to a sinner, already for crimes condemned to hell, and with no means of delivering himself from its punishments : Take thou My Son, and offer Him in thy room? And for the same Son to have said : Take Me, and deliver thyself from hell ? ' What greater mercy can we imagine than that to one who, being a sinner, cannot redeem himself, God the Father should say, Accept of My only-begotten Son, and deliver Him over to be punished in thy stead ; and that the Son should say, Take Me, and redeem thyself?'

Ah, my loving Father, I thank Thee for having given me this Thy Son for my Saviour; I offer to Thee His death ; and for the sake of His merits, I pray Thee for mercy. And ever do I return thanks to Thee, O my Redeemer, for having given Thy Blood and Thy Life to deliver me from eternal death. 'We pray Thee, therefore, help Thy servants, whom Thou hast redeemed with Thy precious Blood.' Help, then, us, Thy rebellious servants, since Thou hast redeemed us at so great a cost. O Jesus, my one and only Hope, Thou dost love me. Thou hast power to do all things : make me a saint. If I am weak, do Thou give me strength ; if I am sick, in consequence of the sins I have committed, do Thou apply to my soul one drop of Thy Blood, and heal me. Give me the love of Thee, and final perseverance, making me die in Thy grace. Give me Paradise ; through Thy merits do I ask it of Thee, and hope to obtain it. I love Thee, O my most lovely God, with all my soul ; and I hope to love Thee always. Oh, help a miserable sinner, who is wishing to love Thee.

6. " Having, therefore, a great High-Priest, who hath penetrated the heavens, Jesus the Son of God, let us hold fast our confession. For we have not a high-priest who cannot have compassion on our infirmities, but one tempted in all things like as we are, yet without sin" (Heb. iv. 14). Since, says the Apostle, we have this Saviour, who has opened to us Paradise, which was at one time closed to us by sin, let us always have confidence in His merits ; because, from having of His goodness willed to suffer in Himself also our miseries, He well knows how to compassionate us : " Let us, therefore, go with confidence to the throne of grace, that we may obtain mercy, and find grace in seasonable aid" (Ibid. 16). Let us, then, go with confidence to the throne of the Divine mercy, to which we have access by means of Jesus Christ, that so we may there find all the graces that we need. And how can we doubt, subjoins St. Paul, but that God, having given us His Son, has given us together with that Son all His goods : " He delivered Him up for us all ; how hath He not, with Him, given us all things?" (Rom. viii. 32.) Cardinal Hugo comments on this : ' He will give the lesser, that is to say, eternal life, who hath given the greater, that is to say, His own Son.' That Lord will not deny us the lesser, which is eternal life, who has gone so far as to give us the greater, which is His own Son Himself.

O my chief and only Good, what shall I render Thee, miserable as I am, in return for so great a gift as that which Thou hast given me of Thy Son ? To Thee will I, with David, say, " The Lord shall repay for me" (Ps. cxxxvii 8). Lord, I have not wherewith to recompense Thee. That same Son of Thine can alone render Thee worthy thanks ; let Him thank Thee in my stead.

O my most merciful Father, by the Wounds of Jesus, I pray Thee to save me. I love Thee, O infinite Goodness ; and because I love Thee, I repent of having offended Thee. My God, my God, I wish to be all Thine own ; accept of me for the sake of the love of Jesus Christ. Ah, my sweet Creator, is it possible that Thou, after having given me Thy Son, shouldst deny me the good things that belong to Thee,—Thy grace, Thy love, Thy Paradise?

7. St. Leo declares that Jesus Christ, by His Death, has brought us more good than the devil brought us evil in the sin of Adam : ' We have gained greater things through the grace of Christ, than we had lost through the envy of the devil.' And this the Apostle distinctly says, when writing to the Romans : " Not as the offence so also is the gift. Where the offence abounded, grace did superabound" (Rom. v. 15, 20). Cardinal Hugo explains it : ' The grace of Christ is of greater efficacy than is the offence.' There is no comparison, says the Apostle, between the sins of man and the gift which God has made us in giving us Jesus Christ ; great as was the sin of Adam, much greater by far was the grace which Jesus Christ, by His Passion, merited for us: "I have come that they may have life, and that they may have it more abundantly" (St. John x. 10). I am come into the world, the Saviour protests, to the end that mankind, who were dead through sin, may receive through Me not only the life of grace, but a life yet more abundant than that which they had lost by sin. Wherefore it is that Holy Church calls the sin happy which has merited to have such a Redeemer : 'O

felix culpa, quœ talem ac tantum meruit habere Redemptorem.'

" Behold, God is my Saviour, I will deal confidently, and will not fear" (Is. xii. 2). If, then, O my Jesus, Thou, who art an omnipotent God, art also my Saviour, what fear shall I have of being damned? If, in time past, I have offended Thee, I repent of it with all my heart. From this time forth I wish to serve Thee, to obey Thee, and to love Thee. I firmly hope that Thou, my Redeemer, who hast done and suffered so much for my salvation, wilt not deny me any grace that I shall need in order to be saved : 'I will act with confidence, firmly hoping that nothing necessary to salvation will be denied me by Him, who has done and suffered so much for my salvation.'

8. "You shall draw water from the fountains of the Saviour, and you shall say in that day, Praise ye the Lord, and call upon His Name" (Is. xii. 3, 4). The Wounds of Jesus Christ are now the blessed fountains from which we can draw forth all graces, if we pray unto Him with faith : " And a fountain shall come forth from the house of the Lord, and shall water the torrent of thorns" (Joel iii. 18). The Death of Jesus, says Isaias, is precisely this promised fountain, which has bathed our souls in the water of grace, and, from being thorns of sins, has, by His merits, transformed them into flowers and fruits of life eternal. He, the loving Redeemer, made Himself, as St. Paul tells us, poor in this world, in order that we, through the merit of His poverty, might become rich: "For your sakes He became poor, that, through His poverty, you might be rich" (2 Cor. viii. 9). By reason of sin we were ignorant, unjust, wicked, slaves of hell; but Jesus Christ, says the Apostle, by dying and. making satisfaction for us, " is by God made for us Wisdom, Justice, Sanctification, and Redemption" (1 Cor. i. 30). That is to say, as St Bernard explains it, 'Wisdom in His preaching, Justice in His absolving, Sanctification in His conduct, Redemption in His Passion.' He has made Himself our Wisdom by instructing us, our Justice by pardoning us, our Sanctity by His example, and our Redemption by His Passion, delivering us from the hands of Lucifer. In short, as St. Paul says, the merits of Jesus Christ have enriched us with all good things; so that we no more want for anything in order to be able to receive all graces : " In all things you are made rich ; so that nothing is wanting to you in any grace" (1 Cor. i. 5, 7).

O my Jesus, my Jesus, what beautiful hopes does Thy Passion give me ! O my beloved Saviour, how much do I owe Thee ! Oh, would that I had never offended Thee ! Oh, pardon me all the wrongs that I have done Thee ; inflame me fully with Thy love, and save me in eternity. And how can I be afraid of not receiving forgiveness, salvation, and every grace, from an omnipotent God who has given me all His Blood ? Ah, my Jesus, my Hope, Thou, in order not to lose me, hast been willing to lose Thy Life ; I will not lose Thee, O infinite Good. If, in time past, I have lost Thee, I repent of it ; I wish, for the future, never to lose Thee more. It is for Thee to aid me, that I may not lose Thee again. O Lord, I love Thee, and I will love Thee always. Mary, thou, next after Jesus, art my hope ; tell thy Son that thou dost protect me, and I shall be safe. Amen. So may it be.

CHAPTER XV. ON THE LOVE OF THE ETERNAL FATHER IN HAVING GIVEN US HIS SON.

1. "God so loved the world, that He gave His only-begotten Son" (St. John iii. 16). God, says Jesus Christ, has loved the world to that degree, that He has given it His own and only Son. In this gift there are three things demanding our consideration : who is the Giver, what is the thing given, and the greatness of the love wherewith He gives it? We are already aware, that the more exalted the donor is, the more to be prized is the gift. One who receives a flower from a monarch, will set a higher value on that flower than on a large amount of money. How much ought we not, then, to prize this gift, coming to us, as it does, from the hands of one who is God ! And what is it that He has given us ? His own Son. The love of this God did not content itself with having given us so many good things of this earth, until it had reached the point of giving us its whole Self in the Person of the Incarnate Word : ' He gave us not a servant, not an Angel, but His own Son,' says St. John Chrysostom. Wherefore Holy Church exultingly exclaims, ' O wondrous condescension of Thy mercy in our regard ! O unappreciable love of charity I that Thou mightest redeem a slave, Thou deliveredst up Thy Son.'

O infinite God, how couldst Thou condescend to exercise towards us so wondrous a compassion ! Who shall ever be able to understand an excess so great as that, in

order to ransom the slave, Thou wert willing to give us Thine only Son? Ah, my kindest Lord, since Thou hast given me the best that Thou hast, it is but just that I should give Thee the most that I can. Thou desirest of me my love : of Thee I desire nothing else, but only Thy love. Behold this miserable heart of mine ; I consecrate it wholly to Thy love. Depart from my heart, all ye creatures; give room to my God, who deserves and desires to possess it wholly, and without companions. I love Thee, O God of love ; I love Thee above everything ; and I desire to love Thee alone, my Creator, my Treasure, my All.

2. God hath given us His Son ; and why ? For love alone. Pilate, for fear of men, gave Jesus up to the Jews: " He delivered Him up to their will" (St. Luke xxiii. 25). But the Eternal Father gave His Son to us for the love which He bore us : " He delivered Him up for us all" . (Rom. viii. 32). St. Thomas says, that Move has the nature of a first gift.' When a present is made us, the first gift that we receive is that of the love which the donor offers us in the thing that he gives : because (observes the angelic Doctor) the one and only reason of every voluntary gift is love ; otherwise, when a gift is made for some other end than that of simple affection, the gift can no longer rightly be called a true gift. The gift which the Eternal Father made us of His Son was a true gift, perfectly voluntary, and without any merit of ours ; and therefore it is said' that the Incarnation of the Word was effected through the operation of the Holy Spirit ; that is, through love alone ; as the same holy Doctor says : ' Through God's supreme love it was brought to pass, that the Son of God assumed to Himself flesh.'

But not only was it out of pure love that God gave unto: us this His Son, He also gave Him to us with an immensity of love. This is precisely what Jesus wished to signify! when He said : " God so loved the world." The word 'so' (says St. John Chrysostom) signifies the magnitude of the love wherewith God made us this great gift : 'The word *so* signifies the vehemence of the love.' And what greater love could one who was God have been able to give us, than was shown by His condemning to death His innocent Son in order to save us miserable sinners ? " Who spared not His own Son, but delivered Him up for us all" Rom. ib.). Had the Eternal Father been capable of suffering pain, what pain would He not have then experienced, when He saw Himself compelled by His justice to condemn that Son, whom He loved with the same love wherewith He loved Himself, to die by so cruel a death in the midst of so many ignominies ? " And the Lord willed to bruise Him in infirmity" (Is. liii. 10). He willed to make Him die consumed by torments and sufferings.

Imagine thyself, then, to behold the Eternal Father, with Jesus dead in His arms, and saying to us : This, O men, is My beloved Son, in whom I have found all My delights : " This is My beloved Son, in whom I am well pleased." Behold how I have willed to see Him ill-treated on account of your iniquities : " For the wickedness of My people have I smitten Him." Behold how I have condemned Him to die upon this Cross, afflicted, and abandoned even by Myself, who love Him so much. This have I done in order that you may love Me.

O infinite goodness ! O infinite mercy ! O infinite love ! O God of my soul ! since Thou didst will that the Object most dear to Thy Heart should die for me, I offer to Thee in my own behalf that great Sacrifice of Himself which this Thy Son made Thee ; and for the sake of His merits I pray Thee to give me the pardon of my sins, Thy love, and Thy Paradise. Great as are these graces which I ask of Thee, the offering which I present unto Thee is greater still. For the love of Jesus Christ, O my Father, pardon me and save me. If I have offended Thee in time past, I repent of it above every evil. I now prize Thee, and love Thee, above every good.

3. Ah, who but a God of infinite love could ever have loved us to such a degree ? St. Paul writes : " But God, who is rich in mercy, on account of the too great love wherewith He loved us when we were dead in sins, quickened us together in Christ" (Ephes. ii. 4). The Apostle calls too great this love which God showed us in giving to men, by means of the Death of His Son, the life of grace which they had lost by their sins. But to God, who is Love itself, this love was not too great : " God is love" (1 John iv. 6). St. John says that herein He wished to make us see the extent to which the greatness of the love of a God towards us reached, in sending His own Son into the world to obtain for us, by His Death, forgiveness and life eternal : " By this hath appeared the charity of God in us, because God hath sent His own only-begotten Son into the world, that we might have life through Him" (1 John iv. 9).

By sin, we were dead to the life of grace ; and Jesus, by His Death, has brought us back to life. We were miserable, deformed objects of abomination ; but God, by means of Jesus Christ, has rendered us pleasing and precious in His Divine sight. "He hath made us" (wrote the Apostle) " acceptable through His beloved Son." He hath made us acceptable, *i. e.* ' He hath made us pleasing,' says the Greek text. And therefore St. John Chrysostom adds, that were there to be a poor leper all covered with wounds and disfigurements, and any one were to heal his body of the leprosy, and make him beautiful and rich besides, how great would be the sense of obligation that he would retain towards this his benefactor ! How much more, then, are we now beholden to God, since, when our souls were disfigured and hateful on account of our sins, He hath, by means of Jesus Christ, not only delivered us from our sins, but has made them beautiful and lovely besides : " He hath blessed us with all spiritual blessings in heavenly places in Christ" (Ephes. i. 3). Cornelius à Lapide comments upon this : ' He hath bestowed upon us every spiritual gift.' God's blessing involves benefaction. The Eternal Father, then, in giving us Jesus Christ, hath loaded us with all gifts, not indeed earthly ones in the body, but spiritual ones in the soul : " In heavenly places giving us, together with His Son, a heavenly life in this world, and a heavenly glory in the other.

Give me, then, thy blessings and thy benefactions, O my most loving God, and may the benediction draw me wholly to Thy love: 'Draw me by the chains of Thy love.' Let the love which Thou hast borne me make me enamoured of Thy goodness. Thou dost deserve an infinite love : I love Thee with all the love I can command ; I love Thee above everything ; I love Thee more than myself. I give Thee my whole will ; and this is the grace that I ask of Thee : make me from this day forth to live and do everything according to Thy Divine will, wherewith Thou desirest nothing but my good, and my eternal salvation.

4. " The King hath brought me into the cellar of wine; He hath set in order charity in me" (Cant. ii. 4). My Lord, said the holy spouse, hath taken me into the cellar of wine ; that is to say, hath placed before mine eyes all the benefits that He hath done me in order that I may be induced to love Him : " He hath set in order charity in me." A certain writer says that God, in order to gain our love, has (so to say) despatched against us an army of the graces of love : ' He drew up charity against me like an armed host.' But, says Cardinal Hugo, the gift of Jesus Christ to us was the reserved arrow of which Isaias prophesied : " He hath made me as a chosen arrow : in His quiver he hath hidden me" (Is. xlix. 2). As the hunter, says Hugo, keeps the best arrow in reserve to give the finishing stroke to his game, so did God, amongst all His other benefits, keep Jesus in reserve, until the time of grace had arrived, and then He sent Him forth, as if to give the finishing stroke of love to the hearts of men : ' The chosen arrow is kept in reserve : so was Christ kept in reserve in the bosom of the Father, until the fullness of time should come ; and then He was sent forth to wound the hearts of the faithful.' St. Peter, wounded by this arrow, says St. John Chrysostom, said to his Master : Lord, Thou knowest well that I love Thee : "Lord, Thou knowest that I love Thee" (John xxi. 15).

Ah, my God, I behold myself surrounded on all sides with the artifices of Thy love. I do, likewise, love Thee ; and if I love Thee, I know that Thou too dost love me. And what power shall ever deprive me of Thy love? Sin only. But from this infernal monster it is for Thee, through Thy mercy, to deliver me. I am content to suffer every evil, the most cruel death, or even to be torn in pieces, sooner than offend Thee by mortal sin. But Thou already knowest my past falls ; Thou knowest my weakness ; help me, O my God, for love of Jesus Christ : " Despise not Thon the work of Thine hands." I am the workmanship of Thy hands ; Thou hast created me ; despise me not. If I merit to be left to myself by reason of my sins, I merit nevertheless that Thou be merciful towards me, for love of Jesus Christ, who hath sacrificed His life ta Thee for my salvation. I offer up to Thee His merits, which all are mine ; and, through them, I ask of Thee, and hope for from Thee, the gift of holy perseverance, together with a good death ; and meanwhile to live the remainder of my life entirely to Thy glory. Long enough have I offended Thee! I now repent of it with all my heart, and I wish to love Thee to the uttermost of my power. I desire no longer to offer resistance to Thy love : I surrender myself wholly unto Thee. Give me Thy grace, and Thy love, and then do with me what Thou wilt. I love Thee, O my God, and I wish, and I ask of Thee, to love Thee always. Oh, for the merits of Jesus Christy hearken unto my prayer. Mary, my Mother, pray to God for me. Amen. So may it be.

CHAPTER XVI. ON THE LOVE OF THE SON OF GOD IN HAVING WILLED TO DIE FOR US.

1. "And behold Thy time was the time of lovers . . . . And Thou wast made exceeding beautiful" (Ezech. xvi. 8, 13). How deeply are we Christians indebted to the Lord, in that He has, caused us to be born after the coming of Jesus Christ. Our time is no longer a time of fear, as wan, that of the Jews, but a time of love ; having seen a God dead for our salvation, and in order to gain our love. It is of faith that Jesus has loved us, and for love of us has given . Himself over unto death : " Christ hath loved us, and hath. delivered Himself up for us" (Ephes. v. 2). And where would ever have been the power to make an omnipotent God die, had not He of Himself voluntarily willed to give His life for us ? "I give My life . . . no one taketh it from Me ; but I lay it down of Myself (St. John x. 17). Wherefore St. John observes, that Jesus, by His Death, gave us the uttermost proof that He could have given us of His love : "Having loved His own, He loved them to the end" (St. John xiii. 1). Jesus, by His Death, says a devout writer, gave us the greatest possible sign of His love, be-yond which there remained for Him nothing that He could do in order to show how much He loved us : 'The highest proof of love was that which He showed forth at the end of His life upon the Cross.'

O my beloved Redeemer, Thou hast for love given Thyself wholly unto me ; for love I give myself wholly unto Thee. Thou for my salvation hast given Thy life ; I for Thy glory wish to die, when and as Thou dost please. There was nothing more that Thou couldst do in order to gain my love ; but I have ungratefully exchanged Thee away for nothing. I repent of it, O my Jesus, with all my heart. Pardon me through Thy Passion ; and, in token of pardon, help me to love Thee. Through Thy grace I feel within myself a great desire of loving Thee, and I resolve to be all Thine own ; but I see my languid-ness and the betrayals of which I have been guilty. Thou alone canst help me and render me happy. Help me, then, O my Love. Make me love Thee : I ask Thee for nothing more.

2. The Blessed Denis, the Carthusian, says that the Passion of Jesus Christ was called an excess,—" And they spake of His excess, which He would accomplish in Jerusalem" (St. Luke ix. 31),—because it was an excess of mercy and of love : ' The Passion of Jesus Christ is said to be an excess, because in it was shown forth an excess of love and of compassion.' O my God, and where is the believer that could live without loving Jesus Christ, if he were frequently to meditate upon His Passion? The wounds of Jesus, says St. Bonaventure, are all of them wounds of love. They are darts and flames which wound the hardest hearts, and kindle into a flame the most frozen souls : ' O Wounds that wound stony hearts, and set frozen minds on fire !' In order the more strongly to impress upon his heart a love towards Jesus in His Passion, the Blessed Henry Suso one day took a knife, and cut out in letters upon his breast the Name of his beloved Lord. And, when thus bathed in blood, he went into the church, and, prostrating himself before the Crucifix, he said, Behold, O Lord, Thou only Love of my soul, behold my desire. I would gladly have written Thee deeper within my heart ; but this I cannot do. Do Thou, who canst do all things, supply what is wanting in my powers, and imprint Thy adorable Name in the lowest depths of my heart, that so it may no more be possible to cancel in it either Thy Name or Thy love.

" My Beloved is white and ruddy, chosen out of thousands" (Cant. v. 10). O my Jesus, Thou art all white through Thy spotless innocence ; but upon this Cross Thou art also all ruddy with wounds suffered for me. I choose Thee for the one and only Object of my love. And whom shall I love, if I love not Thee? What is there that I can find amongst all other objects more lovely than Thee, my Redeemer, my God, my All? I love Thee, O most lovely Lord. I love Thee above everything. Do Thou make me love Thee with all my affection, and without reserve.

3. ' Oh, if thou didst know the mystery of the Cross!' said St. Andrew to the tyrant. O tyrant (it was his wish to say), wert thou to understand the love which Jesus Christ has borne thee, in willing to die upon a Cross to save thee, thou wouldst abandon all thy possessions and earthly hopes, in order to give thyself wholly to the love of this thy Saviour. The same ought to be said to those Catholics who, believing, as they do, the Passion of Jesus, yet do not think of it. Ah, were all men to think upon the love which Jesus Christ has shown forth for us in His Death, who would ever be able not to love Him? It was for this end, says the Apostle, that He, our beloved Redeemer, died for us, that, by the love He displayed towards us in His Death, He might become the Possessor of our hearts : " To this end Christ died, and rose again, that He might be Lord both of the dead and of the living ; therefore, whether we live, or whether we die, we are the Lord's" (Rom. xiv. 9). Whether, then, we die or live, it is but just that we belong wholly to Jesus, who has saved us at so great a cost. Oh, who is there that could say, as did the loving martyr St. Ignatius, whose lot it was to give his life for Jesus Christ.' Let fire, cross, beasts, and torments of every kind come upon me : let me only have fruition of Thee, O Christ.' Let flames, crosses, wild-beasts, and every kind of torture come upon me, provided only that I obtain and enjoy my Jesus Christ.

O my dear Lord, Thou didst die in order to gain my soul ; but what have I done in order to gain Thee, O infinite Good ? Ah, my Jesus, how often have I lost Thee for nothing ! Miserable that I was, I knew at the time that I was losing Thy grace by my sin ; I knew that I was giving Thee great displeasure ; and yet I committed it. My consolation is, that I have to deal with an infinite Goodness, who remembers his offences no more when a sinner repents and loves Him. Yes, my God, I do repent and love Thee. Oh, pardon me ; and do Thou from this day forth bear rule in this rebellious heart of mine. To Thee do I consign it ; to Thee do I wholly give myself. Tell me what Thou dost desire ; wishing, as I do, to perform it all. Yes, my Lord, I wish to love Thee ; I wish to please Thee in everything. Do Thou give me strength, and I hope to do so.

4. Jesus has not, by dying, ceased to love us. He loves us, and seeks us with the selfsame love wherewith He first of all came down from heaven to seek us and to die for us. That artifice of love, too, which was manifested by our Redeemer to St. Francis Xavier, while on his travels, is celebrated far and wide. In a storm at sea there came a wave which carried away from him his Crucifix. As the saint, after landing, was standing upon the shore, sorrowing, and earnestly longing to recover, if he might, the image of his beloved Lord, behold, he saw a crab coming towards him, holding up the Crucifix between its claws. Then, going forwards to meet it with tears of tenderness and love, he received it, and clasped it to his bosom. Oh, with what love does Jesus go to that soul

that seeks Him—" The Lord is good . . . . to the soul that seeketh Him" (Lam. iii.)—to the soul that seeketh Him, however, with true levé ! But can they think that they possess this true love who refuse the crosses which the Lord sends them ?

" Christ pleased not Himself" (Rom. xv. 3). 'Christ (as Cornelius à Lapide explains this passage) served not His own will and convenience ; but all this and His life itself did He expose for our salvation.' Jesus, for love of us, sought not earthly pleasures ; but He sought sufferings and death, all innocent though He was ; yet what is there that we are seeking for love of Jesus Christ ? St. Peter the martyr was one day standing in his prison, complaining of an unjust accusation which had been preferred against him, saying, ' But, Lord, what have I done that I should have had to suffer this persecution?' When the Crucifix made him this reply, · And I, what evil have I done that I should have had to be upon this Cross?'

O my dear Saviour, Thou didst say, what evil hast Thou done ? Too much hast Thou loved us ; since for love of us Thou hast been willing to suffer so much. And shall we, who deserved hell for our sins, refuse to suffer that which Thou dost will for our good ? Thou, my Jesus j art all love with whomsoever seeketh Thee. It is not Thy sweetnesses and consolations that I seek : I seek only Thyself and Thy will. Give me Thy love, and then do with me whatsoever Thou dost please. I embrace all the crosses which Thou wilt send me—poverty, persecutions, sickness, and pain. Deliver me only from the evil of sin, and then lay upon me every other evil. All will be but little in comparison of the evils which Thou hast suffered for love of me.

5. 'That He might redeem a slave, the Father neither spared the Son, nor did the Son spare Himself,' says St. Bernard. To liberate the slave, then, the Father hath not pardoned the Son, neither hath the Son pardoned Himself. And after so great a love to men, will it be possible? for there to be one who loves not this God, so loving as He is ? The Apostle says that Jesus died for us all, to the end that we might live only to Him and to His love : " Christ died for all, that they who live may no longer live unto themselves, but unto Him who died for them" (2 Cor. v. 15). But, alas! the greater portion of mankind, although One who is God has died for them, live unto sin, unto the devil, and not unto Jesus Christ. It was said by Plato, that ' Love is the magnet of love.' And Seneca replied, Do thou love, if thou wouldst be beloved : 'If you would be loved, love.' And how does it happen that Jesus, who, by dying for men, would seem to have gone foolish, as it were, out of love for us—' It seemed foolish that the Author of life should die for all,' says St. Gregory—how does it happen that He, after so many tokens of love on His part, has not been able to draw to Himself our hearts ? How is it that, loving us so much, He has not yet been able to make Himself beloved by us?

Oh, that all men loved Thee, my most lovely Jesus ! Thou art a God worthy of infinite love. But, my poor Lord, —give me leave so to call Thee,—Thou art so lovely, Thou hast done and suffered so much in order to be loved by men ; and, after all, how many are they that do love Thee ? I see almost all men applying themselves to the love— some of their parents, some of their friends, some of wealth, honours, or pleasures, and some even of dumb animals ; but how many are they that love Thee, O infinite Loveliness? O God, too few, indeed, they are; yet amongst these few I wish to be—I, miserable sinner as I am, who at one time also offended Thee by loving that which is but mire, going astray from Thee. But now I love Thee, and I prize Thee above every good ; and Thee only do I wish to love. Do Thou pardon me, O my Jesus, and come to my assistance.

6. God, then, O Christian, says St. Cyprian, rests content with thee, even to dying in order to gain Thy love ; and wilt not thou rest content with God, so that thou wilt love objects other than thy Lord ? ' God is content with thee, and wilt thou not be content with thy God?' Ah, no ; my beloved Jesus, I will not have any love in me which is not for Thee. I am content with Thee ; I renounce all other loves : Thy love alone is enough for me. I hear Thee saying to me, " Put Me as a seal upon thy heart" (Cant. viii. 6). Yes, my crucified Jesus, I do set Thee, and do Thou, too, set Thyself, as a seal upon my heart, that it may remain closed against every other love which tends not to Thee. In time past I have given Thee displeasure by means of other loves ; but, at the present moment, there is no pain that afflicts me excepting the remembrance of having, by my sins, lost my love of Thee. For the future, " Who shall separate me from the love of Christ ?" Who shall ever again separate me from my love for Thee ?

No, my most lovely Saviour, since Thou hast made me know the love which Thou hast borne me, I have not the heart to live any more without loving Thee. I love Thee, my crucified Love ; I love Thee with all my heart ; and I give unto Thee this soul of mine, which Thou hast so much sought and loved. Oh, by the merits of Thy Death, which so painfully separated Thy blessed Soul from Thy Body, do Thou detach me from every love which can hinder me from being all Thine own, and from loving Thee with all my heart. Mary, my hope, do thou help me to love thy sweetest Son alone, that so I may be able with truth, throughout my whole life, ever to repeat : 'My Love is crucified ; my Love is crucified.' Amen.

PRAYER OF ST. BONAVENTURA

O Jesus, who, for my sake, hast not pardoned Thyself, do Thou so impress upon me Thy Passion, that, wheresoever I turn, I may behold Thy Wounds, and find no repose but in Thee, and in the contemplation of Thy sufferings. Amen.

FIFTEEN MEDITATIONS ON THE PASSION OF JESUS CHRIST, TO BE MADE DURING THE FIFTEEN DAYS COMMENCING ON THE SATURDAY BEFORE PASSION SUNDAY, AND ENDING ON HOLY SATURDAY.

MEDITATION I. FOR SATURDAY BEFORE PASSION SUNDAY.

Jesus makes His triumphant entry into Jerusalem.

1. The time of His Passion being now at hand, our Redeemer departs from Bethany to go to Jerusalem. On drawing nigh to that ungrateful city He beheld it, and went : "Beholding the city He wept over it" (St. Luke xix. 41). He wept because He foresaw its ruin, which would be the consequence of the stupendous crime of taking away the life of the Son of God, of which that people would shortly become guilty. Ah, my Jesus, when Thou wert then weeping over that city, Thou wert weeping also over my soul, beholding the ruin which I have brought upon myself by my sins, constraining Thee to condemn me to hell, even after Thy having died to save me. Oh, leave it to me to weep over the great evil of which I have been guilty in despising Thee, the greatest of all good, and do Thou have mercy upon me.

2. Jesus Christ enters into the city : the people go forth to meet Him ; they receive Him with acclamations and rejoicings ; and, in order to do Him honour, some of them strew branches of palms along, the road, whilst others spread out their garments for Him to pass over.

Oh, who would ever then have said that that Lord, now recognised as the Messias, and welcomed with so many demonstrations of respect, the next time that He appeared along the selfsame ways, would be under sentence of death, and with a Cross upon His shoulders. Ah, my beloved Jesus, these people now receive Thee with acclamations, saying, " Hosanna to the Son of David ! Blessed is He that cometh in the name of the Lord !" (St. Matthew xxi. 9.) Glory to the Son of David! Blessed be He who cometh in the name of God for our salvation ! And then they will raise their voices insultingly to Pilate to take Thee out of the world, and cause Thee to die upon a Cross : " Away with Him ! away with Him I crucify Him!" Go, my soul, and do thou too lovingly say to Him, "Blessed is He that cometh in the name of the Lord !" Blessed forever be Thou that art come, O Saviour of the world ! for, otherwise, we had all been lost. O my Saviour, save me !

3. When the evening, however, was come, after all those acclamations, there was no one found who would invite Him to lodge in his house ; so that He was obliged to retrace His steps to Bethany. O my beloved Redeemer, if others will not give Thee a welcome, I desire to welcome Thee into my poor heart. At one time, I, unhappily, expelled Thee from my soul ; but I now prize to have Thee with me more than the possession of all the treasures of earth. I love Thee, O my Saviour; what power shall ever be able to separate me from my love of Thee ? Sin only ; but from this sin it is Thine to deliver me, by Thy help, O my Jesus ; and thine too, by thy intercession, O Mary, my Mother.

MEDITATION II. FOR PASSION SUNDAY.

Jesus prays in the Garden.

1. Jesus, knowing that the hour of his Passion bad now come, after having washed the feet of His disciples and instituted the most Holy Sacrament of the Altar,— wherein He left ne His whole Self,—goes to the Garden of Gethsemani, whither He knew already that His enemies would come to take Him. He there betakes Himself to prayer, and lo ! He finds Himself assailed by a great dread, by a great repugnance, and by a great sadness : "He began to be afraid, to be weary, and sorrowful" (St. Mark xiv. and St. Matt. xxvi.). There came upon Him, first, a great dread of the bitter Death which He would have to suffer on Calvary, and of all the anguish and desolations by which it would be accompanied. During the actual course of His Passion, the scourges, the thorns, the nails, and the rest of His tortures came upon Him but one at a time ; whereas, in the Garden, they all came upon Him together at once, crowding into His memory in order to torment Him. For His love of us He embraced them all; but in embracing them, He trembles and is in agony : "Being in an agony, He prayed the longer" (St. Luke xxii. 43).

2. There comes upon Him, moreover, a great repugnance to that which He has to suffer ; so that He prays His Father to deliver Him from it : " My Father, if it be possible, let this chalice pass away from Me" (St. Matt, xxvi. 39). He prayed thus to teach us that in our tribulations we may indeed beg of God to deliver us from them ; but we ought at the same time to refer ourselves to His will, and to say, as Jesus then said, " Not, however, as I will, but as Thou wilt." Yes, my Jesus, Thy will, not mine, be done. I embrace all the crosses that Thou will send me. Thou, innocent as Thou art, hast suffered so much for love of me ; it is but just that I, who am a sinner, and deserving of hell, should suffer for love of Thee that which Thou dost ordain.

3. There came upon Him, likewise, a sadness so great, that it would have been enough to cause Him to die, had He not, of Himself, kept death away, in order to die for us after having suffered more : "My soul is sorrowful even unto death" (St. Mark xiv. 34). This great sadness was occasioned by the sight of the future ungratefulness of men, who, instead of corresponding to so great a love on His part, would offend Him by so many sins, the sight of which caused Him to sweat in streams of Blood : " And His sweat became as drops of Blood trickling down upon the ground" (St. Luke xxii. 44). So, then, O my Jesus, it is not the executioners, the scourges, the thorns, or the Cross, that have been so cruel : the cruelty lies in my sins, which afflicted Thee so much in the Garden. Do Thou give me, then, a share of that sorrow and abhorrence which Thou didst experience in the Garden, that so, even to my death, I may bitterly weep for the offences that I have given Thee. I love Thee, O my Jesus : do Thou receive with kindness a sinner who wishes to love Thee. Recommend me, O Mary, to this thy Son, who is in affliction and sadness for love of me.

MEDITATION III. FOR PASSION MONDAY.

Jesus is apprehended, and led before Caiphas.

1. The Lord, knowing that the Jews who were coming to take Him were now at hand, rose up from prayer, and went to meet them ; and so, without reluctance, He lets them take Him, and bind Him : " They apprehended Jesus, and bound Him" (St. John xviii. 12). O amazement ! A God bound as a criminal by His own creatures ! Behold, my soul, how some of them seize hold of His hands ; others put the handcuffs on Him ; and others smite Him ; and the innocent Lamb lets Himself be bound and struck at their will, and says not a word : " He was offered because it was His own will, and opened not His mouth. He is led as a sheep to the slaughter" (Is. liii. 7). He neither speaks nor utters complaint, since He bad Himself already offered Himself up to die for us : and, therefore, did that Lamb let Himself be bound and led to death without opening His mouth.

2. Jesus enters Jerusalem bound. Those who were asleep in their beds, at the noise of the crowd passing by, awake, and inquire who that might be whom they are taking along in custody ; and they are told in reply, 'It is Jesus of Nazareth, who has been found out to be an impostor and seducer.' They bring Him up before Caiphas, who is pleased at seeing Him, and asks Him about His disciples, and about His doctrine. Jesus replies, that He has spoken openly; so that He calls upon the Jews themselves, who were standing around Him, to bear their testimony as to what He has said : " Behold, these know what I have said." But upon this reply, one of the officials of the court gives Him a blow in the Face, saying, " Dost Thou answer the high-priest so?" But, O God, how does a reply, so humble and gentle, deserve so great an insult ? Ah, my Jesus, Thou dost suffer it all in order to pay the penalty of the insults that I have offered to Thy Heavenly Father.

3. The high-priest, in the next place, conjures Him, in the name of God, to say whether He be truly the Son of God ? Jesus answered in the affirmative, that such He was ; and Caiphas, on hearing this, instead of prostrating himself upon the floor to adore his God, rends his garments, and, turning to the other priests, says, "What more need have we of witnesses I Behold, ye have now heard His blasphemy : what is your opinion ?" And they unanimously replied, " He is guilty of death." And then, as the Evangelists relate, they all began to spit in His Face, and to abuse Him, slapping Him with their hands, and striking Him with their fists ; and then, tying a piece of cloth over His Face, they turned Him into ridicule, saying, " Prophesy to us, Thou Christ : who is it that smote Thee?" Thus writes St. Matthew (chap. xxvi. 68). And St. Mark writes, "And some began to spit upon Him, and to cover His Face, and to deal upon Him blows, and to say to Him, Prophesy. And the officers did smite Him with the palms of their hands" (Mark xiv. 65). Behold Thyself, O my Jesus, become, upon this night, the butt of the rabble. And how can men see Thee in such humiliation for love of them, and not love Thee ? And how have I been able to go so far as to outrage Thee by so many sins, after that Thou hast suffered so much for me ? Forgive me, O my Love, for I will not displease Thee more. I love Thee, my chiefest Good, and I repent, above every other evil, of having despised Thee. O Mary, my Mother, pray thy ill-treated Son to pardon me.

MEDITATION IV. FOR PASSION TUESDAY.

Jesus is led before Pilate and Herod, and then has Barabbas preferred before Him.

1. The morning being come, they lead Jesus to Pilate, that he may pronounce upon Him the sentence of death. But Pilate is aware that Jesus is innocent, and, therefore, he tells the Jews that he can find no reason why lie should condemn Him. However, on seeing them obstinate in their desire for His death, he referred Him to the court of Herod. Herod, on seeing Jesus before him, desired to see some one of the Lord's great miracles, of which he had heard accounts, wrought in his presence. The Lord would not vouchsafe so much as an answer to the questions of that audacious man. Alas, for that poor soul to which God speaks no more ! O my Redeemer, such too were my deserts, for not having obeyed so many calls of Thine ; I deserved that Thou shouldst not speak to me more, and that Thou shouldst leave me to myself : but no, my Jesus, Thou hast not abandoned me yet. Speak to me, then : "Speak, Lord, for Thy servant heareth ;" tell me what Thou desirest of me, for I will do all to please Thee.

2. Herod, seeing that Jesus gave him no answer, drove Him away from his house with scorn, turning Him into ridicule with all the persons of his court ; and in order to load Him with the greater contempt, he had Him clothed in a white garment, so treating Him like a fool ; and thus he sent Him back again to Pilate : " He despised and mocked Him, putting on Him a white garment, and sent Him again to Pilate" (St. Luke xxiii. 1l). Behold how Jesus, clad in that robe which makes Him a laughingstock, is borne on along the streets of Jerusalem. O my despised Saviour, this additional wrong, of being treated as a fool, was still wanting to Thee ! If then, the Divine Wisdom is so treated by the world, happy is he who cares nothing for the world's approbation, and desires nothing but to know Jesus crucified, and to love sufferings and contempt, saying, with the Apostle : "For I judged not myself to know anything among you, hut Jesus Christ and Him crucified" (1 Cor. ii. 2).

3. The Jews had the right of demanding from the Roman governor the liberation of a criminal on the Feast of the Passover. Pilate, therefore, asked the people which of the two they would wish to have liberated, Jesus or Barabbas : "Whom will you that I release to you, Barabbas or Jesus?" (Matt, xxvii. 17.) Barabbas was a wicked wretch, a murderer, a thief, and held in abhorrence by all : Jesus was innocent ; but the Jews cry aloud for Barabbas to live, and for Jesus to die. Ah, my Jesus, so too have I said, whenever I have deliberately offended Thee for some satisfaction of my own, preferring before Thee that miserable pleasure of mine, and, in order not to lose it, contenting myself to lose Thee, O infinite Good. But now I love Thee above every other good, and more than my life itself. Have compassion upon me, O God of mercy. And do thou, O Mary, be my advocate.

MEDITATION V. FOR PASSION WEDNESDAY.

Jesus is scourged at the Pillar.

1. "Then Pilate, therefore, took Jesus, and scourged Him" (St. John xix. 1). O thou unjust judge, thou hast declared Him innocent, and then thou dost condemn Him to so cruel and so ignominious a punishment! Behold, now, my soul, how, after this unjust decree, the executioners seize hold of the Divine Lamb; they take Him to the pretorium, and bind Him with ropes to the pillar. O ye Blessed Ropes, that bound the hands of my sweet Redeemer to that pillar, bind likewise this wretched heart of mine to His Divine Heart, that so I may, from this day forth, neither seek for, nor desire, anything but what He doth wish.

2. Behold how they now lay hold of the scourges, and, at a given sign, begin to strike, in every part, that Sacred Flesh, which at first assumes a livid appearance, and then is covered all over with Blood, that flows from every pore. Alas, the scourges and the executioners' hands are all now dyed in Blood; and with Blood is the ground all drenched. But, O God, through the violence of the blows, not only does the Blood, but pieces of the very Flesh, of Jesus Christ go flying through the air. That Divine Body is already but one mass of wounds; and yet do those barbarians continue to add blow to blow and pain to pain. And all this while, what is Jesus doing? He speaks not; He complains not; but patiently endures that great torture in order to appease the Divine justice, that was wroth against us: "As a lamb before the shearer is dumb, so opened He not His mouth" (Acts viii. 32). Go quickly, O my soul, go and wash thyself in that Divine Blood. My beloved Saviour, I behold Thee all torn in pieces for me; no longer, therefore, can I doubt that Thou dost love me, and love me greatly, too. Every wound of Thine is a sure token on Thy part of Thy love, which with too much reason demands my love. Thou, O my Jesus, dost, without reserve, give me Thy Blood; it is but just that I without reserve should give Thee all my heart. Do Thou, then, accept of it, and make it to be ever faithful.

3. O my God, had Jesus Christ not suffered more than a single blow for love of me, I ought yet to have been burning with love for Him, saying, A God hath been willing to be struck for me! But no: He contented not Himself with a single blow j but, to pay the penalty due to my sins, He was willing to have His whole Body torn to shreds, as Isaias had already foretold: "He was bruised for our iniquities" (Is. liii. 5); and that even until He looked like a leper covered with wounds from head to foot: " And we thought Him to be, as it were, a leper" (is. liii. 4). While, then, O my soul, Jesus was being scourged, He was thinking of thee, and offering to God those bitter sufferings of His, in order to deliver thee from the eternal scourges of hell. O God of love, how have I been able to live so many years, in time past, without loving Thee? O ye Wounds of Jesus, wound me with love towards a God who has loved me so much! O Mary, O Mother of graces, do thou gain for me this love!

MEDITATION VI. FOR PASSION THURSDAY.

Jesus is crowned with thorns, and treated as a mock king.

1. When the soldiers had finished the scourging of Jesus Christ, they all assembled together in the pretorium, and, stripping His own clothes off Him again, in order to turn Him into ridicule, and to make Him into a mock king, they put upon Him an old ragged mantle, of a reddish colour, to represent the royal purple ; in Hie hand a reed, to represent a sceptre ; and upon His Head a bundle of thorns, to represent a crown, but fashioned like a helmet, so as to fit close upon the whole of His Sacred Head. " Stripping Him, they put a scarlet cloak about Him, and plaiting a crown of thorns they put it upon His Head, and a reed in His right hand" (St. Matt, xxvii. 29). And when the thorns, by the pressure of their hands alone, could not be made to penetrate deeper into that Divine Head which they were piercing, with the selfsame reed, and with all their might, they battered down that barbarous crown : " And spitting upon Him, they took the reed, and struck His Head" (St. Matt, xxvii. 30). O ungrateful Thorns, do you thus torture your Creator ? But what thorns ? what thorns ? You, ye wicked thoughts of mine ; it is you that have pierced the Head of my Redeemer. I detest, O my Jesus, and I abhor, more than I do death itself, those evil consents by which I have so often grieved Thee, my God, who art so good. But since Thou dost make me know how much Thou bast loved me, Thee alone will I love, Thee alone.

2. O my God, how the Blood is now streaming down from that pierced Head over the Face and the breast of Jesus ! And Thou, my Saviour, dost not even utter a complaint of such unjust cruelties ! Thou art the King of heaven and of earth ; but now, my Jesus, Thou art brought down so low as to appear before us a King of derision and of sorrows, being made the laughingstock of all Jerusalem. But the prophecy of Jeremias had to be fulfilled, that Thou wouldst one day have Thy fill of sorrows and shame : " He will give His cheek to the smiter, He will be satiated with reproaches" (Lam. iii. 30). O Jesus, my Love, in time past I have despised Thee ; but now I prize Thee, and I love Thee with all my heart, and I desire to die for love of Thee.

3. But no ; these men for whom Thou art suffering have not yet their fill of torturing and making game of Thee. After having thus tortured Thee, and dressed Thee up as a mock king, they bend their knee before Thee, and scornfully address Thee: "Hail to Thee, O King of the Jews." And then, with shouts of laughter, they deal out more blows upon Thee, thus rendering twofold the anguish of the Head already pierced by the thorns:' "And bowing the knee before Him, they derided Him, saying, Hail, King of the Jews; and they gave Him blows" (St. Matthew xxvii. 29, and St. John xix. 3). Do thou at least go, O my soul, and recognise Jesus for what He is, the King of kings, and Lord of lords ; and return thanks to Him, and love Him, now that thou beholdest Him become, for love of thee, the King of sorrows. O my Lord, keep not in Thy remembrance the griefs which I have caused Thee. I now love Thee more than myself. Thou only dost deserve all my love, and, therefore, Thee only do I wish to love. I fear, on account of my weaknesses ; but it is for Thee to give me the strength to execute my desire. And thou, too, O Mary, must help me by thy prayers.

MEDITATION VII. FOR PASSION FRIDAY.

Pilate exhibits Jesus to the people, saying : " Behold the Man !"
1. Jesus having again been brought and set before Pilate, he beheld Him so wounded and disfigured by the scourges and the thorns, that he thought, by showing Him to them, to move the people to compassion. He therefore went out into the portico, bringing with him the afflicted Lord, and said : "Behold the Man !" As though he would say : Go now, and rest content with that which this poor innocent One has already suffered. Behold Him brought to so low a state that He cannot long survive. Go your way, and leave Him, for He can but have a short time to live. Do thou too, my soul, behold thy Lord in that portico, bound and half naked, covered only with wounds and Blood ; and consider to what thy Shepherd has reduced Himself, in order to save thee, a sheep that was lost.
2. At the same time that Pilate is exhibiting the wounded Jesus to the Jews, the Eternal Father is from heaven inviting us to turn our eyes to behold Jesus Christ in such a condition, and in like manner says to us : " Behold the Man !" O men, this Man whom you behold thus wounded and set at naught, He is My beloved Son, who is suffering all this in order to pay the penalty of your sins ; behold Him, and love Him. O my God and my Father, I do behold Thy Son, and I thank Him, and love Him, and hope to love Him always ; but do Thou, I pray Thee, behold Him also, and for love of this Thy Son have mercy upon me ; pardon me, and give me the grace never to love anything apart from Thee.
3. But what is it that the Jews reply, on their beholding that King of sorrows? They raise a shout and say : " Crucify, crucify Him !" And seeing that Pilate, notwithstanding their clamour, was seeking a means to release Him, they worked upon his fears by telling him : "If thou release this Man, thou art not Caesar's friend" (St. John xix. 12). Pilate still makes resistance, and replies : " Shall I crucify your King ?" And their answer was : " We have no king but Cœsar." Ah, my adorable Jesus, these men will not recognise Thee for their King, and tell Thee that they wish for no other king but Cœsar. I acknowledge Thee to be my King and God ; and I protest that I wish for no other King of my heart but Thee, my Love, and my one and only Good. Wretch that I am, I at one time refused Thee for my King, and declared that I did not wish to serve Thee ; but now I wish Thee alone to have dominion over my will. Do Thou make it obey Thee in all that Thou dost ordain. O Will of God, Thou art my love. Do thou, O Mary, pray for me. Thy prayers are not rejected.

MEDITATION VIII. FOR PASSION SATURDAY.

Jesus is condemned by Pilate.

1. Behold, at last, how Pilate, after having so often declared the innocence of Jesus, declares it now anew, and, protesting that he is innocent of the Blood of that Just Man,—" I am innocent of the Blood of this Just Man" (St. Matt, xxvii 24), after all this he pronounces the sentence, and condemns Him to death. Oh, what injustice—such as the world has never seen ! At the very time that the judge declares the accused One to be innocent, he condemns Him. Ah, my Jesus, Thou dost not deserve death ; but it is I that deserve it. Since, then, it is Thy will to make satisfaction for me, it is not Pilate, but Thy Father Himself, who justly condemns Thee to pay the penalty that was my due. I love Thee, O Eternal Father, who dost condemn Thine innocent Son in order to liberate me, who am the guilty one. I love Thee, O Eternal Son, who dost accept of the death which I, a sinner, have deserved.

2. Pilate, after having pronounced sentence upon Jesus, delivers Him over to the hands of the Jews, to the end that they may do with Him whatsoever they please : " He delivered Jesus up to their will " (St. Luke xxiii. 25). Such truly is the course of things. When an innocent one is condemned, there are no limits to the punishment ; but he is left in the hands of his enemies, that they may make him suffer and die according to their own pleasure. Poor Jews ! you then imprecated chastisement upon yourselves in saying, " His Blood be upon us, and upon our children " (St. Matt, xxvii. 25) ; and the chastisement has come : you now endure, you miserable men, and will endure, even to the end of the world, the penalty of that innocent Blood. Do Thou, O my Jesus, have mercy upon me, who by my sins have also been a cause of Thy Death. But I do not wish to be obstinate, and like the Jews ; I wish to bewail the evil treatment that I have given Thee, and I wish to love Thee—always, always, always !

3. Behold, the unjust sentence of Death upon a Cross is read over in the presence of the condemned Lord. He listens to it ; and, all submissive to the will of the Father, He obediently and humbly accepts it : " He humbled Himself, becoming obedient unto death, and that the death of the Cross " (Phil. ii. 8). Pilate says on earth, ' Let Jesus die and the Eternal Father, in like manner, says from heaven, ' Let My Son die and the Son Himself makes answer, ' Behold Me ! I obey ; I accept of death, and death upon a Cross.' O my Beloved Redeemer, Thou dost accept of the death that was my due. Blessed for evermore be Thy mercy : I return Thee my most hearty thanks for it. But since Thou who art innocent dost accept of the Death of the Cross for me, I, who am a sinner, accept of that death which Thou dost destine to be mine, together with all the pains that shall accompany it ; and, from this time forth, I unite it to Thy Death, and offer it up to Thy Eternal Father. Thou hast died for love of me, and I wish to die for love of Thee. Ah, by the merits of Thy holy Death, make me die in Thy grace, and burning with holy love for Thee. Mary, my hope, be mindful of me.

MEDITATION IX. FOR PALM SUNDAY.

Jesus carries the Cross to Calvary.

1. The sentence upon Our Saviour having been published, they straightway seize hold of Him in their fury : they strip Him anew of that purple rag, and put His own raiment upon Him, to lead Him away to be crucified on Calvary,—the place appropriated for the execution of criminals : " They took off the cloak from Him, and put on Him His own garments, and led Him away to crucify Him" (St. Matt, xxvii. 31). They then lay hold of two rough beams, and quickly make them into a Cross, and order Him to carry it on His shoulders to the place of His punishment. What cruelty, to lay upon the criminal the gibbet on which he has to die ! But this is Thy lot, O my Jesus, because Thou hast taken my sins upon Thyself.

2. Jesus refuses not the Cross; with love He embraces it, as being the Altar whereon is destined to be completed the sacrifice of His life for the salvation of men : "And, bearing His own Cross, He went forth to that place which is called Calvary" (St. John xix. 17). The condemned criminals now come forth from Pilate's residence, and in the midst of them there goes also our condemned Lord. O that sight, which filled both heaven and earth with amazement ! To see the Son of God going to die for the sake of those very men from whose hands He is receiving His Death ! Behold the prophecy fulfilled : "And I was as a meek lamb, that is carried to be a victim" (Jer. xi. 19). The appearance that Jesus made on this journey was so pitiable, that the Jewish women, on beholding Him, followed Him in tears : "They bewailed and lamented Him" (St. Luke xxiii 27). O my dear Redeemer, by the merits of this sorrowful journey of Thine, give me strength to bear my cross with patience. I accept of all the sufferings and contempts which Thou dost destine for me to undergo. Thou hast rendered them lovely and sweet by embracing them for love of us : give me strength to endure them with calmness.

Behold, my soul, now that thy condemned Saviour is passing, behold how He moves along, dripping with Blood that keeps flowing from His still fresh Wounds, crowned with thorns, and laden with the Cross. Alas, how at every motion is the pain of all His Wounds renewed ! The Cross, from the first moment, begins its torture, pressing heavily upon His wounded shoulders, and cruelly acting like a hammer upon the thorns of the crown. O God, at every step, how great are the sufferings ! Let us meditate upon the sentiments of love wherewith Jesus, in this journey, is drawing nigh to Calvary, where Death stands awaiting Him; Ah, my Jesus, Thou art going to die for Us. In time past I have turned my back upon Thee, and would that I could die of grief on this account ! but for the future I have not the heart any more to leave Thee, O my Redeemer, my God, my Love, my AIL O Mary, my Mother, do thou obtain for me strength to bear my cross in peace.

MEDITATION X. FOR HOLY MONDAY.

Jesus is placed upon the Cross.

1. No sooner was the Redeemer arrived, all suffering and wearied out, at Calvary, than they strip Him of His clothes,—that now stick to His wounded Flesh,—and then cast Him down upon the Cross. Jesus stretches forth His holy hands, and at the same time offers up the sacrifice of His life to the Eternal Father, and prays of Him to accept it for the salvation of mankind. In the next place, the executioners savagely lay hold of the nails and hammers, and nailing His hands and His feet, they fasten Him to the Cross. O ye Sacred Hands, which by a mere touch have so often healed the sick, wherefore are they now nailing you upon this Cross? O Holy Feet, which have encountered so much fatigue in your search after us lost sheep, wherefore do they now transfix you with so much pain? When a nerve is wounded in the human body, so great is the suffering, that it occasions convulsions and fits of tainting : what, then, must not the suffering of Jesus have been, in having nails driven through His hands and feet, parts which are most full of nerves and muscles! O my sweet Saviour, so much did the desire of seeing me saved and of gaining my love cost Thee! And I have so often ungratefully despised Thy love for nothing; but now I prize it above every good.

2. The Cross is now raised up, together with the Crucified, and they let it fall with a shock into the hole that had been made for it in the rock. It is then made firm by means of stones and pieces of wood ; and Jesus remains hanging upon it, to leave His life thereon. The afflicted Saviour, now about to die upon that bed of pain, and finding Himself in such desolation and misery, seeks for someone to console Him, but finds none. Surely, my Lord, those men will at least compassionate Thee, now that Thou art dying! But no; I hear some outraging Thee, some ridiculing Thee, and others blaspheming Thee, saying to Thee, 'Come down from the Cross if Thou art the Son of God. He has saved others, and now He cannot save Himself.' Alas, you barbarians, He is now about to die, according as you desire ; at least torment Him not with your revilings.

3. See how much thy dying Redeemer is suffering upon that gibbet. Each member suffers its own pain, and the one cannot come to the help of the other. Alas, how does He experience in every moment the pains of death. Well may it be said that, in those three hours during which Jesus was suffering His Agony upon the Cross, He suffered as many deaths as were the moments that He remained there. He finds not there even the slightest relief or repose, whether He lean His weight upon His hands or upon His feet; wheresoever He leans the pain is increased, His most Holy Body hanging suspended, as it does, from His very Wounds themselves. Go, my soul, and tenderly draw nigh to that Cross, and kiss that Altar, whereon thy Lord is dying a Victim of love for thee. Place thyself beneath His feet, and let that Divine Blood trickle down upon thee. Yes, my dear Jesus, let this Blood wash me from all my sins, and set me all on fire with love towards Thee, my God, who hast been willing to die for love of me. Do Thou, O suffering Mother, who dost stand at the foot of the Cross, pray to Jesus for me.

MEDITATION XI. FOR HOLY TUESDAY.

Jesus upon the Cross.

1. Jesus on the Cross! Behold the proof of the love of a God; behold the final manifestation of Himself, which the Word Incarnate makes upon this earth,—a manifestation of suffering indeed, but, still more, a manifestation of love. St. Francis of Paola, as he was one day meditating upon the Divine Love in the person of Jesus Crucified, rapt in ecstasy, exclaimed aloud three times, in these words, ' O God—Love ! O God—Love ! O God —Love!' wishing hereby to signify that we shall never be able to comprehend how great has been the Divine love towards us, in willing to die for love of us.

2. O my beloved Jesus, if I behold Thy Body upon this Cross, nothing do I see but wounds and Blood ; and then, if I turn my attention to Thy Heart, I find it to be all afflicted and in sorrow. Upon this Cross I see it written up that Thou art a King ; but what tokens of Majesty dost Thou retain? I see not any royal throne save that of this Tree of infamy ; no other purple do I behold save Thy wounded and Bloody Flesh ; no other crown save this band of thorns that tortures Thee. Ah, how it all declares Thee to be King of Love ! yes, for this Cross, these Nails, this Crown, and these Wounds are, all of them, tokens of love.

3. Jesus, from the Cross, asks us not so much for our compassion as for our love ; and, if even He does ask our compassion, He asks it solely in order that the compassion may move us to love Him. As being infinite Goodness, He already merits all our love ; but when placed upon the Cross, it seems as if He sought for us to love Him, at least out of compassion. Ah, my Jesus, and who is there that will not love Thee, while confessing Thee to be the God that Thou art, and contemplating Thee upon the Cross ? Oh, what arrows of fire dost Thou not dart at souls from that Throne of Love ! Oh, how many hearts hast Thou not drawn to Thyself from that Cross of Thine! O Wounds of my Jesus ! O beautiful furnaces of love ! admit me, too, amongst yourselves to burn, not indeed with that fire of hell which I have deserved, but with holy flames of love for that God who has been willing to die for me, consumed by torments. O my dear Redeemer, receive back a sinner, who, sorrowing for having offended Thee, is now earnestly longing to love Thee. I love Thee, I love Thee, O infinite Goodness, O infinite Love. O Mary, O Mother of beautiful love, obtain for me a greater measure of love, to consume me for that God who has died consumed of love for me.

MEDITATION XII. FOR HOLY WEDNESDAY.

The words spoken by Jesus upon the Cross.

1. While Jesus upon the Cross is being outraged by that barbarous populace, what is it that He is doing? He is praying for them, and saying, " O My Father, forgive them ; for they know not what they do." O Eternal Father, hearken to this Thy beloved Son, who, in dying, prays Thee to forgive me too, who have outraged Thee so much. Then Jesus, turning to the good thief, who prays Him to have mercy upon him, replies, "To-day shalt thou be with Me in Paradise." Oh, how true is that which the Lord spake by the mouth of Ezechiel, that when a sinner repents of his faults, He, as it were, blots out from His memory all the offences of which he has been guilty : " But if the wicked do penance . . . .   I will not remember all his iniquities" (Ez. xviii. 21, 22). Oh, would that it were true, my Jesus, that I had never offended Thee I But, since the evil is done, remember no more, I pray Thee, the displeasures that I have given Thee ; and, by that bitter Death which Thou hast suffered for me, take me to Thy kingdom after my death ; and, while I live, let Thy love ever reign within my soul.

2. Jesus, in His Agony upon the Cross, with every part of His Body full of torture, and deluged with affliction in His Soul, seeks for someone to console Him. He looks towards Mary; but that sorrowing Mother only adds by her grief to His affliction. He casts His eyes around Him, and there is no one that gives Him comfort. He asks His Father for consolation ; but the Father, beholding Him covered with all the sins of men, even He too abandons Him : and then it was that Jesus cried out with a loud voice : "Jesus cried out with a loud voice, saying, My God, My God, why hast Thou forsaken Me?" (St. Matt, xxvii. 46.) My God, my God, and why hast Thou also abandoned Me? This abandonment by the Eternal Father caused the Death of Jesus Christ to be more bitter than any that has ever fell to the lot of either penitent or martyr ; for it was a death of perfect desolation, and bereft of every kind of relief. O my Jesus, how is it that I have been able to live so long a time in forgetfulness of Thee? I return Thee thanks that Thou hast not been unmindful of me. Oh, I pray Thee ever to keep me in mind of the bitter Death which Thou hast embraced for love of me, that so I may never be unmindful of the love which Thou hast borne me !

3. Jesus then, knowing that His sacrifice was now completed, said that He was thirsty : " He said, I thirst" (St. John xix. 28). And the executioners then reached Up to His mouth a sponge, filled with vinegar and gall. But, Lord, how is it that Thou dost make no complaint of those many pains which are taking away Thy life, but complainest only of Thy thirst ? Ah, I understand Thee, my Jesus, Thy thirst is a thirst of love ; because Thou lovest us, Thou dost desire to be beloved by us. Oh, help me to drive away from my heart all affections which are not for Thee ; make me to love none other but Thee, and to have no other desire save that of doing Thy will. O Will of God, Thou art my love. O Mary, my Mother, obtain for me the grace to wish for nothing but that which God doth will.

MEDITATION XIII. FOR HOLY THURSDAY.

Jesus dies upon the Cross.

1. Behold how the loving Saviour is now drawing nigh unto death. Behold, my soul, those beautiful eyes growing dim, that face become all pallid, that Heart all but ceasing to beat, and that Sacred Body now disposing itself to the final surrender of its life. After Jesus had received the vinegar, He said, " It is consummated. " He then passed over in review before His eyes all the sufferings that He had undergone during His life, in the shape of poverty, contempt, and pain ; and then offering them all up to the Eternal Father, He turned to Him and said, "It is finished." My Father, behold, by the sacrifice of My Death, the work of the world's redemption, which Thou hast laid upon Me, is now completed. And it seems as though, turning Himself again to us, He repeated, " It is finished ;" as if He would have said, O men, O men, love Me, for I have done all; there is nothing more that I can do in order to gain your love.

2. Behold now, lastly, Jesus dies. Come, ye Angels of heaven, come and assist at the Death of your King. And thou, O sorrowing Mother Mary, do thou draw nearer to the Cross, and fix thine eyes yet more attentively on thy Son, for He is now. on the point of death. Behold Him, how, after having commended His Spirit to His Eternal Father, He calls upon Death, giving it permission to come to take away His life. Come, O Death, says He to it, be quick and perform thine office ; slay Me, and save My flock. The earth now trembles, the graves open, the veil of the Temple is rent in twain. The strength of the dying Saviour is failing through the violence of the sufferings; the warmth of His Body is gradually diminishing; He gives up His Body to death; He bows His Head down upon His breast, He opens His mouth, and dies : " And bowing His head, He gave up the ghost (St. John xix. 30). The people behold Him expire, and, observing that He no longer moves, they say, He is dead, He is dead ; and to them the voice of Mary makes echo, while she too says, "Ah ! my Son, Thou art, then, dead."

3. He is dead ! O God, who is it that is dead ? The Author of life, the only-begotten Son of God, the Lord of the world,—He is dead. O Death, thou wert the amazement of heaven and of all nature ! O infinite Love ! A God to sacrifice His Blood and His life I And for whom? For His ungrateful creatures ; dying in an ocean of sufferings and shame, in order to pay the penalty due to their sins. Ah, infinite Goodness ! O infinite Love ! O my Jesus, Thou art, then, dead, on account of the love which Thou hast borne me ! Oh, let me never again live, even for a single moment, without loving Thee ! I love Thee, my chief and only Good ; I love Thee, my Jesus,—dead for me ! O my sorrowing Mother Mary, do thou help a servant of thine, who desires to love Jesus.

MEDITATION XIV. FOR GOOD FRIDAY.

Jesus hanging dead upon the Cross.

1. Raise up thine eyes, my soul, and behold that crucified Man. Behold the Divine Lamb now sacrificed upon that altar of pain. Consider that He is the beloved Son of the Eternal Father ; and consider that He is dead for the love that He has borne thee. See how He holds His arms stretched out to embrace thee ; His Head bent down to give thee the kiss of peace ; His Side open to receive thee into His Heart. What dost thou say ? Does not a God so loving deserve to be loved? Listen to the words He addresses to thee from that Cross : 'Look, My son, and see whether there be any one in the world who has loved thee more than I have.' No, my God, there is none that has loved me more than Thou. But what return shall I ever be able to make to a God who has been willing to die for me ? what love from a creature will ever be able to recompense the love of his Creator, who died to gain his love ?

2. O God, had the vilest one of mankind suffered for me what Jesus Christ has suffered, could I ever refrain from loving him? Were I to see any man torn to pieces with scourges and fastened to a cross in order to save my life, could I ever bear it in mind without feeling a tender emotion of love? And were there to be brought to me the portrait of him, as he lay dead upon the cross, could I behold it with an eye of indifference, when I considered : ' This man is dead, tortured thus, for love of me. Had he not loved me, he would not so have died.' Ah, my Redeemer, O Love of my soul ! How shall I ever again be able to forget Thee ? How shall I ever be able to think that my sins have reduced Thee so low, and not always bewail the wrongs that I have done to Thy goodness ? How shall I ever be able to see Thee dead of pain on this Cross for love of me, and not love Thee to the uttermost of my power ?

3. O my dear Redeemer, well do I recognise in these Thy wounds, and in Thy lacerated Body, as it were through so many lattices, the tender affection which Thou dost retain for me. Since, then, in order to pardon me, Thou hast not pardoned Thyself, oh, look upon me now with the same love wherewith Thou 'didst one day look upon me from the Cross, whilst Thou wert dying for me. Look upon me and enlighten me, and draw my whole heart to Thyself, that so, from this day forth, I may love none else but Thee. Let me not ever be unmindful of Thy Death. Thou didst promise that, when raised up upon the Cross, Thou wouldst draw all our hearts to Thee. Behold this heart of mine, which, made tender by Thy Death, and enamoured of Thee, desires to offer no further resistance to Thy calls. Oh, do Thou draw it to Thyself and make it all Thine own.

Thou hast died for me, and I desire to die for Thee ; and if I continue to live, I will live for Thee alone. O Pains of Jesus, O Ignominies of Jesus, O Death of Jesus, O Love of Jesus, fix yourselves within my heart, and let the remembrance of you abide there always, to be continually smiting me, and inflaming me with love. I love Thee, O infinite Goodness ; I love Thee, O infinite Love. Thou art, and shalt ever be, my one and only Love. O Mary, Mother of love, do thou obtain me love.

MEDITATION XV. FOR HOLY SATURDAY.

Mary assisting on Calvary at the Death of Jesus.

1. "There stood by the Cross of Jesus His Mother" (St. John xix. 25). We observe in this the Queen of Martyrs, a sort of martyrdom more cruel than any other martyrdom,—that of a Mother so placed as to behold an innocent Son executed upon a gibbet of infamy : " she stood." Ever since Jesus was apprehended in the Garden, He has been abandoned by His disciples ; but Mary abandons Him not. She stays with Him till she sees Him expire before her eyes : " she stood close by." Mothers, in general, flee away from the presence of their sons when they see them suffer, and cannot render them any assistance : content enough would they be themselves to endure their sons' sufferings ; and, therefore, when they see them suffering without the power of succouring them, they have not the strength to endure so great a pain, and consequently flee away, and go to a distance. Not so Mary. She sees her Son in torments ; she sees that the pains are taking His life away ; but she flees not, nor moves to a distance. On the contrary, she draws near to the Cross whereon her Son is dying. O sorrowing Mary, disdain me not for a companion to assist at the Death of thy Jesus and mine.

2. "She stood near to the Cross." The Cross, then, is the bed whereon Jesus leaves His life ; a bed of suffering, where this afflicted Mother is watching Jesus, all wounded as He is with scourges and with thorns. Mary observes how this her poor Son, suspended from those three iron nails, finds neither a position nor repose. She would wish to give Him some relief ; she would wish, at least, since He has to die, to have Him die in her arms. But nothing of all this is allowed her. Ah, Cross ! she says, give me back my Son ! Thou art a malefactor's gibbet; whereas my Son is innocent. But grieve not thyself, O Mother ! It is the will of the Eternal Father that the Cross should not give Jesus back to thee until after He has died and breathed His last. O Queen of Sorrows, obtain for me sorrow for my sins.

3. " There stood by the Cross His Mother!" Meditate, my soul, upon Mary, as she stands at the foot of the Cross watching her Son ! Her Son ! but, O God, what a Son ! a Son who was, at one and the same time, her Son and her God ! a Son who had from all eternity chosen her to be His Mother, and had given her a preference in His love before all mankind and all the Angels ! A Son so beautiful, so holy, and so lovely ; a Son who had been ever obedient unto her; a Son who was her one and only Love, being as He was both her Son and God. And this Mother had to see such a Son die of pain before her very eyes ! O Mary, O Mother, most afflicted of all mothers, I compassionate thy heart more especially when thou didst behold thy Jesus surrender Himself up upon the Cross, open His mouth, and expire : and, for love of this thy Son, now dead for my salvation, do thou recommend unto Him my soul. And do Thou, my Jesus, for the sake of the merits of Mary's sorrows, have mercy upon me, and grant me the grace of dying for Thee, as Thou hast died for me : ' May I die, O my Lord' (will I say unto Thee with St. Francis of Assisi), 'for love of the love of Thee, who hast vouchsafed to die for love of the love of me.'

THREE MEDITATIONS ON PARADISE, FOR THE EASTER FESTIVAL.

MEDITATION I. FOR EASTER SUNDAY.

1. Oh, happy are we, if we suffer with patience on earth the troubles of this present life! Distress of circumstances, fears, bodily infirmities, persecutions, and crosses of every kind, will one day all come to an end ; and if we be saved, they will all become for us subjects of joy and glory in Paradise : " Your sorrow" (says the Saviour to encourage us) " shall be turned into joy" (St. John xvi. *30).* So great are the delights of Paradise, that they can neither be explained nor understood by us mortals : " Eye hath not seen" (says the Apostle), " nor ear heard, neither hath it entered into the heart of man, what things God hath prepared for those who love Him" (1 Cor. ii. 9). Beauties like to the beauties of Paradise, eye hath never seen ; harmonies like unto the harmonies of Paradise, ear hath never heard ; nor hath ever human heart gained the comprehension of the joys which God hath prepared for those that love Him. Beautiful is the sight of a landscape adorned with hills, plains, woods, and views of the sea. Beautiful is the sight of a garden abounding with fruit, flowers, and fountains. Oh, how much more beautiful is Paradise !

2. To understand how great the joys of Paradise are, it is enough to know that in that blessed realm resides a God omnipotent, whose care it is to render happy His beloved souls. St. Bernard says, that Paradise is a place where 'there is nothing that thou wouldst not, and everything that thou wouldst.' There shalt thou not find anything displeasing to thyself, and everything thou dost desire thou shalt find : ' There is nothing that thou wouldst not.' In Paradise there is no night ; no seasons of winter and summer ; but one perpetual day of unvaried serenity, and one perpetual spring of unvaried delight. No more persecutions or jealousies are there ; for there do all in sincerity love one another, and each rejoices in each other's good, as if it were his own. *No* more bodily infirmities or pains are there, for the body is no longer subject to suffering ; no poverty is there, for everyone is rich to the full, not having anything more to desire; no more fears are there, for the soul being confirmed in grace can sin no more, nor lose that supreme good which it possesses.

3. ' There is everything that thou wouldst.' In Paradise thou shalt have whatsoever thou desirest. There the sight is satisfied in beholding that city so beautiful, and its citizens all clothed in royal apparel, for they are all kings of that everlasting kingdom. There shall we see the beauty of Mary, whose appearance will be more beautiful than that of all the Angels and Saints together. We shall see the beauty of Jesus, which will immeasurably surpass the beauty of Mary. The smell will be satisfied with the perfumes of Paradise. The hearing will be satisfied with the harmonies of Heaven and the canticles of the blessed, who will all with ravishing sweetness sing the Divine praises for all eternity. Ah, my God, I deserve not Paradise, but hell ; yet Thy Death gives me a hope of obtaining it. I desire and ask Paradise of Thee, not so much in order to enjoy, as in order to love Thee everlastingly, secure that it will never more be possible for me to lose Thee. O Mary, my Mother, O Star of the Sea, it is for thee, by thy prayers, to conduct me to Paradise.

MEDITATION II. FOR EASTER MONDAY.

1. Let us imagine to ourselves a soul which, on departing out of this world, enters into eternity in the grace of God. All full of humility and of confidence, it presents itself before Jesus, its Judge and Saviour. Jesus embraces it, gives it His benediction, and causes it to hear those words of sweetness : " Come, my spouse, come, thou shalt be crowned." If the soul have need of being purified, He sends it to Purgatory, and, all resigned, it embraces the chastisement, because itself wishes not to enter into Heaven, that land of purity, if it is not wholly purified. The Guardian-Angel comes to conduct it to Purgatory ; it first returns him thanks for the assistance he has rendered it in its lifetime, and then obediently follows him. Ah, my God, when will that day arrive on which I shall see myself out of this world of perils, secure of never being able to lose Thee more? Yes, willingly will I go to the Purgatory which shall be mine ; joyfully will I embrace all its pains ; sufficient will it be for me in that fire to love Thee with all my heart, since there I shall love none else but Thee.

2. The purgation over, the Angel will return and say to it, Come along, beautiful soul, the punishment is at an end ; come, and enjoy the Presence of thy God who is awaiting thee in Paradise. Behold, the soul now passes beyond the clouds, passes beyond the spheres and the stars, and enters into Heaven. O God, what will it say on entering into that beautiful country, and casting its first glance on that city of delights ? The Angels and Saints, and especially its own holy advocates, will go to meet it, and with jubilation will they welcome it, saying, Welcome, O companion of our own ; welcome ! Ah, my Jesus, do Thou make me worthy of it.

3. What consolation will it not feel in there meeting with relations and friends of its own who have previously entered into Heaven ! But greater by far will be its joy in beholding Mary its Queen, and in kissing her feet, while it will thank her for the many kindnesses she has done it. The Queen will embrace it, and will herself present it unto Jesus, who will receive it as a spouse. And Jesus will then present it to His Divine Father, who will embrace and bless it, saying, "Enter thou into the joy of thy Lord." And thus will He beatify it with the same beatitude which He Himself enjoys. Ah, my God, make me love Thee exceedingly in this life, that I may love Thee exceedingly in eternity. Thou art the Object most worthy of being loved ; Thou dost deserve all my love ; I will love none but Thee. Do Thou help me by Thy grace. And, Mary, my Mother, be thou my protectress.

MEDITATION III. FOR EASTER TUESDAY.

1. The beauties of the Saints, the heavenly music, and all the other delights of Paradise, form but the lesser portion of its treasures. The possession which gives to the soul its fullness of bliss is that of seeing a loving God face to face. St. Augustine says, that were God to let His beautiful Face be seen by the damned, hell, with all its torments, would become to them a paradise. Even in this world, when God gives a soul in prayer a taste of His sweet Presence, and by a ray of light discovers to it His goodness and the love which He bears it, so great is the contentment, that the soul feels itself dissolve and melt away in love; and yet, in this life, it is not possible for us to see God as He is ; we behold Him obscured, as if through a thick veil. What, then, will it be, when God shall take away that veil from before us, and shall cause us to behold Him face to face, openly? O Lord, for having turned my back upon Thee, no more should I be worthy to behold Thee ; but, relying on Thy goodness, I hope to see Thee, and to love Thee in Paradise forever. I speak thus, because I am speaking with a God who has died in order to give Paradise to me.

2. Although the souls that love God are the most happy in this world, yet they cannot, here below, enjoy a happiness full and complete : that fear, which arises from not knowing whether they be deserving of the love or the hatred of their beloved Saviour, keeps them, as it were, in perpetual suffering. But in Paradise the soul is certain that it loves God, and is loved by God ; and it sees that that sweet tie of love which holds it united with God will never be loosened throughout all eternity. The flames of its love will be increased by the clearer knowledge which the soul will then possess of what the love of God has been in being made Man, and having willed to die for it ; and in having, moreover, given Himself to it in the Sacrament of the Eucharist. Its love will be increased by then beholding, in all their distinctness, the graces which He has given it, in order to lead it to Heaven ; it will see that the crosses sent to it in lifetime have all been artifices of His love to render it happy. It will see, besides, the mercies He has granted it, the many lights and calls to penance. From the summit of that blessed Mount will it behold the many lost souls now in hell for sins less than its own, and it will behold itself now saved, possessed of God, and certain that it can never more lose Him throughout all eternity. My Jesus, my Jesus, when will that too happy day for me arrive?

3. The happiness of the blessed soul will be perfected by knowing with absolute certainty that that God whom it then enjoys it will have to enjoy for all eternity. Were there to be any fear in the blessed that they might lose that God whom they now enjoy, Paradise would no more be Paradise. But no ; the blessed soul is certain, with the certainty which it has of the existence of God, that that supreme Good which it enjoys, it will enjoy forever. That joy, moreover, will not grow less with time ; it will be ever new. The blessed one will be ever happy, and ever thirsting for that happiness ; and, on the other hand, while ever thirsting, will be ever satiated.

When, therefore, we see ourselves afflicted with the troubles of this life, let us lift up our eyes unto heaven, and console ourselves by saying, Paradise. The sufferings will one day come to an end ; nay, they will themselves become objects over which to rejoice. The Saints await us ; the Angels await us ; Mary awaits us : and Jesus stands with the crown in His hand wherewith to crown us, if we shall be faithful to Him. Ah, my God, when will come that day on which I shall arrive at possessing Thee, and be able to say unto Thee, My Love, I cannot lose Thee more ? O Mary, my hope, never cease from praying for me, until thou dost see me safe at thy feet in Paradise !

NOVENA TO THE SACRED HEART OF JESUS.

NOTICE ON THE DEVOTION TO THE ADORABLE HEART OF JESUS.

The devotion of all devotions is love for Jesus Christ, and frequent meditation on the love which this amiable Redeemer has borne and still bears to us. A devout author laments, and most justly, the sight of so many persons who pay much attention to the practice of various devotions, but neglect this ; and of many preachers and confessors, who say a great many things, but speak little of love for Jesus Christ : whereas love for Jesus Christ ought to be the principal, indeed the only, devotion of a Christian ; and therefore the only object and care of preachers and confessors towards their hearers and penitents ought to be to recommend to them constantly, and to inflame their hearts with, the love of Jesus Christ. This neglect is the reason why souls make so little progress in virtue, and remain grovelling in the same defects, and even frequently relapse into grievous sins, because they take but little care, and are not sufficiently admonished to acquire the love of Jesus Christ, which is that golden cord which unites and binds the soul to God. For this sole purpose did the Eternal Word come into this world, to make Himself loved : "I am come to cast fire on the earth, and what will I but that it be kindled?" (St. Luke xii. 49.) And for this purpose also did the Eternal Father send Him into the world, in order that He might make known to us His love, and thus obtain ours in return ; and He protests that He will love us in the same proportion as we love Jesus Christ : " For the Father Himself loveth you, because you have loved Me" (St. John xvi. 27). Moreover, He gives us His graces as far as we ask for them in the name of His Son : " If you ask the Father an thing in My name, He will give it you" (St. John xvi. 23). And He will admit us to the eternal beatitude in so far only as He finds us conformable to the life of Jesus Christ : "For whom He foreknew, He also predestinated to be made conformable to the image of His Son" (Rom. viii. 29). But we shall never acquire this conformity, nor even ever desire it, if we are not attentive to meditate upon the love which Jesus Christ has borne to us.

For this same purpose it is related in the life of the Venerable Sister Margaret Alacoque, a nun of the Order of the Visitation, that our Saviour revealed to this His servant His wish that in our times the Devotion and Feast of His Sacred Heart should be established and propagated in the Church, in order that devout souls should by their adoration and prayer make reparation for the injuries His Heart constantly receives from ungrateful men when He is exposed in the Sacrament upon the Altar. It is also related in the life of the same venerable sister, written by the learned Monseigneur Languet, Bishop of Sens, that while this devout virgin was one day praying before the most Holy Sacrament, Jesus Christ showed her His Heart surrounded by thorns, with a cross on the top and in a throne of flames; and then He said thus to her, 'Behold the Heart that has so much loved men, and has spared nothing for love of them, even to consuming itself to give them pledges of its love, but which receives from the majority of men no other recompense but ingratitude, and insults towards the Sacrament of love ; and what grieves Me most is, that these hearts are consecrated to Me.' And then He desired her to use her utmost endeavours in order that a particular Feast should be celebrated in honour of His Divine Heart on the first Friday after the Octave of Corpus Christi. And this for three reasons : 1. in order that the faithful would return thanks to Him for the great gift which He has left them in the adorable Eucharist ; 2. in order that loving souls should make amends by their prayers and pious affections for the irreverences and insults which He has received and still receives from sinners in this most Holy Sacrament ; 3. in order that they might make up also for the honour which He does not receive in so many churches where He is so little adored and reverenced. And He promised that He would make the riches of His Sacred Heart abound towards those who should render Him this honour, both on the day of this Feast, and on every other day when they should visit Him in the most Holy Sacrament. So that this devotion to the Sacred Heart of Jesus Christ is nothing more than an exercise of love towards this amiable Saviour.

But as to the principal object of this Devotion, the *spiritual* object is the love with which the Heart of Jesus Christ is inflamed towards men, because love is generally attributed to the heart, as we read in many places of Scripture : "My son, give Me thy heart" (Prov. xxiii. 26). " My heart and my flesh have rejoiced in the living God" (Ps. lxxxiii. 3). " The God of my heart, and the God that is my portion forever" (Ps. lxxii. 26). " The charity of God is poured forth in our hearts by the Holy Ghost who is given to us" (Rom. v. *5)*. But the *material* or sensible object is the most Sacred Heart of Jesus, not taken separately by itself, but united to His Sacred Humanity, and consequently to the Divine Person of the Word.

This Devotion in the course of a short time has been so extensively propagated, that besides having been introduced into many convents of holy virgins, there have been about 400 confraternities erected of the Sacred Heart of Jesus, established with the authority of the Prelates in France, in Savoy, in Flanders, in Germany, in Italy, and even in many heathen countries ; and these confraternities have also been enriched by the Holy See with many indulgences, and also with the faculty of erecting chapels and churches with the title of the Sacred Heart, as it appears from the brief of Clement X. in the year 1674, mentioned by Father Eudes in his book (page 468), and referred to by Father Gallifet, of the Company of Jesus, in his work on the " Excellence of the Devotion to the Heart of Jesus."

And many devout persons hope that the Holy Church may someday grant permission for the Office, and proper Mass, in honour of the most Sacred Heart of Jesus Christ. We know, indeed, that even in the year 1726 this request was made through the medium of the same Father Gallifet, who was the postulator of it ; he explained that the Sacred Heart of Jesus deserved this special veneration, because it was the sensible origin and the seat of all the affections of the Redeemer, and especially that of love ; and because it was also the centre of all the interior sorrows which He suffered during His life. But, as far as my weak judgment goes, I believe that this good religious did not obtain his petition because he urged it upon grounds which were dubiously tenable. It was therefore justly objected to his views that it was a great question as to whether the affections of the soul were found in the heart or in the brain ; and even the most modern philosophers, with Lewis Muratori in his moral philosophy, adopt the second opinion, viz. of the brain. And that therefore, as there had been no judgment pronounced concerning this disputed point by the Church, which prudently abstains from such decisions, the request made was not to be granted, inasmuch as it was grounded on an uncertain opinion of the ancients. And it was moreover said, that as this special motive for the veneration of the Sacred Heart had failed, it would not be right to grant the petition for the Office and Mass ; because otherwise this might be a precedent for similar requests in favour of the most Holy Side, of the Tongue, the Eyes, and other members of Jesus Christ's Body. This is the sum of what I find recorded in the celebrated work of Benedict XIV., of blessed memory (*De Canoniz. Sanct*, tom. iv. lib. iv. pars 2, cap. 31).

But the hope we entertain that this concession will someday be granted in favour of the Heart of our Lord, is not built upon the above-mentioned opinion of the ancients, but on the common opinion of philosophers, both ancient and modern, that the human heart, even though it may not be the seat of the affections and the principle of life, is, notwithstanding, as the most learned Muratori writes in the same place, · One of the primary fountains and organs of the life of man.' For the generality of modern physicians agree in saying that the fountain and the principle of the circulation of the blood is the heart, to which are attached the veins and arteries ; and therefore there is no doubt that the other parts of the body receive their principle of motion from the heart. If, therefore, the heart is one of the ' primary fountains' of human life, it cannot be doubted that the heart has a principal share in the affections of man. And, indeed, one may observe from experience, that the internal affections of sorrow and love produce a much greater impression on the heart than on all the other parts of the body. And especially with regard to love, without naming many other saints, it is recorded of St. Philip Neri, that in his fervours of love towards God, heat came forth from his heart so that it might be felt on his chest, and his heart palpitated so violently that it beat against the head of any one that approached him ; and by a supernatural prodigy our Lord enlarged the ribs of the saint round his heart, which, agitated by the ardour he felt, required a greater space to be able to move. St. Teresa writes herself, in her life, that God sent several times an Angel to pierce her heart, so that she remained afterwards inflamed with Divine love, and felt herself sensibly burning and fainting away,—a thing to be well pondered on, as we perceive from this that the affections of love are in a special manner impressed by God in the hearts of the saints ; and the Church has not objected to grant to the Discalced Carmelites the proper Mass in honour of the wounded heart of St. Teresa.

It may be added, that the Church has declared worthy of particular veneration the instruments of the Passion of Christ, such as the Lance, the Nails, and the Crown of Thorns, granting a particular Office and Mass for their special veneration, as is mentioned by Benedict XIV. in the work and place referred to (n. 18), where he quotes particularly the words of Innocent VI., who granted the Office for the Lance and the Nails of our Lord, and these are the words : 'We think it right that a special Feast were celebrated in honour of the special Instruments of His Passion, and particularly in those countries in which those Instruments are said to be, and that we should encourage the faithful servants of Christ in devotion to them by concession of the Divine Offices.' If, therefore, the Church has judged it right to venerate by a special Office the Lance, the Nails, the Thorns, because they came in contact with." those parts of Christ's Body which were particularly tormented in the Passion, how much more have we not reason to hope that a special Office may be granted in honour of the most Sacred Heart of Jesus Christ, which had such a great share in His affections, and in the immense internal sorrows that He suffered in seeing the torments that were prepared for Him, and the ingratitude which, after all His love for them, would be shown Him by men? This was the cause of the Bloody Sweat which our Lord afterwards endured in the Garden, because such a sweat can only be explained by a strong compression of the heart, by which the blood, being impeded in its course, was forced to diffuse itself through the exterior parts ; and this compression of the Heart of Jesus Christ could not arrive from any other cause than from the internal pains of fear, of weariness, and of sorrow, according as the Evangelists write : "He began to fear, and to be heavy and sad" (St Matt. xxvi. 37 ; St. Mark xiv. 33).

But, however this may be, let us now endeavour to satisfy the devotion of souls enamoured of Jesus Christ, who are desirous to honour Him in the most Holy Sacrament, by a Novena of holy meditations and affections to His Sacred Heart.

MEDITATION I. ON THE AMIABLE HEART OF JESUS.

He who shows himself amiable in everything must necessarily make himself loved. Oh, if we only applied ourselves to discover all the good qualities by which Jesus (Christ renders Himself worthy of our love, we should all be under the happy necessity of loving Him. And what heart among all hearts can be found more worthy of love than the Heart of Jesus ? A Heart all pure, all holy, all full of love towards God and towards us ; because all His desires are only for the Divine glory and our good. This is the Heart in which God finds all His delight. Every perfection, every virtue reign in this Heart ;—a most ardent love for God, His Father, united to the greatest humility and respect that can possibly exist ; a sovereign confusion for our sins, which He has taken upon Him, united to the extreme confidence of a most affectionate Son ; a sovereign abhorrence of our sins, united to a lively compassion for our miseries ; an extreme sorrow, united to a perfect conformity to the Will of God : so that in Jesus is found everything that there can be most amiable. Some are attracted to love others by their beauty, others by their innocence, others by living with them, others by devotion. But if there were a person in whom all these and other virtues were united, who could help loving him? If we heard that there was in a distant country a foreign prince who was handsome, humble, courteous, devout, full of charity, affable to all, who rendered good to those who did him evil ; then, although we knew not who he was, and though he knew not us, and though we were not acquainted with him, nor was there any possibility of our ever being so, yet we should be enamoured of him, and should be constrained to love him. How is it, then, possible that Jesus Christ, who possesses in Himself all these virtues, and in the most perfect degree, and who loves us so tenderly, how is it possible that He should be so little loved by men, and should not be the only Object of our love? O my God, how is it that Jesus, who alone is worthy of love, and who has given us so many proofs of the love that He bears us, should be alone, as it were, the unlucky one with us, who cannot arrive at making us love Him ; as if He were not sufficiently worthy of our love ! This is what caused floods of tears to St. Bose of Lima, St. Catherine of Genoa, St. Teresa, St. Mary Magdalen of Pazzi, who, on considering the ingratitude of men, exclaimed, weeping, 'Love is not loved, Love is not loved.'

AFFECTIONS AND PRAYERS.

O my amiable Redeemer, what object more worthy of love could Thy Eternal Father command me to love than Thee? Thou art the beauty of Paradise, Thou art the love of Thy Father, Thy Heart is the throne of all virtues. O amiable Heart of my Jesus, Thou dost well deserve the love of all hearts ; poor and wretched is that heart which loves Thee not ! Thus miserable, O my God, has my heart been during all the time in which it hath not loved Thee. But I will not continue to be thus wretched ; I love Thee, I will always continue to love Thee, O my Jesus. O my Lord, I have hitherto forgotten Thee, and now what can I expect ? That my ingratitude will oblige Thee to forget me entirely and forsake me forever ? No, my Saviour, do not permit it. Thou art the Object of the love of God ; and shalt Thou not, then, be loved by a miserable sinner, such as I am, who have been so favoured and loved by Thee ? O lovely flames that burnt in the loving Heart of my Jesus, enkindle in my poor heart that holy fire which Jesus came down from heaven to kindle on earth. Consume and destroy all the impure affections that dwell in my heart, and prevent it from being entirely His. O my God, grant that it may only exist to love Thee, and Thee alone, my dearest Saviour. If at one time I despised Thee, Thou art now the only Object of my love. I love Thee, I love Thee, I love Thee, and I will never love any but Thee. My beloved Lord, do not disdain to accept the love of a heart which has once afflicted Thee by my sins. Let it be Thy glory to exhibit to the angels a heart now burning with the love of Thee, which hitherto shunned and despised Thee. Most holy Virgin Mary, my hope, do thou assist me, and beseech Jesus to make me, by His grace, all that He wishes me to be.

MEDITATION II. ON THE LOVING HEART OF JESUS.

Oh, if we could but understand the love that burns in the Heart of Jesus for us ! He has loved us so much, that if all men, all the angels, and all the saints were to unite, with all their energies, they could not arrive at the thousandth part of the love that Jesus bears to us. He loves us infinitely more than we love ourselves. He has loved us even to excess : " They spoke of His decease (excess) which He was to accomplish in Jerusalem" (St. Luke ix. 31). And what greater excess of love could there be than for God to die for His creatures ? He has loved us to the greatest degree : "Having loved His own . . . . He loved them unto the end" (St. John xiii. 1) ; since, after having loved us from eternity,—for there never was a moment from eternity when God did not think of us and did not love each one of us: "I have loved thee with an everlasting love,"—for the love of us He made Himself man, and chose a life of sufferings and the death of the Cross for our sakes. Therefore He has loved us more than His honour, more than His repose, and more than His life ; for He sacrificed everything to show us the love that He bears us. And is not this an excess of love sufficient to stupefy with astonishment the Angels of Paradise for all eternity? This love has induced Him also to remain with us in the Holy Sacrament as on a throne of love ; for He remains there under the appearance of a small piece of bread, shut up in a ciborium, where He seems to remain in a perfect annihilation of His Majesty, without movement, and without the use of His senses; so that it seems that He performs no other office there than that of loving men. Love makes us desire the constant presence of the object of our love. It is this love and this desire that makes Jesus Christ reside with us in the most Holy Sacrament.

It seemed too short a time to this loving Saviour to have been only thirty-three years with men on earth ; therefore, in order to show His desire of being constantly with us, He thought right to perform the greatest of all miracles, in the institution of the Holy Eucharist. But the work of redemption was already completed, men had already become reconciled to God; for what purpose, then, did Jesus remain on earth in this Sacrament ? Ah, He remains there because He cannot bear to separate Himself from us, as He has said that He takes a delight in us. Again, this love has induced Him even to become the Food of our souls, so as to unite Himself to us, and to make His Heart and ours as one : " He that eateth My Flesh and drinketh My Blood, abideth in Me and I in him" (St. John vi. 57). O wonder ! O excess of Divine love ! It was said by a servant of God, If anything could shake my faith in the Eucharist, it would not be the doubt as to how the bread could become Flesh, or how Jesus could be in several places and confined into so small a space, because I should answer, that God can do everything; but if I were asked how He could love men so much as to make Himself their food, I have nothing else to answer but that this is a mystery of faith above my comprehension, and that the love of Jesus cannot be understood. O Love of Jesus, do Thou make Thyself known to men, and do Thou make Thyself loved !

AFFECTIONS AND PRAYERS.

O adorable Heart of my Jesus, Heart inflamed with the love of men, Heart created on purpose to love them, how is it possible that Thou canst be despised, and Thy love so ill corresponded to by men ? Oh, miserable that I am, I also have been one of those ungrateful ones that have not loved Thee. Forgive me, my Jesus, this great sin of not having loved Thee, who art so amiable, and who hast loved me so much that Thou canst do nothing more to oblige me to love Thee. I feel that I deserve to be condemned not to be able to love Thee, for having renounced Thy love, as I have hitherto done. But no, my dearest Saviour, give me any chastisement, but do not inflict this one upon me. Grant me the grace to love Thee, and then give me any affliction Thou pleasest. But how can I fear such a chastisement, whilst I feel that Thou continuest to give me the sweet, the pleasing precept of loving Thee, my Lord and my God ? " Love the Lord thy God with thy whole heart." Yes, O my God, Thou wouldst be loved by me, and I will love Thee ; indeed, I will love none but Thee, who hast loved me so much. O Love of my Jesus, Thou art my Love. O burning Heart of my Jesus, do thou inflame my heart also. Do not permit me in future, even for a single moment, to live without Thy love ; rather kill me, destroy me ; do not let the world behold the spectacle of such horrid ingratitude as that I, who have been so beloved by Thee, and received so many favours and lights from Thee, should begin again to despise Thy love. No, my Jesus, permit it not. I trust in the Blood that Thou hast shed for me, that I shall always love Thee, and that Thou wilt always love me, and that this love between Thee and me will not be broken off for eternity. O Mary, Mother of fair love, thou who desirest so much to see Jesus loved, bind me, unite me with thy Son ; but bind me to Him, so that we may never again be separated.

MEDITATION III. ON THE HEART OF JESUS PANTING TO BE LOVED.

Jesus has no need of us ; He is equally happy, equally rich, equally powerful with or without our love ; and yet, as St. Thomas says, He loves us so, that He desires our love as much as if man was His God, and His felicity depended on that of man. This filled holy Job with astonishment : "What is man that thou shouldst magnify him? or why dost Thou set Thy heart upon him?" (Job vii. 17.) What ! can God desire or ask with such eagerness for the love of a worm ? It would have been a great favour if God had only permitted us to love Him. If a vassal were to say to his king, ' Sire, I love you,' he would be considered impertinent. But what would one say if the king were to tell his vassal, 'I desire you to love me' ? The princes of the earth do not humble themselves to this ; but Jesus, who is the King of Heaven, is He who with so much earnestness demands our love: "Love the Lord thy God with thy whole heart." So pressingly does He ask for our heart : " My son, give Me thy heart" (Prov. xxiii. 26). And if He is driven from a soul, He does not depart, but He stands outside of the door of the heart, and He calls and knocks to be let in : "I stand at the gate and knock" (Apoc. iii. 20). And He beseeches her to open to Him, calling her sister and spouse : " Open to Me, My sister, My love" (Cant. v. 5). In short, He takes a delight in being loved by us, and is quite consoled when a soul says to Him, and repeats often, ' My God,' my God, I love Thee.' All this is the effect of the great love He bears us. He who loves necessarily desires to be loved. The heart requires the heart ; love seeks love : ' Why does God love, but that He might be loved Himself,' said St. Bernard ; and God Himself first said, " What doth the Lord thy God require of thee, but that thou fear the Lord thy God, . . and love Him" (Deut. x. 12). Therefore He tells us that He is that Shepherd who, having found the lost sheep, calls all the others to rejoice with Him : " Rejoice with Me, because I have found My sheep that was lost" (St. Luke xv. 6). He tells us that He is that Father who, when His lost son returns and throws himself at His feet, not only forgives him, but embraces him tenderly. He tells us, that he that loves Him not is condemned to death : " He that loveth not abideth in death" (1 St. John iii. 14). And, on the contrary, that He takes him that loves Him and keeps possession of him : " He that abideth in charity, abideth in God, and God in him" (1 St. John iv. 16). Oh, will not such invitations, such entreaties, such threats, and such promises move us to love God, who so much desires to be loved by us?

AFFECTIONS AND PRAYERS.

My dearest Redeemer, I will say to Thee, with St. Augustine, Thou dost command me to love Thee, and dost threaten me with hell if I do not love Thee; but what more dreadful hell, what greater misfortune, can happen to me, than to be deprived of Thy love? If, therefore, Thon desirest to frighten me, Thou shouldst threaten me only that I should live without loving Thee; for this threat alone will frighten me more than a thousand hells. If, in the midst of the flames of hell, the damned could hum with Thy love, O my God, hell itself would become a paradise; and if, on the contrary, the blessed in Heaven could not love Thee, Paradise would become hell. Thus says St. Augustine.

I see, indeed, my dearest Lord, that I, on account of my sins, did deserve to be forsaken by Thy grace, and at the same time condemned to be incapable of loving Thee; but still I understand that Thou dost continue to command me to love Thee, and I also feel within me a great desire to love Thee. This my desire is a gift of Thy grace, and it comes from Thee. Oh, give me also the strength necessary to put it into execution, and make me, from this day forth, say to Thee earnestly, and from the bottom of my heart, and to repeat to Thee always, My God, I love Thee, I love Thee, I love Thee. Thou desirest my love; I also desire Thine. Blot out, therefore, from Thy remembrance; O my Jesus, the offences that in past times I have committed against Thee; let us love each other henceforth forever. I will not leave Thee, and Thou wilt not leave me. Thou wilt always love me, and I will always love Thee. My dearest Saviour, in Thy merits do I place my hope; oh, do Thou make Thyself to be loved forever, and loved greatly, by a sinner who has offended Thee greatly. O Mary, Immaculate Virgin, do thou help me, do thou beseech Jesus for me.

MEDITATION IV. ON THE SORROWFUL HEART OF JESUS.

It is impossible to consider how afflicted the Heart of Jesus was for love of us and not to pity Him. He Himself tells us that His Heart was overwhelmed with such sorrow, that this alone would have sufficed to take His life away, and to make Him die of pure grief, if the virtue of His Divinity had not, by a miracle, prevented His death : "My soul is sorrowful even unto death" (St. Mark xiv. 34). The principal sorrow which afflicted the Heart of Jesus so much, was not the sight of the torments and infamy which men were preparing for Him, but the sight of their ingratitude towards His immense love. He distinctly foresaw all the sins which we should commit after all His sufferings and such a bitter and ignominious death. He foresaw, especially, the horrible insults which men would offer to His adorable Heart, which He has left us in the most Holy Sacrament as a proof of His affection. O my God, what affronts has not Jesus Christ received from men in this Sacrament of love ? One has trampled Him under foot, another has thrown Him into the gutters, others have availed themselves of Him to pass homage to the devil ! And yet the sight of all these insults did not prevent Him from leaving us this great pledge of His love. He has a sovereign hatred of sin ; but still it seems as if His love towards us had overcome the hatred. He bore to sin, since He was content to permit these sacrileges, rather than to deprive the souls that love Him of this Divine food. Shall not all this suffice to make us love a Heart that has loved us so much ? Has not Jesus Christ done enough to deserve our love ? Ungrateful that we are, shall we still leave Jesus forsaken on the Altar, as the majority of men do ? And shall we not unite ourselves to those few souls who acknowledge Him, and melt with love more even than the torches melt away which burn round the ciborium? The Heart of Jesus remains there burning with love for us; and shall we not, in His Presence, burn with love for Jesus ?

AFFECTIONS AND PRAYERS.

My adorable and dearest Jesus, behold at Thy feet one who has caused so much sorrow to Thy amiable Heart. O my God, how could I grieve this Heart, which has loved me so much, and has spared nothing to make itself loved by me ? But console Thyself, I will say, O my Saviour, for my heart having been wounded, through Thy grace, with Thy most holy love, feels now so much regret for the offences I have committed against Thee, that it would fain die of sorrow. Oh, who will give me, my Jesus, that sorrow for my sins which Thou didst feel for them in Thy life ! Eternal Father, I offer Thee the sorrow and abhorrence Thy Son felt for my sins ; and, for His sake, I beseech Thee to give me so great a sorrow for the offences I have committed against Thee, that I may lead an afflicted and sorrowful life at the thought of having once despised Thy friendship. And Thou, O my Jesus, do Thou give me, from this day forth, such a horror of sin, that I may abhor even the lightest faults, considering that they dis" please Thee, who dost not deserve to be offended much or little, but dost deserve an infinite love. My beloved Lord, I now detest everything that displeases Thee, and in future I will love only Thee, and that which Thou lovest. Oh, help me, give me the strength, give me the grace to invoke Thee constantly, O my Jesus, and always to repeat to Thee this petition: My Jesus, give me Thy love, give me Thy love, give me Thy love. And thou, most holy Mary, obtain for me the grace to pray to thee continually, and to say to Thee, O my Mother, make me love Jesus Christ.

MEDITATION V. ON THE COMPASSIONATE HEART OF JESUS.

Where shall we ever find à heart more compassionate or tender than the Heart of Jesus, or one that had a greater feeling for our miseries ? This pity induced Him to descend from heaven to this earth ; it made Him say that He was that Good Shepherd who came to give His life to save His sheep. In order to obtain the pardon of our sins, He would not spare Himself, but would sacrifice Himself on the Cross, that by His sufferings He might satisfy for the chastisement that we have deserved. This pity and compassion makes Him say even now: " Why will ye die, O house of Israel? return ye, and live" (Ezech. xviii. 31, 32). O men, He says, my poor children, why will you damn yourselves by flying from Me ? Do you not see that by separating yourselves from Me you are hastening to eternal death ? I desire not to see you lost; do not despair; as often as you wish to return, return, and you shall recover your life : "Return, and live." This compassion even makes Him say that He is that loving Father who, though He sees Himself despised by His son, yet, if that son returns a penitent, He cannot reject him, but embraces him tenderly and forgets all the injuries He has received :

" I will not remember all his iniquities." It is not thus that men behave ; for though they may forgive, yet they nevertheless retain the remembrance of the offence received, and feel inclined to revenge themselves ; and even if they do not revenge themselves, because they fear God, at least they always feel a great repugnance against conversing and entertaining themselves with those persons who have vilified them. O my Jesus, Thou dost pardon the penitent sinners, and dost not refuse in this world to give them everything in Holy Communion during their life, and everything in the other world, even in heaven, with eternal glory, without retaining the slightest repugnance towards being united to the soul that has offended Thee, for all eternity. Where, then, is there to be found a heart so amiable and compassionate as Thine, O my dearest Saviour ?

AFFECTIONS AND PRAYERS.

O compassionate Heart of my Jesus, have pity on me : ' Most sweet Jesus, have mercy on me.' I say so now, and beseech Thee to give me the grace always to say to Thee, ' Most sweet Jesus, have mercy on me.' Even before I offended Thee, O my Redeemer, I certainly did not deserve any of the favours Thou hast bestowed upon me. Thou hast created me, Thou hast given me so much light and knowledge ; and all without any merit of mine. But after I had offended Thee, I not only did not deserve Thy favour, but I deserved to be forsaken by Thee and cast into hell. Thy compassion has made Thee wait for me, and preserve my life even when I had offended Thee. Thy compassion has enlightened me, and offered me pardon ; it has given me sorrow for my sins, and the desire of loving Thee ; and now I hope from Thy mercy to remain always in Thy grace. O my Jesus, cease not to show Thy compassion towards me. The mercy which I implore of Thee is that Thou wouldst grant me light and strength to be no longer ungrateful towards Thee. No, O my Love, I do not expect that Thou shouldst again forgive me, if I again turn my back towards Thee; this would be presumption, and would prevent Thy showing mercy to me anymore. For what pity could I expect any more from Thee if I were so ungrateful as to despise Thy friendship again, and to separate myself from Thee. No, my Jesus, I love Thee, and I will always love Thee ; and this is the mercy which I hope for and seek from Thee : ' Permit me not to be separated from Thee, permit me not to be separated from *Thee.*' And I beseech Thee also, O Mary my Mother, permit me not to be ever again separated from my God.

MEDITATION VI. ON THE GENEROUS HEART OF JESUS.

It is the characteristic of good-hearted people to desire to make everybody happy, and especially those most distressed and afflicted. But who can ever find one who has a better heart than Jesus Christ? He is infinite Goodness, and has therefore a sovereign desire to communicate to us His riches : " With Me are riches, ... that I may enrich them that love Me" (Prov. viii. 18, 21). He for this purpose made Himself poor, as the Apostle says, that He might make us rich : " He became poor for your sakes, that through His poverty you might be rich" (2 Cor. viii. 9). For this purpose also He chose to remain with us in the most Holy Sacrament, where He remains constantly with His hands full of graces, as was seen by Father Balthazar Alvarez, to dispense them to those who come to visit Him. For this reason also He gives Himself wholly to us in Holy Communion, giving us to understand from this that He cannot refuse us any good gifts, since He even gives Himself entirely to us : " How hath He not also, with Him, given us all things" (Rom. viii. 32). For in the Heart of Jesus we receive every good, every grace that we desire : " In all things you are made rich in Christ, . . . so that nothing is wanting to you in any grace" (1 Cor. i. 6, 7). And we must understand that we are debtors to the Heart of Jesus for all the graces we have received— graces of redemption, of vocation, of light, of pardon, the grace to resist temptations, and to bear patiently with contradictions ; for without His assistance we could not do anything good : " Without Me you can do nothing" (St. John XV. 5). And if hitherto, says our Saviour, you have not received more graces, do not complain of Me, but blame yourself, who have neglected to seek them of Me : " Hitherto you have not asked anything . . . . ask, and you shall receive" (St. John xvi. 24). Oh, how rich and liberal is the Heart of Jesus towards every one that has recourse to Him ! "Rich unto all that call upon Him" (Rom. x. 12), Oh, what great mercies do those souls receive who are earnest in asking help of Jesus Christ. David said, "For Thou, O Lord, art sweet and mild, and plenteous to all who call upon Thee" (Ps. lxxxv. 5). Let us therefore always go to this Heart, and ask with confidence, and we shall obtain all we want.

AFFECTIONS AND PRAYERS.

Ah, my Jesus, Thou hast not refused to give me Thy Blood and Thy Life, and shall I refuse to give Thee my miserable heart ? No, my dearest Redeemer, I offer it entirely to Thee. I give Thee all my will ; do Thou accept it, and dispose of it at Thy pleasure. I can do nothing, and have nothing ; but I have this heart which Thou hast given me, and of which no one can deprive me. I may be deprived of my goods, my blood, my life, but not of my heart. With this heart I can love Thee ; with this heart I will love Thee.

I beseech Thee, O my God, teach me a perfect forgetfulness of myself ; teach me what I must do to arrive at Thy pure love, of which Thou in Thy goodness hast inspired me with the desire. I feel in myself a determination to please Thee ; but in order to put my resolve into execution, I expect and implore help from Thee. It depends on Thee, O loving Heart of Jesus, to make entirely Thine my poor heart, which hitherto has been so ungrateful, and through my own fault deprived of Thy love. Oh, grant that my heart may be all on fire with the love of Thee, even as Thine is on fire with the love of me. Grant that my will may be entirely united to Thine, so that I may will nothing but what Thou willest, and that from this day forth Thy holy will may be the rule of all my actions, of all my thoughts, and of all my desires. I trust, O my Saviour, that Thou wilt not refuse me Thy grace to fulfil this resolution which I now make prostrate at Thy feet, to receive with submission whatever Thou mayest ordain for me and my affairs, as well in life as in death. Blessed art thou, O Immaculate Mary, who hadst Thy Heart always and entirely united to the Heart of Jesus ; obtain for me, O my Mother, that in future I may wish and desire that which Jesus wills and thou willest.

MEDITATION VII. ON THE GRATEFUL HEART OF JESUS.

The Heart of Jesus is so grateful, that it cannot behold the most trifling works done for the love of Him—our smallest word spoken for His glory, a single good thought directed towards pleasing Him—without giving to each its own reward. He is besides so grateful, that He always returns a hundredfold for one : "You shall receive a hundredfold." Men, when they are grateful, and recompense any benefit done to them, recompense it only once ; they, as it were, divest themselves of all the obligation, and then they think no more of it. Jesus Christ does not do thus with us : He not only recompenses a hundredfold in this life every good action that we perform to please Him, but in the next life He recompenses it an infinite number of times throughout eternity. And who will be so negligent as not to do as much as he can to please this most grateful Heart ? But, O my God, how do men try to please Jesus Christ ? Or rather, I will say, how can we be so ungrateful towards this our Saviour? If He had only shed a single drop of Blood, or one tear alone for our salvation, yet we should be under infinite obligation to Him ; because this drop and this tear would have been of infinite value in the sight of God towards obtaining for us every grace. But Jesus would employ for us every moment of His life. He has given us all His merits, all His sufferings, all His ignominies, all His Blood, and His Life ; so that we are under, not one, but infinite, obligations to love Him.

But alas ! we are grateful even towards animals : if a little dog shows us any sign of affection, it seems to constrain us to love it. How, then, can we be so ungrateful towards God? It seems as if the benefits of God towards men change their nature, and become ill-usage ; for, instead of gratitude and love, they obtain nothing but offences and injuries. Do Thou, O Lord, enlighten these ungrateful ones, to know the love that Thou bearest them.

AFFECTIONS AND PRAYERS.

O my beloved Jesus, behold at Thy feet an ungrateful sinner. I have been grateful indeed towards creatures ; but to Thee alone I have been ungrateful—to Thee, who hast died for me, and hast done the utmost that Thou couldst do to oblige me to love Thee. But the thought that I have to do with a Heart full of goodness and infinite in mercy, of One who proclaims that He forgives all the offences of the sinner who repents and loves Him, consoles me and gives me courage. My dearest Jesus, I have in times past offended Thee and despised Thee ; but now I love Thee more than everything—more than myself. Tell me what Thou wouldst have me to do ; for I am ready to do everything with Thy help. I believe that Thou hast created me. Thou hast given Thy Blood and Thy Life for the love of me. I believe also that for my sake Thou dost remain in the Blessed Sacrament ; I thank Thee for it, O my Love. Oh, permit me not to be ungrateful in future for so many benefits and proofs of thy love. Oh, bind me, unite me to Thy Heart; and permit me not, during the years that remain to me, to offend Thee or grieve Thee any more. I have displeased Thee sufficiently. O my Jesus, it is time that I should love Thee now. Oh, that those years that I have lost would return ! But they will return no more, and the life that remains for me may be short; but whether it be short or long, my God, I desire to spend it all in loving Thee, my sovereign Good, who dost deserve an eternal and infinite love. O Mary, my Mother, let me never again be ungrateful to thy Son. Pray to Jesus for me.

MEDITATION VIII. ON THE DESPISED HEART OF JESUS.

There is not a greater sorrow for a heart that loves, than to see its love despised ; and so much the more when the proofs given of this love have been great, and, on the other hand, the ingratitude great. If every human being were to renounce all his goods, and to go and live in the desert, to feed on herbs, to sleep on the bare earth, to macerate himself with penances, and at last give himself up to be murdered for Christ's sake, what recompense could he render for the sufferings, the Blood, the life that this great Son of God has given for his sake ? If we were to sacrifice ourselves every moment unto death, we should certainly not recompense in the smallest degree the love that Jesus Christ has shown us, by giving Himself to us in the most Holy Sacrament. Only conceive that God should conceal Himself under the species of bread to become the food of one of His creatures ! But, O my God, what recompense and gratitude do men render to Jesus Christ? What but ill-treatment, contempt of His laws and His maxims,—injuries such as they would not commit towards their enemy, or their slave, or the greatest villain upon earth. And can we think upon all these injuries which Jesus Christ has received, and still receives every day, and not feel sorrow for them ? and not endeavour, by our love, to recompense the infinite love of His Divine Heart, which remains in the most Holy Sacrament, inflamed with the same love towards us, and anxious to communicate every good gift to us, and to give Himself entirely to us, ever ready to receive us into His Heart whenever we go to Him ? " Him that cometh to Me, I will not cast out" (St. John vi. 37). We have been accustomed to hear of the Creation, Incarnation, Redemption, of Jesus born in a stable, of Jesus dead on the Cross. O my God, if we knew that another man had conferred on us any of these benefits, we could not help loving him. It seems that God alone has, so to say, this bad luck with men, that, though He has done His utmost to make them love Him, yet He cannot attain this end, and, instead of being loved, He sees Himself despised and neglected. All this arises from the forgetfulness of men of the love of God.

AFFECTIONS AND PRAYERS.

O Heart of Jesus, abyss of mercy and love, how is it that, at the sight of the goodness Thou hast shown me, and of my ingratitude, I do not die of sorrow? Thou, O my Saviour, after having given me my being, hast given me all Thy Blood and Thy life, giving Thyself up, for my sake, to ignominy and death ; and, not content with this, Thou hast invented the mode of sacrificing Thyself every day for me in the Holy Eucharist, not refusing to expose Thyself to the injuries which Thou shouldst receive, and which Thou didst foresee, in this Sacrament of love. O my God, how can I see myself so ungrateful to Thee without dying with confusion ! O Lord, put an end, I pray Thee, to my ingratitude, by wounding my heart with Thy love, and making me entirely Thine. Remember the Blood and the tears that Thou hast shed for me, and forgive me. Oh, let not all Thy sufferings be lost upon me. But though Thou hast seen how ungrateful and unworthy of Thy love I have been, yet Thou didst not cease to love me even when I did not love Thee, nor even desire that Thou shouldst love me ; how much rather, then, may I not hope for Thy love, now that I desire and sigh after nothing but to love Thee, and to be loved by Thee. Oh, do Thou fully satisfy this my desire ; or rather this Thy desire, for it is Thou that hast given it to me. Grant that this day may be the day of my thorough conversion ; so that I may begin to love Thee, and may never cease to love Thee, my sovereign Good. Make me die in everything to myself, in order that I may live only to Thee, and that I may always burn with Thy love. O Mary, thy heart was the blessed altar that was always on fire with Divine love : my dearest Mother, make me like to thee ; obtain this from thy Son, who delights in honouring thee, by denying thee nothing that thou askest of Him.

MEDITATION IX. ON THE FAITHFUL HEART OF JESUS.

Oh, how faithful is the beautiful Heart of Jesus towards those whom He calls to His love : " He is faithful who hath called you, who also will perform" (1 Thes, v. 24). The faithfulness of God gives us confidence to hope all things, although we deserve nothing. If we have driven God from our heart, let us open the door to Him, and He will immediately enter, according to the promise He has made : " If any one open to Me the door, I will come into him, and will sup with him" (Apoc. iii. 20). If we wish for graces, let us ask for them of God, in the name of Jesus Christ, and He has promised us that we shall obtain them : " If you shall ask the Father anything in My name, He will give it you" (St. John xvi. 23). If we are tempted, let us trust in His merits, and He will not permit our enemies to strive with us beyond our strength : " God is faithful, who will not suffer you to be tempted above that which you are able"(I Cor. x. 13). Oh, how much better it is to have to do with God than with men ! How often do men promise and then fail, either because they tell lies in making their promises, or because, after having made the promise, they change their minds : " God is not as man," says the Holy Spirit, " that He should lie ; or as the son of man, that He should be changed" (Numb, xxiii. 19). God cannot be unfaithful to His promises, because, being Truth itself, He cannot lie ; nor can He change His mind, because all that He wills is just and right. He has promised to receive all that come to Him, to give help to him that asks it, to love him that loves Him ; and shall He then not do it? " Hath He said, then, and will He not do it ?" Oh, that we were as faithful with God as He is with us ! Oh, how often have we, in times past, promised Him to be His, to serve Him and love Him ; and then have betrayed Him, and, renouncing His service, have sold ourselves as slaves to the devil ! Oh, let us beseech Him to give us strength to be faithful to Him for the future! Oh, how blessed shall we be if we are faithful to Jesus Christ in the few things that He commands us to do ; He will, indeed, be faithful in remunerating us with infinitely great rewards ; and He will declare to us what He has promised to His faithful servants : " Well done, good and faithful servant ; because thou hast been faithful over a few things, I will place thee over many things ; enter thou into the joy of thy Lord" (St. Matt. xxv. 21).

AFFECTIONS AND PRAYERS.

Oh, that I had been as faithful towards Thee, my dearest Redeemer, as Thou hast been faithful to me. Whenever I have opened my heart to Thee, Thou hast entered in, to forgive me and to receive me into Thy favour ; whenever I have called Thee, Thou hast hastened to my assistance. Thou hast been faithful with me, but I have been exceedingly unfaithful towards Thee. I have promised Thee my love, and then have many times refused it to Thee ; as if Thou, my God, who hast created and redeemed me, wert less worthy of being loved than Thy creatures and those miserable pleasures for which I have forsaken Thee. Forgive me, O my Jesus. I know my ingratitude, and abhor it. I know that Thou art infinite Goodness, who deservest an infinite love, especially from me, whom Thou hast so much loved, even after all the offences I have committed against Thee. Unhappy me if I should damn myself; the graces Thou hast vouchsafed to me, and the proofs of the singular affection which Thou hast shown me, would be, O God, the hell of hells to me. Ah, no, my Love, have pity on me ; suffer me not to forsake Thee again, and then by damning myself, as I should deserve, continue to repay in hell with injuries and hatred the love that Thou hast borne me. O loving and faithful Heart of Jesus, inflame, I beseech Thee, my miserable heart, so that it may burn with love for Thee, as Thine dost for me. My Jesus, it seems to me that now I love Thee ; but I love Thee but little. Make me love Thee exceedingly, and remain faithful to Thee until death. I ask of Thee this grace, together with that of always praying to Thee for it. Grant that I may die rather than ever betray Thee again. O Alary, my Mother, help me to be faithful to thy Son.

EXERCISE OF THE WAY OF THE CROSS.

This Exercise of the Way of the Cross represents to us the sorrowful journey which Jesus made to Calvary, when, with the Cross on His shoulders, He went to die for love of us. We ought, then, to practise this devotion with all possible tenderness, imagining we accompany our Saviour weeping, compassionating His sufferings, and thanking Him for suffering on our behalf.

In making the following Stations, we gain the same Indulgences as if they were made at Jerusalem, on the very spot where our Saviour suffered.

MANNER OF PRACTISING THIS EXERCISE.

Let each one, kneeling before the High Altar, make an act of contrition, and form the intention of gaining the Indulgences, whether for himself or for the souls in Purgatory. Then say : My Lord Jesus Christ, Thou hast made this journey to die for me with love unutterable, and I have so many times unworthily abandoned Thee ; but now I love Thee with ray whole heart, and because I love Thee I repent sincerely for having ever offended Thee. Pardon me, my God, and permit me to accompany Thee on this journey. Thou goest to die for love of me; I wish also, my beloved Redeemer, to die for love of Thee. My Jesus, I will live and die always united to Thee.

  Dear Jesus, Thou dost go to die
   For very love of me :
  Ah ! let me bear Thee company,
  I wish to die with Thee.

FIRST STATION.
JESUS IS CONDEMNED TO DEATH.

V. We adore Thee, O Christ, and praise Thee.
R. Because by Thy holy Cross Thou hast redeemed the world.

Consider how Jesus, after having been scourged and crowned with thorns, was unjustly condemned by Pilate to die on the Cross.

My adorable Jesus, it was not Pilate, no, it was my sins, that condemned Thee to die. I beseech Thee, by the merits of this sorrowful journey, to assist my soul in its journey towards eternity. I love Thee, my beloved Jesus ; I love Thee more than myself ; I repent with my whole heart of having offended Thee. Never permit me to separate myself from Thee again. Grant that I may love Thee always ; and then do with me what Thou wilt.

  Our Father. Hail Mary. Glory be, &c.
  Dear Jesus, Thou dost go to die
   For very love of id e :
  Ah ! let me bear Thee company,
  I wish to die with Thee.

SECOND STATION.
JESUS IS MADE TO BEAR HIS CROSS.

V. We adore Thee, O Christ, and praise Thee.
R. Because by Thy holy Cross Thou hast redeemed the world.

Consider how Jesus, in making this journey with the Cross on His shoulders, thought on us, and offered for us to His Father the Death He was about to undergo.

My most beloved Jesus, I embrace all the tribulations Thou hast destined for me until death. I beseech Thee, by the merits of the pain Thou didst suffer in carrying Thy Cross, to give me the necessary help to carry mine with perfect patience and resignation. I love Thee, Jesus, my Love ; I repent of having offended Thee. Never permit me to separate myself from Thee again. Grant that I may love Thee always, and then do with me what Thou wilt. Our Father. Hail Mary. Glory be, &c.

  Dear Jesus, Thou dost go to die
   For very love of me :
  Ah ! let me bear Thee company,
  I wish to die with Thee.

THIRD STATION.
JESUS FALLS THE FIRST TIME UNDER HIS CROSS.

V. We adore Thee, O Christ, and praise Thee.
R. Because by Thy holy Cross Thou hast redeemed the world.

Consider this first fall of Jesus under His Cross. His Flesh was torn by the scourges, His Head crowned with thorns, and He had lost a great quantity of Blood. He was so weakened He could scarcely walk, and yet He had to carry this great load upon His shoulders. The soldiers struck Him rudely, and thus He fell several times in His journey.

My beloved Jesus, it is not the weight of the Cross, but of my sins, which has made Thee suffer so much pain. Ah, by the merits of this first fall, deliver me from the misfortune of falling into mortal sin. I love Thee, O my Jesus, with my whole heart ; I repent of having offended Thee. Never permit me to offend Thee again. Grant that I may love Thee always ; and then do with me what Thou wilt.

Our Father. Hail Mary. Glory be, &c.

> Dear Jesus, Thou dost go to die
> For very love of me :
> Ah ! let me bear Thee company,
> I wish to die with Thee.

FOURTH STATION.
JESUS MEETS HIS AFFLICTED MOTHER.

V. We adore Thee, O Christ, and praise Thee.
R. Because by Thy holy Cross Thou hast redeemed the world.

Consider the meeting of the Son and the Mother, which took place on this journey. Jesus and Mary looked at each other, and their looks became as so many arrows to wound those Hearts which loved each other so tenderly.

My most loving Jesus, by the sorrow Thou didst experience in this meeting, grant me the grace of a truly devoted love for Thy most holy Mother. And thou, my Queen, who wast overwhelmed with sorrow, obtain for me by thy intercession a continual and tender remembrance of the Passion of thy Son. I love Thee, Jesus, my Love ; I repent of ever having offended Thee. Never permit me to offend Thee again. Grant that I may love Thee ; and then do with me what Thou wilt.

Our Father. Hail Mary. Glory be, &c.

> Dear Jesus, Thou dost go to die
> For very love of me :
> Ah ! let me bear Thee company,
> I wish to die with Thee.

FIFTH STATION.

THE CYRENEAN HELPS JESUS TO CARRY HIS CROSS.

V We adore Thee, O Christ, and praise Thee. *R.* Because by Thy holy Cross Thou hast redeemed the world.

Consider how the Jews, seeing that at each step Jesus from weakness was on the point of expiring, and fearing He would die on the way, when they wished Him to die the ignominious death of the Cross, constrained Simon the Cyrenean to carry the Cross behind our Lord.

My most sweet Jesus, I will not refuse the Cross as the Cyrenean did ; I accept it, I embrace it. I accept in particular the death Thou hast destined for me, with all the pains which may accompany it ; I unite it to Thy Death, I offer it to Thee. Thou hast died for love of me ; I will die for love of Thee, and to please Thee. Help me by Thy grace. I love Thee, Jesus, my Love ; I repent of having offended Thee. Never permit me to offend Thee again.

Grant that I may love Thee ; and then do with me what Thou wilt.

Our Father. Hail Mary. Glory be, &c.
Dear Jesus, Thou dost go to die
For very love of me :
Ah ! let me bear Thee company,
I wish to die with Thee.

SIXTH STATION.
VERONICA WIPES THE FACE OF JESUS.

V. We adore Thee, O Christ, and praise Thee.
R. Because by Thy holy Cross Thou hast redeemed the world.

Consider how the holy woman named Veronica, seeing Jesus so afflicted, and His Face bathed in sweat and Blood, presented Him with a towel, with which He wiped His adorable Face, leaving on it the impression of His holy Countenance.

My most beloved Jesus, Thy Face was beautiful before, but in this journey it has lost all its beauty, and wounds and blood have disfigured it. Alas! my soul also was once beautiful, when it received Thy grace in baptism ; but I have disfigured it since by my sins ; Thou alone, my Redeemer, canst restore it to its former beauty. Do this by Thy Passion, and then do with me what Thou wilt.

Our Father. Hail Mary. Glory be, &c.
Dear Jesus, Thou dost go to die
For very love of me :
Ah ! let me bear Thee company,
I wish to die with Thee.

SEVENTH STATION.
JESUS FALLS THE SECOND TIME.

V. We adore Thee, O Christ, and praise Thee.
R. Because by Thy holy Cross Thou hast redeemed the world.

Consider the second fall of Jesus under the Cross,—a fall which renews the pain of all the wounds of the Head and members of our afflicted Lord.

My most gentle Jesus, how many times Thou hast pardoned me, and how many times have I fallen again, and begun again to offend Thee ! Oh, by the merits of this new fall, give me the necessary helps to persevere in Thy grace until death. Grant that in all temptations which assail me I may always commend myself to Thee. I love Thee, Jesus, my Love, with my whole heart ; I repent of having offended Thee. Never permit me to offend Thee again. Grant that I may love Thee always ; and then do with me what Thou wilt.

Our Father. Hail Mary. Glory be, &c.
Dear Jesus, Thou dost go to die
For very love of me :
Ah ! let me bear Thee company,
I wish to die with Thee.

EIGHTH STATION.
JESUS SPEAKS TO THE DAUGHTERS OF JERUSALEM.

V. We adore Thee, O Christ, and praise Thee.
R. Because by Thy holy Cross Thou hast redeemed the world.

Consider how those women wept with compassion at seeing Jesus in such a pitiable state, streaming with Blood, as He walked along. But Jesus said to them, " Weep not for Me, but for your children."

My Jesus, laden with sorrows, I weep for the offences I have committed against Thee, because of the pains they have deserved, and still more because of the displeasure they have caused Thee, who hast loved me so much. It is Thy love, more than the fear of hell, which causes me to weep for my sins. My Jesus, I love Thee more than myself ; I repent of having offended Thee. Never permit me to offend Thee again. Grant that I may love Thee always ; and then do with me what Thou wilt.

Our Father. Hail Mary. Glory be, &c.
Dear Jesus, Thou dost go to die
For very love of me :
Ah ! let me bear Thee company,

I wish to die with Thee.

NINTH STATION.
JESUS FALLS THE THIRD TIME.

V. We adore Thee, O Christ, and praise Thee.
R. Because by Thy holy Cross Thou hast redeemed the world.

Consider the third fall of Jesus Christ. His weakness was extreme, and the cruelty of His executioners excessive, who tried to hasten His steps when He had scarcely strength to move.

Ah, my outraged Jesus, by the merits of the weakness Thou didst suffer in going to Calvary, give me strength sufficient to conquer all human respect and all my wicked passions, which have led me to despise Thy friendship. I love Thee, Jesus, my Love, with my whole heart ; I repent of having offended Thee. Never permit me to offend Thee again. Grant that I may love Thee always ; and then do with me what Thou wilt.

Our Father.   Hail Mary.   Glory be, &c.

Dear Jesus, Thou dost go to die
For very love of me :
Ah ! let me bear Thee company,
I wish to die with Thee.

TENTH STATION.
JESUS IS STRIPPED OF HIS GARMENTS.

V. We adore Thee, O Christ, and praise Thee.
R. Because by Thy holy Cross Thou hast redeemed the world.

Consider the violence with which the executioners stripped Jesus. His inner garments adhered to His torn Flesh, and they dragged them off so roughly that the skin came with them. Compassionate your Saviour thus cruelly treated, and say to Him : My innocent Jesus, by the merits of the torment Thou hast felt, help me to strip myself of all affection to things of earth, in order that I may place all my love in Thee, who art so worthy of my love. I love Thee, O Jesus, with my whole heart ; I repent of having offended Thee. Never permit me to offend Thee again. Grant that I may love Thee always ; and then do with me what Thou wilt.

Our Father.   Hail Mary.   Glory be, &c.

Dear Jesus, Thou dost go to die
For very love of me :
Ah ! let me bear Thee company,
I wish to die with Thee.

ELEVENTH STATION.

JESUS IS NAILED TO THE CROSS.

V. We adore Thee, O Christ, and praise Thee.
R. Because by Thy holy Cross Thou hast redeemed the world.

Consider how Jesus, after being thrown on the Cross, extended His hands, and offered to His Eternal Father the sacrifice of His life for our salvation. These barbarians fastened Him with nails ; and then, raising the Cross, leave Him to die with anguish on this infamous gibbet.

My Jesus, loaded with contempt, nail my heart to Thy feet, that it may ever remain there to love Thee, and never quit Thee again. I love Thee more than myself ; I repent of having offended Thee. Never permit me to offend Thee again. Grant that I may love Thee always ; and then do with me what Thou wilt.

Our Father. Hail Mary. Glory be, &c.

Dear Jesus, Thou dost go to die
For very love of me :
Ah ! let me bear Thee company,
I wish to die with Thee.

TWELFTH STATION.
JESUS DIES ON THE CROSS.

V. We adore Thee, O Christ, and praise Thee.
R. Because by Thy holy Cross Thou hast redeemed the world.

Consider how thy Jesus, after three hours' Agony on the Cross, consumed at length with anguish, abandons Himself to the weight of His Body, bows His Head, and dies.

O my dying Jesus, I kiss devoutly the Cross on which Thou didst die for love of me. I have merited by my sins to die a miserable death ; but Thy Death is my hope. Ah, by the merits of Thy Death, give me grace to die embracing Thy feet and burning with love to Thee. I commit my soul into Thy hands. I love Thee with my whole heart ; I repent of ever having offended Thee. Permit not that I ever offend Thee again. Grant that I may love thee always ; and then do with me what Thou wilt.

Our Father. Hail Mary. Glory be, &c.

Dear Jesus, Thou dost go to die
For very love of me :
Ah ! let me bear Thee company,
I wish to die with Thee.

THIRTEENTH STATION.
JESUS IS TAKEN DOWN FROM THE CROSS.

V. We adore Thee, O Christ, and praise Thee.
R. Because by Thy holy Cross Thou hast redeemed the world.

Consider how, our Lord having expired, two of His disciples, Joseph and Nicodemus, took Him down from the Cross, and placed Him in the arms of His afflicted Mother, who received Him with unutterable tenderness, and pressed Him to her bosom.

O Mother of sorrow, for the love of this Son, accept me for thy servant, and pray to Him for me. And Thou, my Redeemer, since Thou hast died for me, permit me to love Thee ; for I wish but Thee, and nothing more. I love Thee, my Jesus, and I repent of ever having offended Thee. Never permit me to offend Thee again. Grant that I may love Thee always ; and then do with me what Thou wilt.

Our Father. Hail Mary. Glory be, &c.

Dear Jesus, Thou dost go to die
For very love of me : Ah ! let me bear Thee company,
I wish to die with Thee.

FOURTEENTH STATION.
JESUS IS PLACED IN THE SEPULCHRE.

V. We adore Thee, O Christ, and praise Thee.
R. Because by Thy holy Cross Thou hast redeemed the world.

Consider how the disciples carried the Body of Jesus to bury it, accompanied by His holy Mother, who arranged it in the sepulchre with her own hands. They then closed the tomb, and all withdrew.

Ah, my buried Jesus, I kiss the stone that encloses Thee. But Thou didst rise again the third day. I beseech Thee, by Thy resurrection, make me rise glorious with Thee at the last day, to be always united with Thee in heaven, to praise Thee, and love Thee forever. I love Thee, and I repent of ever having offended Thee. Permit not that I ever offend Thee again. Grant that I may love Thee ; and then do with me what Thou wilt.

Our Father. Hail Mary. Glory be, &c.

Dear Jesus, Thou dost go to die
For very love of me :
Ah ! let me bear Thee company,
I wish to die with Thee.

After this, return to the High Altar, and say, Our Father, Hail Mary, and Glory be, &c. five times, in honour of the Passion of Jesus Christ, to gain the other Indulgences granted to those who recite them.

PRAYERS TO JESUS BY THE MERIT OF EACH PARTICULAR PAIN WHICH HE SUFFERED IN HIS PASSION.

O my Jesus, by that humiliation which Thou didst practise in washing the feet of Thy disciples, I pray Thee to bestow upon me the grace of true humility, that I may humble myself to all, especially to such fus treat me with contempt.

My Jesus, by that sorrow which Thou didst suffer in the Garden, sufficient, as it was, to cause Thy Death, I pray Thee to deliver me from the sorrow of hell, from living for evermore at a distance from Thee, and without the power of ever loving Thee again.

My Jesus, by that horror which Thou hadst of my sins, which were then present to Thy sight, give me a true sorrow for all the offences which I have committed against Thee.

My Jesus, by that pain which Thou didst experience at seeing Thyself betrayed by Judas with a kiss, give me the grace to be ever faithful unto Thee, and never more to betray Thee, as I have done in time past.

My Jesus, by that pain which Thou didst feel at seeing Thyself bound like a culprit to be taken before the judges, I pray Thee to bind me to Thyself by the sweet chains of holy love, that so I may never more see myself separated from Thee, my only Good.

My Jesus, by all those insults, buffetings, and spittings which Thou didst on that night suffer in the house of Caiaphas, give me the strength to suffer in peace, for love of Thee, all the affronts which I shall meet with from men.

My Jesus, by that ridicule which Thou didst receive from Herod in being treated as a fool, give me the grace to endure with patience all that men shall say of me, treating me as base, senseless, or wicked.

My Jesus, by that outrage which Thou didst receive from the Jews in seeing Thyself placed after Barabbas, give me the grace to suffer with patience the dishonour of seeing myself placed after others.

My Jesus, by that pain which Thou didst suffer in Thy most holy Body when Thou wast so cruelly scourged, give me the grace to suffer with patience all the pains of my sicknesses, and especially those of my death.

My Jesus, by that pain which Thou didst suffer in Thy most sacred Head when it was pierced with the thorns, give me the grace never to consent to thoughts displeasing unto Thee.

My Jesus, by that act of Thine by which Thou didst accept of the death of the Cross, to which Pilate condemned Thee, give me the grace to accept of my death with resignation, together with all the other pains which shall accompany it.

My Jesus, by the pain which Thou didst suffer in carrying Thy Cross on Thy journey to Calvary, give me the grace to suffer with patience all my crosses in this life.

My Jesus, by that pain which Thou didst suffer in having the nails driven through Thy Hands and Thy Feet, I pray Thee to nail my will unto Thy Feet, that so I may will nothing save that which Thou dost will.

My Jesus, by the affliction which Thou didst suffer in having gall given Thee to drink, give me the grace not to offend Thee by intemperance in eating and drinking.

My Jesus, by that pain which Thou didst experience in taking leave of Thy holy Mother upon the Cross, deliver me from an inordinate love for my relations, or for any other creature, that so my heart may be wholly and always Thine.

My Jesus, by that desolation which Thou didst suffer in Thy Death in seeing Thyself abandoned by Thine Eternal Father, give me the grace to suffer all my desolations with patience, without ever losing my confidence in Thy goodness.

My Jesus, by those three hours of affliction and agony which Thou didst suffer when dying upon the Cross, give me the grace to suffer with resignation, for love of Thee, the pains of my agony at the hour of death.

My Jesus, by that great sorrow which Thou didst feel when Thy most holy Soul, on Thy expiring, separated itself from Thy most Sacred Body, give me the grace to breathe forth my soul in the hour of my death, offering up my sorrow then to Thee, together with an act of perfect love, that so I may go to love Thee in heaven, face to face, with all my strength, and for all eternity.

And thee, most holy Virgin, and my Mother Mary, by that sword which pierced thine heart when thou didst behold thy Son bow down His Head and expire, do I pray to assist me in the hour of my death, that so I may come to praise thee and to thank thee in Paradise for all the graces which thou hast obtained for me from God.

STEPS OF THE PASSION.

My sweetest Jesus, who, while praying in the Garden, didst sweat Blood, wast in agony, and didst suffer a sorrow so great as to suffice to cause Thee death, have mercy on us.

R. Mercy on us, O Lord, have mercy on us.

My sweetest Jesus, who wast betrayed by Judas with a kiss, and delivered over into the hands of Thine enemies, and then wast taken prisoner by them and bound, and abandoned by Thy disciples, have mercy on us.

R. Mercy on us, O Lord, &c.

My sweetest Jesus, declared by the council of the Jews guilty of death, and in the house of Caiaphas blindfolded with a piece of cloth, and then buffeted, spit at, and derided, have mercy on us.

R. Mercy on us, O Lord, &c.

My sweetest Jesus, led away as a malefactor to Pilate, and then turned by Herod into ridicule, and treated as a madman, have mercy on us.

R. Mercy on us, O Lord, &c.

My sweetest Jesus, stripped of Thy garments, and bound to the pillar, and so cruelly scourged, have mercy on us.

R. Mercy on us, O Lord, &c.

My sweetest Jesus, crowned with thorns, covered with a red mantle, buffeted, and in mockery saluted as King of the Jews, have mercy on us.

R. Mercy on us, O Lord, &c.

My sweetest Jesus, rejected by the Jews, and placed after Barabbas, and then unjustly condemned by Pilate to die upon a Cross, have mercy on us. *R.* Mercy on us, O Lord, &c.

My sweetest Jesus, laden with the wood of the Cross, and as an innocent Lamb led away unto death, have mercy on us.

R. Mercy on us, O Lord, &c.

My sweetest Jesus, nailed upon the Cross, placed between two thieves, ridiculed and blasphemed, and for three hours in an agony of the most horrible torments, have mercy on us.

R. Mercy on us, O Lord, &c.

My sweetest Jesus, dead upon the Cross, and in sight of Thy holy Mother, transfixed in Thy side with the spear, from whence there issued forth Blood and Water, have mercy on us.

R. Mercy on us, O Lord, &c.

My sweetest Jesus, taken down from the Cross, and placed in the bosom of Thine afflicted Mother, have mercy on us.

R. Mercy on us, O Lord, &c.

My sweetest Jesus, who, torn with stripes and stamped
with Thy five Wounds, wast laid in the sepulchre, have mercy on us.

R. Mercy on us, O Lord, &c.

V. Surely He hath borne our infirmities.

R. And He hath carried our sorrows.

Let us pray.

O God, who, for the Redemption of the world, didst will to be born, to be circumcised, rejected by the Jews, betrayed by the traitor Judas with a kiss, bound with cords, led as an innocent Lamb to the sacrifice, and with so many insults taken before Annas, Caiaphas, Pilate, and Herod, accused by false witnesses, beaten with scourges and buffetings, overwhelmed with ignominies, spit upon, crowned with thorns, smitten with the reed, blindfolded, stripped of Thy raiment, fastened with nails to the Cross, lifted up on the Cross, numbered amongst thieves, with gall and vinegar given Thee to drink, and wounded with the spear,—do thou, Lord, by these Sacred Pains, which I, unworthy, venerate, and by Thy holy Cross and Death, deliver me from hell, and vouchsafe to conduct me whither Thou didst conduct the thief that was crucified with Thee : Thou, who livest and reignest with the Father and the Holy Spirit for ever and ever. Amen. So do I hope ; and so may it be.

LITTLE CHAPLET OF THE FIVE WOUNDS OF JESUS CRUCIFIED.

O my Lord Jesus Christ, I adore the wound in Thy left Foot. I thank Thee for having suffered it for me with so much sorrow and with so much love. I compassionate Thy pain, and that of Thine afflicted Mother. And, by the merit of this sacred wound, I pray Thee to grant me the pardon of my sins, of which I repent with all my heart, because they have offended Thine infinite goodness. O sorrowing Mary, pray to Jesus for me. Our Father, Hail Mary, Glory, &c.

> By all the wounds which Thou didst bear
> With so much love and so much pain,
> Oh, let a sinner's prayer
> Thy mercy, Lord, obtain.

O my Lord Jesus Christ, I adore the wound in Thy right Foot. I thank Thee for having suffered it for me with so much sorrow and with so much love. I compassionate Thy pain, and that of Thine afflicted Mother. And, by the merit of this sacred wound, I pray Thee to give me the strength not to fall into mortal sin for the future, but to persevere in Thy grace unto my death. O sorrowing Mary, pray to Jesus for me.

Our Father, &c.

> By all the wounds which Thou didst bear
> With so much love and so much pain,
> Oh, let a sinner's prayer
> Thy mercy, Lord, obtain.

O my Lord Jesus Christ, I adore the wound in Thy left Hand. I thank Thee for having suffered it for me with so much sorrow and with so much love. I compassionate Thy pain, and that of Thine afflicted Mother. And, by the merit of this sacred wound, I pray Thee to deliver me from hell, which I have so often deserved, where I could never love Thee more. O sorrowing Mary, pray to Jesus for me.

Our Father, &c.

> By all the wounds which Thou didst bear
> With so much love and so much pain,
> Oh, let a sinner's prayer
> Thy mercy, Lord, obtain.

O my Lord Jesus Christ, I adore the wound in Thy right Hand. I thank Thee for having suffered it for me with so much sorrow and with so much love. I compassionate Thy pain, and that of Thy most afflicted Mother. And, by the merit of this sacred wound, I pray Thee to give me the glory of Paradise, where I shall love Thee perfectly, and with all my strength. O sorrowing Mary, pray to Jesus for me.

Our Father, &c.

> By all the wounds which Thou didst bear
> With so much love and so much pain,
> Oh, let a sinner's prayer
> Thy mercy, Lord, obtain.

O my Lord Jesus Christ, I adore the wound in Thy Side. I thank Thee for having willed, even after Thy Death, to suffer this additional injury, without pain indeed, yet with consummate love. I compassionate Thine afflicted Mother, who alone felt all its pain. And, by the merit of this sacred wound, I pray Thee to bestow upon me the gift of holy love for Thee, that so I may ever love Thee in this life, and in the other, face to face, for all eternity, in Paradise. O sorrowing Mary, pray to Jesus for me.

Our Father, &c.

> By all the wounds which Thou didst bear
> With so much love and so much pain, Oh, let a sinner's prayer
> Thy mercy, Lord, obtain.

HYMNS ON THE PASSION OF JESUS.

NO. I.
Gesù mio, *con dure funi.*

I.

My Jesus ! say, what wretch has dared
Thy Sacred Hands to bind ?
And who has dared to buffet so
Thy Face so meek and kind ?
'Tis I have thus ungrateful been,
    Yet, Jesus, pity take !
    Oh, spare and pardon me, my Lord,
    For Thy sweet mercy's sake !

II.

My Jesus ! who with spittle vile
Profaned Thy Sacred Brow?
Or whose unpitying scourge has made
Thy Precious Blood to flow ?
'Tis I have thus ungrateful been,
    Yet, Jesus, pity take !
    Oh, spare and pardon me, my Lord,
    For Thy sweet mercy's sake !

III.

My Jesus ! whose the hands that wove
    That cruel thorny crown ?
    Who made that hard and heavy cross
    That weighs Thy Shoulders down ?
'Tis I Lave thus ungrateful been,
    Yet, Jesus, pity take !
    Oh, spare and pardon me, my Lord,
    For Thy sweet mercy's sake !

IV.

My Jesus ! who has mocked Thy thirst
    With vinegar and gall?
    Who held the nails that pierced Thy Hands,
    And made the hammer fall ?
'Tis I have thus ungrateful been,
    Yet, Jesus, pity take !
    Oh, spare and pardon me, my Lord,
    For Thy sweet mercy's sake !

V.

My Jesus! say, who dared to nail
    Those tender Feet of Thine ?
    And whose the arm that raised the lance
    To pierce that Heart Divine ?
'Tis I have thus ungrateful been,
    Yet, Jesus, pity take !
    Oh, spare and pardon me, my Lord,
    For Thy sweet mercy's sake !

VI.

And, Mary ! who has murdered thus
    Thy loved and only One *!*
    Canst thou forgive the bloodstained hand
    That robbed thee of thy Son *!*
'Tis I have thus ungrateful been
    To Jesus and to thee ;
    Forgive me for thy Jesus' sake,
    And pray to Him for me.

NO. II.
O fieri flagelli che al mio *buon Signore.*

I.

Oh, ruthless Scourges, with what pain you tear
My Saviour's Flesh, so innocent and fair !
    Oh, cease to rend that Flesh Divine,
    My loving Lord torment no more ;
    Wound rather, wound this heart of mine,
    The guilty cause of all He bore !

II.

Ye cruel Thorns, in mocking wreath entwined,
My Saviour's Brow in agony to bind !
    Oh, cease to rend that Flesh Divine,
    My loving Lord torment no more ;
    Wound rather, wound this heart of mine,
    The guilty cause of all He bore !

III.

Unpitying Nails, whose points, with anguish fierce,
The Hands and Feet of my Redeemer pierce!
    Oh, cease to rend that Flesh Divine,
    My loving Lord torment no more ;
    Wound rather, wound this heart of mine,
    The guilty cause of all He bore !

IV.

Unfeeling Lance, that dar'st to open wide
The sacred temple of my Saviour's Side !
    Oh, cease to wound that Flesh Divine,
    My loving Lord torment no more ;
    Pierce rather, pierce this heart of mine,
    The guilty cause of all He bore !

THE AUTHOR'S PROTEST.

In obedience to the decrees of Urban VIII., I declare that I have no intention of attributing any other than a purely human authority to the miracles, revelations, favours, and particular cases recorded in this book ; and the same as regards the titles of saints and blessed, applied to servants of God not yet canonised, except in those cases which have been confirmed by the Holy Roman Catholic Church and the Apostolic See, of which I declare myself to be an obedient son ; and therefore I submit myself, and all that I have written in this book, to her judgment.